D1527591

The Structure of Tone

THE STRUCTURE OF TONE

Zhiming Bao

New York   Oxford
Oxford University Press
1999

Oxford University Press

Oxford   New York
Athens   Auckland   Bangkok   Bogotá   Buenos Aires   Calcutta
Cape Town   Chennai   Dar es Salaam   Delhi   Florence   Hong Kong   Istanbul
Karachi   Kuala Lumpur   Madrid   Melbourne   Mexico City   Mumbai
Nairobi   Paris   São Paulo   Singapore   Taipei   Tokyo   Toronto   Warsaw

and associated companies in
Berlin   Ibadan

Copyright © 1999 by Zhiming Bao

Published by Oxford University Press, Inc.
198 Madison Avenue, New York, New York 10016

Oxford is a registered trademark of Oxford University Press

Library of Congress Cataloging-in-Publication Data
Bao, Zhiming, 1957–
The structure of tone / Zhiming Bao.
p.   cm.
Includes bibliographical references and index.
ISBN 0-19-511880-4
1. Chinese language—Tone.   2. Tone (Phonetics)   I. Title.
PL1213.B36   1999
495.1'16—dc21   99-19275

1 3 5 7 9 8 6 4 2

Printed in the United States of America
on acid-free paper

For my parents, and Kar Lin

Preface

This book is based on my 1990 MIT dissertation, *On the Nature of Tone*, completed under the supervision of Morris Halle. I decided to retain the bulk of the dissertation, in order to keep its theoretical concern, and the overall structure of its argumentation. I have, however, incorporated works on tone that have been published since 1990. Revising the dissertation forced me to think more carefully about some of the controversial issues in tonology, and scholarly critique allows me to see my own work in a new light. I hope the present volume represents an improvement over the dissertation.

During the writing of the dissertation, I have benefited from formal or informal discussions with various people. In particular, I would like to thank my committee members, Francois Dell, Ken Hale, and Morris Halle; and other phonologists who have influenced me in one way or another: Matthew Chen, Michael Kenstowitcz, Duanmu San, Donca Steriade, and Moira Yip. The dissertation could not have been written without their input. Francois readily shared with me his knowledge of Southeast Asian languages and Chinese dialects, and his theoretical insights. Ken drew my attention to more global issues, and to the formal similarities among different branches of linguistics. Morris's guidance improved the quality of my argument enormously. In fact, the dissertation took shape as much in the talks I had with him as in the time between the talks. Donca and Michael taught me phonology, and discussed with me some of the issues that eventually found their way into the dissertation. To Moira I owe an enormous intellectual debt, which is obvious in the following pages. And finally, I feel encouraged by Matthew's sharp-minded critique of my work, and by his continued interest in tonological issues.

I am grateful to my former teachers and colleagues at Fudan University, Shanghai, especially Cheng Yumin and Xu Liejiong. I am also grateful to two scholars of Chinese philosophy, Henry Rosemont, Jr. and Chad Hansen. They may not be aware of it, but their influence on me, linguistic or otherwise, has been enormous.

Finally, I thank Oxford University Press for giving me the opportunity to publish this book and the editors Peter Ohlin and MaryBeth Branigan for their fine work.

Zhiming Bao
Singapore, December 1998

Contents

Chapter Six: The Mid Tone   181

Chapter Seven: Epilogue   200

The Structure of Tone

1

Introduction

This book is a study on the internal structure of tone. It addresses two issues that are at the center of research in nonlinear phonology: (1) the internal structure of phonological elements, such as segments and tones; and (2) the overall structure of phonological representation. The book deals with the geometry of tone and how it fits into the geometry of laryngeal features. It also addresses the relationship between tone and other autosegments, particularly syllable structure. In this chapter, I sketch in general terms the theoretical results of this study.

1.1　The Geometry of Tone

The geometry of tone is the central concern of this book. Tone consists of register and contour, formally represented in (1):

(1)　

The register node and the contour node play different conceptual roles. The register node specifies the pitch level of the tone, whereas the contour node specifies how the pitch of the tone behaves over the temporal duration of the tone-bearing unit. The register is therefore tone's static aspect, whereas the contour is its dynamic aspect. These two components are encoded in the structure in (1) as sister nodes dominated by the tonal root node. (Henceforth, I will use the letters t, r, and c to represent tone, register, and contour, respectively.) I will argue that the structure in (1) accounts for a wide range of phonological phenomena of tone sandhi found in various dialects of Chinese and other Asian languages.

The r node is specified by the laryngeal feature [stiff vocal cords], or [stiff] for short, proposed by Halle and Stevens (1971). Formally, it is a non-terminal node that dominates a single feature:

(2)

The contour node c is specified by the laryngeal feature [slack vocal cord], or [slack]. Following Yip (1980, 1989), the contour node may dominate a single [slack] specification, or a sequence of [slack] specifications. The c node has two formal configurations:

(3)   a.   c
               |
             [slack]

         b.   c

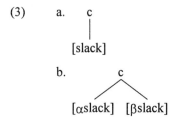

              [αslack] [βslack]

(3a) is the configuration for an even (or level) tone, and (3b) is the configuration for a contour tone. The values of the feature [slack] in any given sequence are different. It is assumed that the configurations in (4) are conceptually equivalent to (3a).

(4)   a.   c

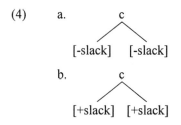

              [-slack]   [-slack]

         b.   c

              [+slack] [+slack]

In articulatory terms, the features provide articulatory instructions to the relevant articulators. Since the branching of the c node is temporal, the sequences of [slack] in (4) provide the same articulatory instructions to the same laryngeal articulators over time. Similarly, in configuration (3a), the single feature [slack] provides the same articulatory instructions over time. The articulatory effect produced by the configurations in (4) and (3a) are identical. An articulatorily meaningful branching structure involving a single feature must have different specifications of that feature.[1] Throughout this book, I will use H, L, h, and l to specify the internal structure of tone. These symbols have the following meanings.

(5)   H = [+stiff]   ([+upper])
         L = [-stiff]   ([-upper])
         h = [-slack]   ([+raised])
         l = [+slack]   ([-raised])

Functionally, the features [stiff] and [slack] are equivalent to [upper] and [raised] as proposed by Yip (1980, 1989). The formal apparatus postulated so far gives the following structures:

(6)   Registers

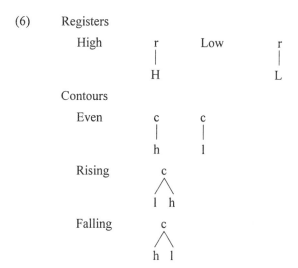

Since tone is phonetically executed by the vocal cords, the geometry of tone is a substructure of the geometry of laryngeal features. Out of the four laryngeal features of Halle and Stevens (1971), two concern the tension of the vocal cords and two concern the state of the glottis. I propose that these four features have the following structure:

(7)

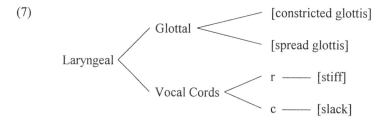

The geometry of tone is the geometry of the vocal cords, which I take to be the articulators that execute tone in addition to voicing. I will not address the structure of the glottal features [constricted glottis] and [spread glottis].

1.2   Tone as Autosegmental Tier

The claim that the geometry of tone is part of the geometry of laryngeal features commits one to the view that tone is phonetically realized on segments. I assume that tone is realized on segments that serve as syllabic nucleus. The canonical tone-bearing segments are vowels.

At the level of representation prior to phonetic execution, tones must be represented as autosegments that are independent from the segments on which they are realized. The tone-segment segregation accounts for the phenomenon known as tone stability—tone often survives segmental deletion. In nonlinear phonology in which phonological representation is rich in structure, the notion of tone-segment segregation can be formally captured in two ways: tone as an autosegmental plane, or tone as an autosegmental tier on the syllabic plane. Planes and tiers are distinct formal entities, as shown by the biplanar representation in (8):

(8)

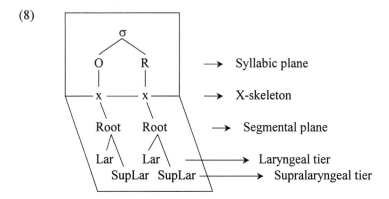

The terms "plane" and "tier" have many different uses in the literature. According to Archangeli (1985:336), tiers are "plane-internal sequences of matrices parallel to the core skeleton," while planes are the entire melodies anchored on the x-skeleton. My use of the terms essentially follows this definition. Since segments are no longer conceived as feature matrices, but rather as root nodes having internal geometrical structure, the term "tier" is used to refer to sequences of nodes of the same type. In (8), the laryngeal nodes of the onset and nucleus form the laryngeal tier. The same is true of the supralaryngeal nodes. The laryngeal and supralaryngeal nodes do not form a tier, because they are of different types. Tiers are internal to planes, which in turn link directly to the x-slots.[2]

Tone can be represented as an autosegmental tier on the syllabic plane, as in (9a), or as an autosegmental plane anchored on the x-skeleton, as in (9b).

(9)   a. Tone as autosegmental tier

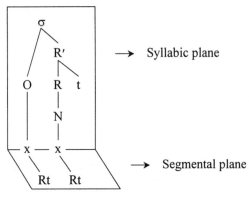

b. Tone as autosegmental plane

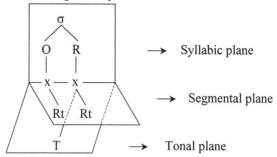

→ Syllabic plane

→ Segmental plane

→ Tonal plane

In both representations only relevant nodes are shown. Tone mapping may be governed by the same set of association conventions and well-formedness conditions that have been introduced in autosegmental phonology. In (10), the conventions and condition are due to Pulleyblank (1986:11):

(10) *Association Conventions*:
   Map a sequence of tones onto a sequence of tone-bearing units:
   (a) from left to right;
   (b) in a one-to-one relation.

   Well-Formedness Condition:
   Association lines do not cross.

I have nothing to say about the empirical validity of the *Association Conventions*, particularly the directionality of mapping (10a). The *Well-Formedness Condition* may be derivable from extra-linguistic considerations; see Hammond (1988) and Sagey (1988).

In structure (9a), tone is adjoined to the tone-bearing unit, which in this book is argued to be the rime (R). The syllabic elements are temporally ordered by virtue of their x-skeleton positions. Onset (O) necessarily precedes R in time. Tone, when adjoined to the R node, does not precede rime in time. It is "simultaneous" with the rime to which it is adjoined. In structure (9b), tone is associated with the x-slot of the nucleus segment. Tone is an element on the tone plane, which is anchored on the x-skeleton.

In Chapter 5 I argue that tone stability is structure-dependent and can be explained only by assuming the structure in (9a). To derive the structure in (9a), I assume that tone mapping is an adjunction process: it adjoins tone t to R, creating a new segment of the rime node, R′:

(11)   R′

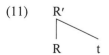

   R   t

Tones form an autosegmental tier on the syllabic plane; they do not form an autosegmental plane.

1.3   A Brief Note on Chinese Dialects

This book draws most of its data from Chinese dialects. A brief sketch of the conventional classification of Chinese dialects may be useful for readers who are not familiar with Chinese. For general references in English, Chao (1968) is the standard grammar of Chinese, although its description of dialect differentiation and classification is quite sketchy. DeFrancis (1984), Ramsey (1987), and Norman (1989) provide good diachronic and synchronic introductions to the Chinese language; Norman (1989) provides a particularly valuable introduction to Chinese dialectology in English.

Geographically, most major Chinese dialects are concentrated in the southern provinces of China, especially along the Pacific coast. It is generally accepted that there are eight major dialect groups in Chinese that are mutually unintelligible. These groups, or "families," are as follows (adapted from DeFrancis 1984:58):

(12)	Dialect Group	Speakers	Percent of Population
	Mandarin	715 million	71.5
	Wu	85 million	8.5
	Yue (Cantonese)	50 million	5.0
	Xiang (Hunan)	48 million	4.8
	Kejia (Hakka)	37 million	3.7
	Southern Min	28 million	2.8
	Gan (Jiangxi)	24 million	2.4
	Northern Min	13 million	1.3

By far, the Mandarin dialect group is spoken by more people and over a larger geographical area than any other major dialect group. The Wu region comprises the city of Shanghai and the provinces of Zhejiang and Jiangsu south of the Yangtze River. The Yue (better known as Cantonese), Xiang, Gan, Northern Min, and Southern Min dialect groups are spoken in the provinces for which they are the historical names: Yue in Guangdong Province (Canton), Xiang in Jiangxi Province, Gan in Hunan Province, and Northern and Southern Min in Fujian Province. This, of course, does not mean that other dialects are not spoken in these provinces. Guangdong, for example, is home not only for the Yue dialect family, but for a sizable Southern Min-speaking area; and in a few of its counties the majority speak Kejia (X.-K. Li 1994). Southern Min, mainly confined to southern Fujian, is also spoken in Taiwan and Hainan and quite extensively in Southeast Asian countries such as Malaysia and Singapore. Within Fujian itself, the dialect situation is very diverse. The Northern-Southern division is only a rough approximation (Yuan et al. 1960, Zhan 1981, Chen and Li 1991). Unlike other dialect groups, Kejia (or Hakka), literally "guest people," is not confined to any single geographical region; its speakers are scattered in various provinces south of the Yangtze River and in Southeast Asia. Except Kejia, all other dialect groups or dialect families are identified with geographical regions of China. For this reason, DeFrancis (1984) calls them "regionalects."

The regionalects are mutually unintelligible. For all practical purposes, they can be considered separate languages. However, throughout history, people speaking different regional dialects in China have been united by common political, ethnic, and cultural ties. In addition, a shared literary heritage ensures a large core vocabulary common to all Chinese dialects. To varying degrees, the non-Mandarin dialects maintain two distinct registers, the literary register and the colloquial register. The two registers not only contain distinct vocabulary items, but have distinct phonology as well. A character is pronounced quite differently depending on the register. For example, in the Wu dialect of Shanghai, the character *da* "big" is pronounced as [da 35] in the literary reading, but as [du 13] in the colloquial reading. By and large, the literary register is closer in phonology to Mandarin than is the colloquial reading.

In this book, I use the term "dialect." In the Chinese linguistics circle, the term "dialect" is ambiguously applied to the dialect groups and to the individual dialects within each group. This degree of ambiguity is acceptable for our purposes. Following conventional practice, I will continue to use "dialect" to refer to dialect groups and to individual dialects as well; context of use will disambiguate it. When context warrants it, the term "dialect" will be applied only to individual dialects; the term "dialect group" or "dialect family" will be used with its intended meaning.

2

Theories of Tone: A Survey

2.1 *Yin-Yang* Registers

In Chinese philological and linguistic literature tones are classified into the *yin* and *yang* registers. Historically the *yin* tones occur on syllables with voiceless initial obstruents, and the *yang* tones occur on syllables with voiced initial obstruents. The voiced obstruents of Middle Chinese (ca. 600 A.D.) are lost in many modern dialects, mostly of the Mandarin variety. But many dialects, particularly those spoken in the southern coastal regions, still maintain voicing as a distinctive feature among obstruents. From the perspective of phonetics, it is well known that voiceless consonants induce higher pitch in the following vowel, and voiced consonants induce lower pitch (see, for example, Haudricourt 1954; Halle and Stevens 1971; Maddieson 1974, 1978; and Hombert et al. 1979). The correlation between *yin* and *yang* on the one hand, and the pitch of tone on the other, does not present a clear pattern over modern Chinese dialects. In some dialects with voiced obstruents, notably those in the Wu dialect family, the *yin* tones are higher in pitch than their *yang* counterparts. But in other dialects, such as those in the Southern Min dialect family, the situation is reversed: in the dialect of Chaoyang, and in many other Southern Min dialects spoken in southern Fujian Province and northern Guangdong Province, high-pitched tones are found in syllables with voiced initials, and low-pitched tones on syllables with voiceless initials (W. S.-Y. Wang 1967, Yue-Hashimoto 1986). In tone languages, tones are not necessarily correlated with consonant voicing.

The tones are further classified into four tonal categories: *ping* "even," *shang* "rising," *qu* "departing," and *ru* "entering." Each of the four tonal categories can be realized in both the *yin* and *yang* registers, giving a total of eight tones:[1]

(1)   Traditional Classification of Tones
        a. *yin ping* (even)
        b. *yin shang* (rising)
        c. *yin qu* (departing)
        d. *yin ru* (entering)
        A. *yang ping* (even)
        B. *yang shang* (rising)
        C. *yang qu* (departing)
        D. *yang ru* (entering)

The *ru* tones are the so-called checked tones, because they are realized on syllables ending in the voiceless stops /p, t, k, ?/, depending on the dialect. As we will see later, on the basis of sandhi facts, the *ru* tones are derivable from either the *ping*, *shang*, or *qu* tones.

The historical classification in (1) does not give the phonetic pitch of the tones. The meanings of the tonal labels are obscure at best, and we have no clear idea how the tones in classical Chinese were realized phonetically (see, for example, Mei 1970; K. Chang 1975; Ting 1982, 1989; and Hashimoto 1991). According to Mei (1970:104), the tones in Middle Chinese can be characterized as follows:

ping: long, level, and low, with a higher and a lower allotone, i.e. *yin* and *yang* allotones

shang: short, level, and high, its lower allotone having merged with the departing, i.e. *qu*, tone

qu: slightly drawn out and hence longish

ru: short

These descriptions are not explicit enough to allow a precise determination of the pitch height and contour of the tones. The labels may reflect the phonetic properties of the tones at the time when they were coined, but, judging by the tones of modern dialects, the names are hardly an indication of their pitch height or contour. For instance, the *yin ping* (1a) is realized as high level, 55, in Beijing Mandarin, but in Tianjin, a port city about a hundred miles southeast of Beijing, the same tone is realized as low fall, 21. Both Beijing and Tianjin dialects belong to the Mandarin family.

The system in (1) is non-phonetic in character, since it specifies eight tones without giving their phonetic pitch values. The insight of the system as an abstract representation is that it explicitly recognizes no more than two pitch registers, the *yin* and the *yang*, which are correlated with the voicing qualities of the syllable-initial consonants. The system serves a diachronic purpose by helping us identify the historical origin of tones in modern dialects. Although it fails as a phonetic tool for synchronic analysis, the *yin/yang* registers prove to be a viable theoretical device to capture the phonological regularities of tone sandhi. Attempts have been made, notably by Yip (1980) and Pulleyblank (1986), to formalize pitch registers in terms of tonal features, as we will see later in this chapter.

2.2   Chao (1930)

The numbers by which the two *yin ping* tones were represented in the preceding section, the high level 55 and the low falling 21, are the relative pitch values of the tones. The numeric notational system was first introduced by Chao (1930) as a systematic method of transcribing the phonetic pitch of tones, and it has since been widely used in Chinese linguistics literature. Chao's system divides a pitch scale into five distinct levels, ranging from 1 (the lowest) to 5 (the highest). It provides a convenient method of phonetically transcribing auditory impressions of tone height. A high falling tone may be transcribed as 53, a high concave tone as 535, and so on. Short tones are represented with a single digit if they are level, and with underlined digits if contour. So a high short tone may be 5, and a high falling short tone, 5̲3̲. It must be pointed out that the numbers represent relative pitch values. For phonological purposes, a 42 in one tone system may be a high falling tone, but in another it may be low falling.

With five digits, Chao's notation provides up to five tones with distinct pitch levels. Ever since Chao (1930), the number five has enjoyed a special status in the investigation of tonal systems, particularly in the field of Chinese dialectology. Languages with five distinct level tones phonetically *and* phonologically remain to be documented.

Using the number notation, the tonal inventory of Songjiang, spoken in the suburb of Shanghai, is as follows (Jiangsu 1960).

(2)   Tonal inventory of Songjiang
        Yin-register
        a. *ping*   53   t'i   "ladder"
                           ti   "low"
        b. *shang*   44   t'i   "body"
                           ti   "bottom"
        c. *qu*   35   t'i   "tear"
                           ti   "emperor"
        d. *ru*   5   p'aʔ   "tap"
                           paʔ   "hundred"

        Yang-register
        A. *ping*   31   di   "lift"
        B. *shang*   22   di   "brother"
        C. *qu*   13   di   "field"
        D. *ru*   3   baʔ   "white"

The tonal inventory of Songjiang is quite unusual in that it contains all the tones of classical Chinese and clearly shows the impact of syllable-initial voicing on tonal registers. Most modern Chinese dialects do not have tonal inventories as neatly patterned as Songjiang's.

The number notation is inadequate for two reasons. First, the system generates too many tones. By W. S.-Y. Wang's (1967:98) calculation, there will be a total of 125 theoretically possible tones if up to three positions are allowed for tonal specification.[2] No tone language actually contains so many distinctive tones in its tonal inventory. Second, the numbers fail to give a straightforward account of phonologically relevant tonal alternations, among them the correlation between syllable-initial consonant voicing and tone pitch (see the tone inventory of Songjiang above). Despite these shortcomings, however, the Chao numbers provide a convenient and effective tool to represent the phonetic realization of tone, a task the traditional labels fail to accomplish.

2.3 Tone in Chinese Linguistics

The names of the four tones of Chinese—*ping, shang, qu* and *ru*—were first established in the fifth century A.D. (L. Wang 1957; K. Chang 1975; and E. Pulleyblank 1978, 1984). Traditional philologists are preoccupied mainly with the classification of characters in terms of their tones. Dictionaries compiled on the basis of tones often serve as philological tools for students and poets. In regulated poetry, a literary genre popularized in the Tang Dynasty (618–907 A.D.), it is the tones that are metrically "regulated" (L. Wang 1979, Chen 1979). The philological importance of tone cannot be overemphasized. Little attention was paid to the internal make-up of tone or to tonological processes. Although the four terms, plus the registers *yin* and *yang*, are more than adequate for philological purposes, they are nevertheless insufficient as a systematic account of tone and tonological phenomena. It is only in modern times that questions of pitch and pitch contour have been raised.

In current Chinese linguistics, a tone is often described in terms of its pitch height, and the pitch shape it has over the duration of the syllable. This is the position of such standard works on tone as L. Wang (1956), Luo and Wang (1981), and Wu (1984), and of many introductory texts on Chinese linguistics. The traditional register notions *yin* and *yang*, and the tonal labels *ping, shang, qu*, and *ru*, are also employed, but they refer to "tonal categories" of classical Chinese; they are used for the convenience of cross-dialectal or diachronic comparison. The "tonal values" of the categories differ from dialect to dialect. The tones of a dialect are therefore described in terms of their tonal values—the pitch height and shape, and the tonal categories to which they correspond diachronically. The tonal values are transcribed in the numeric notation introduced in Chao (1930). In (2), we have seen the tonal inventory of Songjiang, in which tonal categories (*ping, shang, qu*, and *ru*) are presented together with their tonal values in numeric form. Thus, in Songjiang, the tonal value of the category *yin ping* is 53, and that of *yang ping*, 31. Tonal inventories vary greatly among modern Chinese dialects. Beijing Mandarin has only four tones, shown below (Wu 1984).

(3) | Tonal categories | Tonal values |
|---|---|
| *yin ping* | 55 |
| *yang ping* | 35 |
| *shang* | 214 |
| *qu* | 51 |

Beijing Mandarin does not have syllables that end in voiceless stops, so the *ru* tones of classical Chinese have merged into the remaining tones, and the *yin-yang* distinction is lost on *shang* and *qu*. Only four tones remain.

The dialect of Tianjin, a metropolitan port city not far from Beijing, has a rather different tone inventory. It has four tones, which result from somehow different historical development. The four tones are as follows (Luo and Wang 1981:129).

(4)   Tonal categories   Tonal values
         yin ping   11
         yang ping   55
         yin shang   24
         qu   42

Comparing the tonal inventories of Beijing and Tianjin, we can see that the tones denoted by the classical tonal categories have rather different phonetic realizations in modern dialects. The classical labels thus serve as a good guide for dialectal comparison. Diachronic change follows different courses in different dialects. In Beijing Mandarin, for example, the *yin-yang* distinction is lost on *shang*; in Tianjin Mandarin, *yang shang* is merged into other tonal categories, whereas *yin shang* remains as a distinct tone. For synchronic description of tone, notions like pitch height and pitch shape are inherently present in the numeric notation. However, it is not clear how the two notions should be interpreted in light of the theories of tone that have been developed within the American structuralist tradition.

Two characteristics of work on tone in Chinese linguistics are worth noting. First, the notions of pitch height or tone height and pitch shape or tone shape are part of the descriptive vocabulary of Chinese linguistics. They are extensively used in experimental and phonological work on tone (for example, Luo and Wang 1981, Wu 1984, Guo 1993, and Shi and Liao 1994). However, there has been very little discussion on the ontological status of the two notions in linguistic theory, nor has there been any attempt to use these notions to explain the range of tonological processes that have been extensively documented in Chinese dialectological literature.

Second, contemporary work on tone does not attempt to relate tonal pitch to the *yin/yang* registers of traditional philology. The terms "pitch height" and "pitch shape" are used for the description of the phonetic realization of tone in synchronic tonology, while the traditional terms are used for purposes of historical tonology. Although they have been recognized and accepted as part of the received theory of tone in Chinese linguistics, these notions have not been scrutinized in the Chinese linguistics circle for their theoretical roles and empirical implications. The notions remain very much at the descriptive level.

2.4   Wang (1967)

In Chao's numeric representation, the tones are conceived to be single, atomic entities. 53 does not imply that the high falling tone is composed of the high point 5 followed by the mid point 3. Rather, 53 is a unitary high falling tone, and its *yang*-register counterpart, 31, a unitary low falling tone. With the introduction of distinctive features (oppositions) into phonological theory (Trubetzkoy 1969), segments were no longer primitive entities which were not further decomposable. In the framework of generative phonology, as spelled out particularly in the influential work of Chomsky and Halle (1968), segments such as vowels and consonants are conceived to be bundles of features. The work of Wang (1967) is a systematic attempt in this direction. He decomposes tones into seven features. Example (5) is the feature specification of thirteen tones (Wang 1967:97).

(5)   Table of tones and their features

	a	b	c	d	e	f	g	h	i	j	k	l	m
contour	-	-	-	-	-	+	+	+	+	+	+	+	+
high	+	-	+	-	-	+	-	+	-	+	-	+	-
central	-	-	+	+	+	-	-	-	-	-	-	-	-
mid	-	-	-	-	+	-	-	-	-	-	-	-	-
rising	-	-	-	-	-	+	+	-	-	+	+	+	+
falling	-	-	-	-	-	-	-	+	+	+	+	+	+
convex	-	-	-	-	-	-	-	-	-	-	-	+	+

Among the seven features, [high], [central], and [mid] are responsible for pitch levels, and [contour], [rising], [falling], and [convex] give the pitch contours of the thirteen tones. Wang does not postulate the feature [concave]. As can be seen from the table, concave tones are specified as [+rising, +falling, -convex] (5j,k). Since seven features can specify up to 128 distinct tones, excessive ones are trimmed by means of redundancy conventions.

Like the Chao numbers, Wang's feature system generates five distinct pitch levels, but two tones are theoretically possible for each of the [+contour] tones. As the tone table in (5) indicates, the pitch level opposition among the [+contour] tones is that between high and nonhigh. The other two features, [central] and [mid], play no role in defining [+contour] tones. This implies that a tone language can have only two falling tones that are phonologically distinct, and the difference in their pitch levels is high versus non-high. The same is true of the other contour tones. The feature [high] has special status in Wang's system in that it draws the basic distinction in a tone language, at least among the [+contour] tones. This is consistent with the traditional binary grouping of tones into the *yin* (high) and *yang* (low) registers, although the *yin/yang* division extends to all tones in the traditional analysis, not just to contour tones. Since a single [high] feature can specify only two tonal levels, the inclusion of [central] and [mid] is motivated solely by the descriptive need to represent five distinct tonal levels.

The thirteen tones that Wang's system provides are distributed as follows.

(6)   Number of tones in Wang's system
    a. Level tones   5
    b. Rising tones   2
    c. Falling tones   2
    d. Convex tones   2
    e. Concave tones   2

Using Wang's features, the Songjiang non-checked (i.e. non-*ru*) tones can be specified minimally as follows.

(7)   Tonal inventory of Songjiang
        Yin-register
        a. 53   ⌈ +contour ⌉
                                 | +high |
                                 ⌊ +falling ⌋
        b. 44   ⌈ −contour ⌉
                                 | +high |
                                 ⌊ +central ⌋
        c. 35   ⌈ +contour ⌉
                                 | +high |
                                 ⌊ +rising ⌋
        Yang-register
        A. 31   ⌈ +contour ⌉
                                 | −high |
                                 ⌊ +falling ⌋
        B. 22   ⌈ −contour ⌉
                                 | −high |
                                 ⌊ +central ⌋
        C. 13   ⌈ +contour ⌉
                                 | −high |
                                 ⌊ +rising ⌋

The short tones (2d,D) are derived from (7a,A); the shortening can be attributed to the obstruents in syllable coda position.[3]

Two properties may be noted concerning Wang's features. First, as in Chao (1930), up to five distinct pitch levels are made available for any given tone language; however, the theory has no formal device that correlates the pitch levels with the voicing qualities of the initial consonants of the syllables on which the tones are realized. This differs from the traditional analysis, which groups tones into the *yin* and *yang* registers—although, as we have mentioned earlier, Wang's treatment of contour tones bears resemblance to the binary opposition. The *yin/yang* registers in their historical context have a strict correlation with the voicing qualities of the initial consonants. Second, in order to describe the contour tones that exist abundantly in Chinese and other languages of Southeast Asia, Wang's system makes use of temporally dynamic features such as [falling] and [rising] as theoretical primitives. This postulation is necessary in part because the three level features are unstructured, and tones are conceived to be matrices (or vectors) of features lacking in internal organization. If the features were allowed to occur in temporally meaningful sequence at some level of representation, contour features as primitives could be avoided. Theoretically, however, this did not become practicable until several years later, with the advent of autosegmental phonology (cf. Williams 1971; Leben 1973; Goldsmith 1976; McCarthy 1979; Halle and Vergnaud 1980, 1982; and Yip 1980). Wang's system is consonant with the general theoretical temperament of its time. After all, early *SPE*-style generative phonology treated a phoneme as a bundle of features, and an unstructured bundle at that.

2.5   Woo (1969)

The postulation of dynamic features generates a great deal of controversy. The success of describing tonal phenomena of African languages in terms of pitch levels leads one to expect that languages such as Chinese might be analyzed in the same way, and that contour tones (what Woo calls "dynamic tones") in those languages may simply be the result of concatenating two level tones on a single, sufficiently long syllable. For instance, a high level tone followed by a low level tone on the same syllable creates the dynamic contour of falling. This is precisely the approach Woo takes in her analysis of contour tones. But in the kind of linear representation that Woo's theory assumes, tones must be realized on segments, and there can only be one tone per segment. In featural representation, tonal features must be arrayed in the same matrices as the other features that together define the segments. A contour tone on a single syllable therefore requires that the syllable be long. In Woo's theory, contour tones do not occur in short syllables; short syllables have only level tones.

Three features—[high tone], [low tone], and [modify]—are proposed to specify five distinct pitch levels. Contour tones are concatenations of the five level tones. Example (8) displays the feature specification of the level tones (Woo 1969:146); the corresponding Chao numbers are added for clarity.

(8)

	55	44	33	22	11
high tone	+	+	-	-	-
low tone	-	-	-	+	+
modify	-	+	-	+	-

The features in (8) are functionally similar to [high], [central] and [mid] of Wang (1967). Redundancy rules are needed to trim the number of level tones down to five. For comments on Wang's and Woo's features, and a survey of other feature systems not discussed here, see Fromkin (1972, 1974).

What sets Woo's theory apart from Wang's is the treatment of the dynamic aspect of tone. In Wang's system, contour tones are specified in terms of the dynamic features [contour], [fall], and [rise]; the length of the syllable is irrelevant. Woo, by contrast, represents contour tones as concatenations of level tones. Syllable length becomes important in justifying the existence of contour tones. In syllables of the form CV, Woo treats the vowel as a geminate cluster; CV is in effect CVV. This allows a sequence of two level tones to be realized on a single syllable. The claim, as we have noted earlier, is that contour tones can occur in long syllables (either geminate vowels CVV or CVS, where S represents a sonorant other than a vowel), but not on short syllables (Woo 1969:62).

This claim, however, is not empirically supported. In Beijing Mandarin Woo's theory does not appear to be problematic, since the coda of a Beijing Mandarin syllable can only be a nasal or glide. When we consider dialects with syllables ending in obstruents such as /p t k ʔ/, however, we discover a whole range of dynamic tones realized on short syllables. Pingyao is a case in point. This dialect has five tones, as shown in (9) (all Pingyao data are cited from Hou 1980).

(9)   a. 13   pu   "hatch"
       b. 35   pu   "cloth"
       c. 53   pu   "mend"
       d. <u>23</u>   pʌʔ   "push aside"
       e. <u>54</u>   pʌʔ   a musical instrument

The short tones are underlined. In citation form, we see two falling tones, 53 and
<u>54</u>, and three rising tones, 13, 35, and <u>23</u>. The short tones, which are dynamic
(falling in <u>54</u> and rising in <u>23</u>), are realized on syllables ending in glottal stop.
Consider now the following sandhi data.

(10)   a. 13 53 → 31 53
          tɕi t'uæ   "chicken leg"
          sa t'u   "sandy earth"
          ku kuæ   "ankle"
          tɕ'iŋ iəu   "relative"
       b. <u>23</u> 53 → <u>32</u> 53
          sʌʔ k'əu   "mouthpiece for draft animal"
          k'uʌʔ tɕ'i   "start crying"
          xuʌʔ t'iɔ   "mix"
          tsʌʔ pɔ   "tie"
       c. 53 53 → 35 423
          ta tiŋ   "take a nap"
          mæ ɕi   "curry favor"
          tɕ'i ts'ɔ   "in heat"
          ər nzuaŋ   "soft ear"
       d. 53 <u>54</u> → 35 <u>423</u>
          ts'uaŋ niʌʔ   "establish"
          səŋ liʌʔ   "save strength"
          ts'æ yʌʔ   "gather herbs"
       e. <u>54</u> <u>54</u> → <u>45</u> <u>423</u>
          ʂʌʔ miʌʔ   "gather wheat"
          xuʌʔ yʌʔ   "take medication"
          tuʌʔ sʌʔ   "fight for food"
          xuʌʔ iʌʔ   "military service"

The sandhi patterns exemplified in (10a,b) are what Hou (1980) calls Type A
patterns, and those exemplified in (10c,d,e) are Type B patterns. Phrases of the
verb-object or subject-predicate construction exhibit Type A tone sandhi, and
phrases of other syntactic constructions exhibit Type B tone sandhi. The sandhi
patterns in (10) show that the tones <u>23</u> and 13, as well as <u>54</u> and 53, are derived
from the same underlying tones, since they exhibit the same sandhi behavior.
What is of interest to us is the distribution of the short (*ru*) tones. Notice that
more dynamic short tones are generated through sandhi: a fall <u>32</u> (10b) and a
concave <u>423</u> (10d,e). These two tones, as well as 31 and 423, do not occur in
citation forms. I arrange the two series of tones in (11).

(11)   Tones realized on long syllables

13   35   31   53   423

Tones realized on short syllables

<u>23</u>   <u>45</u>   <u>32</u>   <u>54</u>   <u>423</u>

The contour in dynamic tones tends to level off when realized on short syllables, except for the concave <u>423</u>, of which the concavity remains the same when realized on both types of syllable, if the numerals are to be taken seriously. As for the rising and falling tones, the contour does not level off completely. Detailed analysis of Pingyao tone sandhi will be presented in section 3.3.2.1. Here, it is sufficient to point out that the two series of tones in (11) present a problem for Woo's theory, which predicts that dynamic tones cannot occur on short syllables. The contour of a tone is in fact not directly related to the length of the tone-bearing unit.

Another problem for Woo's treatment of dynamic tones has to do with the interaction between the voicing qualities of syllable-initial consonants and the pitch height of tones. Consider the two falling tones of Songjiang 53 versus 31 (cf. (2)). In Woo's theory the two tones can be represented as in (12).

(12)   a. 53   C V V
                    | |
                    H M

         b. 31   C V V
                    | |
                    M L

In Songjiang, 53 and 31 are in complementary distribution: 53 occurs with voiceless consonants in syllable-initial position, whereas 31 occurs with voiced consonants. Suppose that 53 is the underlying tone. Voicing depresses the tone's pitch height (the register) without changing its dynamic aspect. Both tones are falling in contour. This fact cannot be captured in Woo's model because the voicing of syllable-initial consonants influences not only the pitch of the adjacent H, but also the pitch of the nonadjacent M, as shown in (13).

(13)   C   V V   (surface: C   V V)
             | | | | | |
          [+voice] H M   [+voice] M L

To derive 31 within Woo's model, the syllable-initial consonant voicing must condition the H→M sandhi and the M→L sandhi simultaneously. In Halle and Stevens (1971), voiced consonants and low pitch are both specified as [-stiff]. The phenomenon illustrated in (13) is a case of assimilation. If we treat the assimilation as a single process, then the M→L alternation violates the locality requirement on phonological rules (McCarthy 1989, McCarthy and Prince 1997).

To avoid violating the locality condition, we have to account for the phenomenon as a case of "domino" effect: the voicing of the consonants lowers the pitch of the adjacent H, which in turn lowers the pitch of the adjacent M. This account is counterintuitive. The phenomenon is a simple case of tonal assimilation; a two-step analysis complicates the matter.

We conclude that Woo's theory is inadequate to explain the distribution of contour tones, and the interaction between the voicing of syllable-initial consonants and the pitch of tones. The facts discussed here will present a serious challenge to any theory that correlates tone with the length of the tone-bearing unit.

2.6   Halle and Stevens (1971)

Halle and Stevens (1971) propose a set of binary features to characterize the laryngeal effects in speech sounds, which include voicing and pitch. Two properties of the Halle-Stevens features need to be emphasized, since they play a crucial role in the theory of tone to be developed in Chapter 3. The Halle-Stevens system is articulatory in nature, unlike most work on tone features. The features they posit do not describe auditory impressions of pitch, but rather provide articulatory instructions to the relevant articulators for the actualization of pitch (i.e. tone). This view of the laryngeal features follows the general thrust of distinctive feature theories developed in Jakobson, Fant, and Halle (1952), and especially in Chomsky and Halle (1968).

The second important property of the Halle-Stevens system is that it treats voicing in consonants and pitch in vowels as featurally the same phenomenon. The tonal features proposed in various theories lack a phonetic basis, partly because the phonetic mechanism of pitch control is poorly understood (see, for example, Ladefoged 1973; Maddieson 1974; Fujimura 1977, 1981; Ohala 1972, 1977; Stevens 1977, 1981; and Sawashima and Hirose 1983). Despite the fact that many factors are involved in pitch regulation, there is strong linguistic evidence, both synchronic and diachronic, to show that the voicing of a consonant and the pitch of the following vowel are correlated. This is demonstrated not only in Chinese dialects but in many other tone languages of Asia as well (see K. Chang 1953, 1975; Haudricourt 1954; and Matisoff 1973). This correlation is not captured in a theory that makes use of tonal features unrelated to voicing. The Halle-Stevens system captures this correlation by using the same set of laryngeal features for both vowel pitch and consonant voicing. In other words, the laryngeal musculature whose activities lead to voicing in consonants is also responsible for pitch in vowels. Vowel pitch and consonant voicing are thus the same laryngeal phenomenon (but see critical discussions in Ladefoged 1973 and Gandour 1974).

The four laryngeal features that Halle and Stevens (1971) propose are based on two independently controllable parameters—the stiffness of the vocal cords and the degree of glottal opening. The parameters are controlled by intrinsic laryngeal muscles. The description of the features is as follows.

1. *Spread glottis.* By rotation and displacement of the arytenoid cartilages, the vocal cords can be displaced outward relative to their positions for normal voicing, leaving a large glottal width. If the vocal-cord stiffness is sufficiently large, the combination of wide glottis and stiff glottal walls inhibits vocal-cord vibration. On the other hand, slackening of the glottal walls by reducing the stiffness can lead to a condition in which vocal-cord vibration will occur, even with a relatively wide glottal opening.

2. *Constricted glottis.* Adduction of the arytenoid cartilages relative to the position for normal voicing (accomplished, perhaps, by fibers of the thyro-arytenoid muscles, as well as by the lateral cricoarytenoid muscles) can cause the vocal cords to be pressed together and the glottis to narrow or to close. When the vocal-cord stiffness is large in this situation, vocal-cord vibration does not occur, and no air passes through the glottis. For a lower coupling stiffness, vocal-cord vibration can be initiated, probably with relatively narrow, peaked pulses.

3. *Stiff vocal cords.* Increasing the stiffness of the vocal cords makes the coupling between upper and lower edges of the vocal cords larger. Stiffening of the vocal cords affects glottal vibration, regardless of the size of the glottal aperture. When the vocal cords are in a configuration for normal voicing (neither spread nor constricted), the rate of vocal-cord vibrations increases with increasing stiffness. Increased stiffness of the vocal cords will inhibit vocal-cord vibration under the following circumstances: (a) when an obstruction in the vocal tract causes the intraoral pressure to build up and hence the pressure across the glottis to decrease; (b) when the glottis is spread to cause a wide aperture or when it is constricted. Thus an increased stiffness of the vocal cords tends to narrow the range of transglottal pressures and glottal apertures over which vocal-cord vibration occurs.

4. *Slack vocal cords.* The vocal cords can be made more slack by decreasing the coupling between upper and lower edges of the vocal cords. This is probably accomplished by a decrease in the tension of the vocal cords, as well as by a decreased stiffness of the walls of the glottis. Slackness of the vocal cords can allow glottal vibration to occur even with a spread or constricted glottis. When the vocal cords are slackened, there is a decrease in the frequency of glottal vibration. (201–202)

Two laryngeal features, [stiff vocal cords] and [slack vocal cords] (henceforth [stiff] and [slack]) are primarily responsible for the pitch of vowels and the voicing of consonants. The two vocal cord features define three states of vocal cord tension; their effects on obstruents and vowels are listed below. The more common feature [voice] is added for comparison.

(14)

		M	L	H
Vowels				
Obstruents		b_1	b	p
Stiff		-	-	+
Slack		-	+	-
Voice			+	-

Halle and Stevens rule out the feature combination [+stiff] and [+slack] on logical and physiological grounds, claiming that the vocal cords can not be both stiff and slack at the same time. Notice that voiced obstruents have the same laryngeal feature matrices as low-pitched vowels, and voiceless obstruents have the same laryngeal feature matrices as high-pitched vowels. This readily accounts for the lowering effect of voiced consonants on the pitch of the following vowel that is found in many tone languages.

The two features [stiff] and [slack] allow three distinct vocal cord states, which correspond to three distinct pitch levels. A common criticism of the Halle-Stevens system is that it provides only three pitch levels, which is not sufficient (Fromkin 1972, Ladefoged 1973, Anderson 1978, and Yip 1980). In Chapter 3, I will reinterpret the features [stiff] and [slack] as features that are independently controllable, so that the feature combination [+stiff] and [+slack] is permissible. A total of four pitch levels is specified with two features [stiff] and [slack]. Under this interpretation, the two laryngeal features would be functionally equivalent to the features [upper] and [raised] proposed in Yip (1980), which I discuss in the next section.

2.7   Yip (1980)

The two systems of tonal representation we have reviewed here, Wang (1967) and Woo (1969), are representative of the work in this area, particularly with respect to the treatment of dynamic tones. Since Chao (1930), linguists have appeared to agree that any feature system must be capable of providing at least five distinct levels to be descriptively adequate. This necessitates the postulation of at least three features, with excessive tonal specifications to be trimmed by redundancy rules or conventions. True to the theoretical spirit of early generative phonology, the three level features, [high], [central], and [mid] in Wang's theory, and [high tone], [low tone], and [modify] in Woo's theory, are arranged into matrices, and there is no internal structure among the features. In this regard, Yip (1980) represents a significant theoretical departure in the number of features postulated (two) and their relationship (one dependent on the other).

Yip's work must be understood against the theoretical background of auto-segmental phonology with its vastly enriched phonological representation. The meager, single-tiered representation of early generative phonology gives way to multi-tiered representation with intricate internal structure. Tones are viewed as independent entities on a tier separate from that of the tone-bearing units, and the two tiers are linked by means of the universal association conventions. Early work in autosegmental phonology drew its data mainly from African languages, whose tonology, according to Pike (1948), is typologically different from that of Asian languages. Yip (1980) draws most of the data from Chinese; as such, it represents a valuable contribution to the development of autosegmental phonology.

In Yip's theory, a tone is not an indivisible entity in phonological represent-ation. Rather, it consists of two parts, Register and Tone. Register indicates the imagined band of pitch in which a tone is realized, and Tone specifies the way the tone behaves over the duration of the tone-bearing unit. These two features are to be interpreted in autosegmental terms; in other words, they do not form a "simultaneous" bundle that defines the tone, in the classic *SPE* sense. Rather, they are conceived as autosegments that occupy their own levels in the phonological representation. Through their interaction, four pitch levels are possible (Yip 1980:196),[4] as shown in (15).

(15)   Register   Tone

	+upper		+raised
			-raised
	-upper		+raised
			-raised

Yip's theory is innovative in two ways. First, the two features play different theoretical roles. The Register feature first splits the entire pitch range into two halves, each of which is in turn subdivided by the feature [raised]. Although both [upper] and [raised] are binary features that bisect a certain pitch range, the operation of [raised] depends on [upper]. In Yip's (1980:196) terms, the Register feature is "dominant" over the Tone feature.

Second, the two features are distinct autosegments associated with a single tone-bearing unit (TBU). The relationship between the TBU and Register is one-to-one, and that between the TBU and Tone is one-to-many. In other words, the Tone feature can occur in sequences of two (or possibly more) that are associated with a single TBU, but the Register feature cannot. The sequence of the Tone features gives rise to the contour of the tone. The relationship among Register, Tone, and TBU is illustrated in the representations of a high falling tone and a high rising tone in (16).

(16)   a. High fall

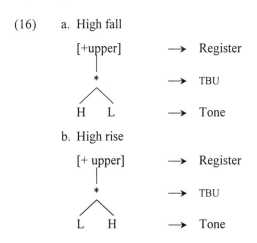

    [+upper]   ⟶   Register

       *   ⟶   TBU

    H   L   ⟶   Tone

    b. High rise

    [+ upper]   ⟶   Register

       *   ⟶   TBU

    L   H   ⟶   Tone

Here, H are L are [+raised] and [-raised], respectively. The two pitch registers specified by the feature [upper] can be seen as functionally equivalent to the *yin* and *yang* registers we have discussed earlier. In Yip's theory, these notions of traditional Chinese philology are reinterpreted and accorded a position of theoretical importance. This move is significant in light of the fact that the *yin/yang* registers play no role in most contemporary theories of tone—either the number notations of Chao (1930), or the feature theories of Wang (1967) and Woo (1969).

Since the sequence of the Tone features gives the tone its contour, Yip's feature system makes the claim that the contour of a tone is relativized to its pitch register. The register itself, in Yip's words, "remains constant over the morpheme" (1980:196). Languages that contain 51 and 15 as contrastive tones are rare. Typically, among Chinese dialects that have two contrastive falling or rising tones, we find 53 (or 42) in opposition to 31. Given sufficient idealization, the high variant is in the *yin* register, and the low variant is in the *yang* register.[5]

Yip's system is highly restrictive. The representation of contours as sequences of specifications of the feature [raised] puts an upper limit on the number of contours that can be created. In the unmarked case, contours are restricted to the register specified by [upper]. In all, Yip's theory gives twelve tones, as shown in (17).

(17)   a. Level   [+upper, H]   [-upper, H]
                        [+upper, L]   [-upper, L]
        b. Rising   [+upper, LH]   [-upper, LH]
        c. Falling   [+upper, HL]   [-upper, HL]
        d. Concave   [+upper, HLH]   [-upper, HLH]
        e. Convex   [+upper, LHL]   [-upper, LHL]

Yip's position on the concave and convex tones is not clearly spelled out. In her analysis of Fuzhou, the tone 242 is represented as [+upper, LHL] (Yip 1980:341), so at least she allows sequences of three Tone feature specifications. It may be observed that no language contains tones with pitch contours more complex than convexity or concavity. This is explicit in Wang's (1967) feature system, which is incapable of featurally specifying a fall-rise-fall-rise contour. Such contours are theoretically possible in Woo's (1969) theory; since contour tones are represented as sequences of level tones, the sequence HLHL, all associated with one sufficiently long syllable, is expected to occur. The same is true of Yip's (1980) theory, in which the Tone feature sequence of HLHL is possible. To avoid over-generation, Yip's system needs the following stipulation.

(18)   The maximum number of Tone feature occurrences in sequence is three.

This stipulation allows concave tones such as [+upper, LHL], but it rules out non-occurring tones such as [+upper, LHLH] and [+upper, HLHL], as well as even more complex ones.

By now the differences and similarities between Yip's theory and that of Woo (1969) should be clear. In terms of the tonal inventory generated, a major difference between Yip's system and that of Woo's lies in the number of possible level tones. Yip's system can generate four distinct level tones, whereas Woo's system generates five. The representations of contour are similar in that neither theory makes use of primitive contour features, and both theories represent contours as clusters. In Woo's model, the clusters consist of feature matrices; in Yip's model, they consist of sequences of the feature [raised] on the Tone tier. The two representations of the high falling tone in (19) illustrate this point (* is the tone-bearing unit).

(19)   a. Woo's Representation

       b. Yip's Representation

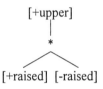

2.8   Clements (1983)

In the feature systems surveyed so far, tones are specified by binary features. Clements's theory provides for multiple tone heights without the express use of binary features. Recall that in Yip's theory the two features [upper] and [raised] bisect their respective pitch scales. The feature [upper] is dominant in that it divides the pitch into two registers, which are then further divided by the feature [raised] into two sub-registers. The feature [raised] is dependent on the feature [upper]. In Clements's (1983) theory of tone hierarchy, the dominance relationship between the two features is made explicit and encoded in the notion of rows. Clements defines tones as "tonal matrices which consist of ordered rows of the elements *h*, *l*, or 0" (1983:150). The element *h* is relatively high pitch, and the element *l* relatively low pitch. The exact number of rows is dependent on the tonal inventories of individual languages, and, theoretically, it is limited only by human perception. Two-level, three-level, and four-level tone systems are specified as follows.

(20)   a. Two-level system

	H	L
row 1	h	l

b. Three-level system

	H	M	L
row 1	h	l	l
row 2		h	l

c. Four-level system

	H	HM	M	L
row 1	h	h	l	l
row 2	h	l	h	l

In (20b), the low register is further divided into two row 2 pitches, which Clements considers as the unmarked case. This expresses the fact that the primary opposition among tones is that between high tones (H) and non-high tones (M and L). Note that in a four-level system (20c), Clements's system is identical to Yip's: row 1 features correspond to Yip's [upper], and row 2 features correspond to Yip's [raised]. Thus, H in (20c) is equivalent to [+upper, +raised], HM to [+upper, -raised], M to [-upper, +raised], and L to [-upper, -raised], which is lowest on the pitch scale. Despite the ready correspondence, there are major conceptual differences between Yip's features and Clements's rows. I will have more to say on the notion of row shortly.

In Clements (1989), the tonal matrices are represented in a tree notation in which occurrences of *h* and *l* on each row are linked to a class node called the "tonal node." The four-level system in (20c) has the tree structure shown in (21):

(21)   tonal node   a. *   b. *   c. *   d. *

        row 1   h   h   l   l

        row 2   h   l   h   l

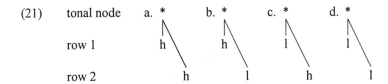

The tree notation captures an often-observed fact of tone sandhi: the features that define tones spread as a unit. If row 1 occurrences of *h/l* and row 2 occurrences of *h/l* are not linked to a single tonal node, tone spreading would have to be expressed as the simultaneous spreading of row 1 and row 2 occurrences of *h/l*. This is also a consequence of Yip's (1980) theory. In Yip (1980), [upper] and [raised] are two independent autosegments associated with a single tone-bearing unit (TBU). This structure runs into difficulty in accounting for the facts of tone spreading. The difficulty does not arise in a representation such as that in (21), where the two rows (or [upper] and [raised] features) are sister nodes under the tonal nodes.

The tree notation is not merely a notational variant of the matrix notation first proposed in Clements (1983). Compare the representations of a four-level system in (20c) and (21). In (20c), row 1 dominates row 2 within the tonal matrices. The matrices are linked to the TBUs, not the individual rows that make up the matrices. In (21), the two rows stand in a sisterhood relationship under the tonal node, which is linked to TBUs.

One important feature of Clements's theory needs to be emphasized. Although the elements *h* and *l* can be characterized in terms of a single binary feature—for example, [+high] for *h* and [-high] for *l*—the organization of the rows is hierarchical. The occurrence of *h* and *l* on row *n* depends on the occurrence of *h* and *l* on row *n–1*. In other words, the structure in (22a) below is interpretable, but (22b) is not, whether it is underlying or generated by rule.

(22)   a. tonal node   *

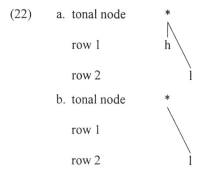

The representation of tone heights in terms of feature trees makes it difficult to interpret the hierarchical property of rows. There are three areas where the hierarchy of rows may meet with difficulty. First, in the tree structure in (21), row 1 elements of *h* and *l* technically do not dominate row 2 elements of *h* and *l* in the tree-theoretic sense. However, row 1 is dominant because it is "higher" on the hierarchy than row 2. Tree structures are ordinarily not able to express Clements's notion of rows. Second, no other phonological features are hierarchical in this manner, which makes tone features special within a general theory of features. With the notion of rows, tone features are in effect multi-valued, while features in general are binary. Finally, features can spread. Given the representation in (21), we expect row *n+1* elements to spread independently of row *n* elements. However, if row *n* elements spread to an adjacent tonal node, does the spreading carry row *n+1* elements? The answer to this question is a bit tricky. On the one hand, if row *n* and row *n+1* are sister nodes under the tonal node, the elements on the two rows are independent of each other. Therefore, row *n+1* elements are not expected to spread with row *n* elements. On the other hand, row *n* elements are conceptually dominant over row *n+1* elements on the pitch hierarchy. We would expect row *n+1* elements to spread along with row *n* elements, which contradicts our earlier conclusion. The tree representation of tone heights and the hierarchical nature of rows are thus incompatible.

Conceptual and empirical problems notwithstanding, the tree representation of features underscores an important insight into the organization of tonal features. Features have internal structure, as various works on segmental features have shown (for example, Halle 1983, 1989, 1992, 1995; Clements 1985; Sagey 1986; Steriade 1986; McCarthy 1989; Goldsmith 1990; and Kenstowicz 1993). The tree in (21) provides a structured model of tones. In Chapter 3, we will use the tree notation to organize the tonal features. The features, however, are strictly binary, and the row hierarchy is abandoned.

2.9   Hyman (1986)

The representation of tones as matrices of tonal features is a common practice in many works on tone, such as Wang (1967), Woo (1969), and Clements (1983), reviewed above. One disadvantage of matrix representation is that we are unable to account for partial assimilation as the spreading of a component tonal feature. As a result, theories that make use of matrices have an inherent weakness—a weakness that led to the development of autosegmental phonology in the first place. Hyman (1986) departs from this practice. He postulates a single tone feature T, which means "effect a tone modification" (Hyman 1986:115). The positive value of T (represented as H) effects an upward change of one step; the negative value (represented as L) effects a downward change of one step. The feature is arranged hierarchically, as in Clements (1983, 1989), except that in Hyman's theory, the hierarchical relationship is expressed as dominance on a tree structure. The notion of ordered rows in a matrix is replaced with multiple tiers filled with occurrences of the tone feature T. A four-level system would have the structures shown in (23).

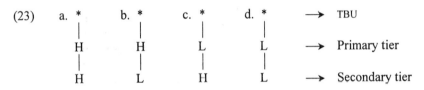

(23)   a. *   b. *   c. *   d. *   →   TBU

          H   H   L   L   →   Primary tier

          H   L   H   L   →   Secondary tier

Note that H is [+T] and L is [-T]. In the structures in (23), * is the tone-bearing unit; the tier that is directly linked to TBUs is the primary tier; and the H and L elements on the primary tier are primary Hs and Ls. The tier dominated by the primary tier is the secondary tier, made up of secondary Hs and Ls. The number of tiers required apparently depends on the tonal system of the language in question.

  The advantage of Hyman's representation over Clements's (1983) matrix representation is that it enables us to express the spreading of secondary Hs/Ls, as shown in (24).

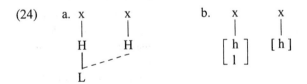

(24)   a. x   x   b. x   x

          H   H $\begin{bmatrix} h \\ l \end{bmatrix}$ [h]
          L- - - -
          L

In (24a), the spreading of L to the neighboring H produces the structure of a downstepped H. The *h* and *l* elements in Clements's theory are functionally equivalent to Hs and Ls in Hyman's. However, the element *l* in (24b) cannot spread to the following tone because it is bound to the feature matrix of the preceding tone. Note that the spreading of primary H/L—that is, the entire feature specification of a tone—can be expressed in both representations. To the extent that empirical evidence of secondary H/L spreading is attested, as in downstep, downdrift, and the so-called "depressor effect" (cf. Laughren 1984), Hyman's tier representation is superior to the matrix representation. This model of tone is, however, abandoned in Hyman (1993), discussed in section 2.12.

2.10 Shih (1986)

The central theme of Shih's (1986) work is the prosodic nature of tone sandhi, rather than the feature representation of tone per se. How tones are represented is related to the theoretical account of their prosodic behavior. Therefore, a prosodic theory of tone must also address the issue of tonal representation. Exactly how Shih represents tone is not entirely clear to me, and I will try to piece together an account that would be consistent with her analysis of the prosody of tone sandhi.

Shih adopts the register feature [upper] of Yip (1980) but rejects the Tone feature and its sequential properties. In this regard, she seems to favor the "unitary" approach, meaning that contour tones are non-decomposable units, rather than combinations of level tones as in Woo's theory, or sequences of the Tone feature [raised] as proposed in Yip (1980). This is at least implicit in the "hierarchically organized system" in (25) (Shih 1986:24).

(25)

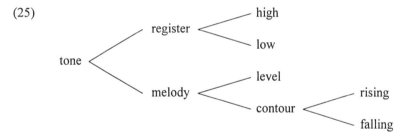

The terminal labels, *high, low, level, rising,* and *falling,* are reminiscent of Wang's (1967) features. If I read Shih correctly, this hierarchy postulates pitch contours as part of the theory; as such, (25) appears to impose some organizational structure on the features of Wang (1967), particularly the contour features. While Wang's features can specify five distinct pitch levels, the tone hierarchy is able to specify only two level tones. No convex or concave tones occur on the hierarchy.

But this hierarchy appears to play no theoretical role in Shih's account of tone sandhi phenomena. She cautions that features like register and contour are not primitive features, but "meta-" or "macro-features." The difference between features and macro-features, however, is not explained. In formulating rules for the Zhangping bisyllabic tone sandhi, the macro-features are used in the same way other tone features are used. To see this, consider the Zhangping bisyllabic tone sandhi facts in (26), along with the rules in (27) (Z.-X. Zhang 1982:267, Shih 1986:24).

(26)   Zhangping tone sandhi

a.

$$
\left\{ \begin{array}{c} 24 \\ 11 \\ 21 \\ 55 \end{array} \right\} \rightarrow
\left\{ \begin{array}{l}
33 \; / \; \_ \left\{ \begin{array}{c} 24 \\ 11 \\ 55 \\ 53 \end{array} \right\} \\[2em]
55 \; / \; \_ \left\{ \begin{array}{c} 31 \\ 21 \end{array} \right\}
\end{array} \right.
$$

b. $\left\{ \begin{array}{c} 31 \\ 53 \end{array} \right\} \rightarrow 21 \; / \; \_ \; X$

(27)   Tone sandhi rules

a. [-fall] $\rightarrow$ $\left[\begin{array}{c} +\alpha\text{mid} \\ +\text{level} \\ -\text{low} \end{array} \right]$ / $\_$ [-αmid]

b. [+fall] $\rightarrow$ [+low] / $\_$ X

(27a) accounts for the facts in (26a), and (27b) for those in (26b). We are concerned not with the sandhi facts but with the rules that account for them. The rules make specific reference to features that occur on the tone hierarchy, such as [fall], [low], and [level], as well as features that do not occur, such as [mid]. Notice that the use of [low] in the two rules suggests that it is used as a feature which, with [high], defines tonal pitch. If so, it would appear that, contrary to her claim, Shih's conception of register is not the same as that of Yip (1980) at all. Recall that in Yip's system, the Register feature [upper] defines only two pitch registers. The two features [high] and [low] in (25) are capable of defining three distinct pitch registers (assuming that the feature combination [+high, +low] is logically ruled out), giving rise to three level tones, and three distinct contour tones as well. In this regard, Shih's theory differs not only from Yip's but also from the theories of Wang (1967) and Woo (1969). Shih is not explicit about the roles of (25) in the specification of tones; it is therefore difficult to investigate its empirical consequences.

2.11 Inkelas (1987)

Research in nonlinear phonology in the 1980s and early 1990s shifted its focus from the planar structure of phonological representation to the internal organization of phonological features. Most work in this area, stimulated by the pioneering work of Clements (1985) and Sagey (1986), has been concerned with the geometry of supralaryngeal features. Inkelas (1987)—along with Snider (1988, 1990) and Yip (1989), to be discussed in sections 2.12 and 2.15 respectively—is among the first serious attempts to provide a structured model of tone features.

In early work on tone within the autosegmental framework, tones, specified by tonal features such as [high tone], are mapped onto tone-bearing units directly. Tone is a unitary object, arrayed on a single tier in the phonological representation. Yip (1980) proposes a two-tiered approach, representing Register and Tone on separate tiers. Tone is now treated as a composite object, arising from the interaction of the two features Register and Tone, which are mapped onto the same tone-bearing unit. Inkelas (1987) further develops this idea and articulates a model which contains two tiers of the same tone feature linked to a tonal node tier, which is mapped onto the tone-bearing unit, here the skeletal tier. The model is shown below (Inkelas 1987:223).

(28)
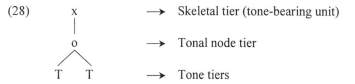

Conceptually, Inkelas's model follows in the tradition of Africanist tonological work. The tone tiers are specified with elements such as H and L, which can be specified with binary features such as [high], or with Hyman's (1986) feature [T]. Although the two tone tiers bear the same features, they can play different roles in pitch-changing processes such as downstep and downdrift, which Hyman (1986) treats as the result of lowering the H on one tier by the presence of an L on another tier (see section 2.9). In fact, the tone model in (28) is similar to Hyman's (1986), except for the presence of the additional tonal node tier, which serves as a class node that "organizes" the two tone tiers. This is a major difference, however. In Hyman's model, the primary Hs and Ls spread with the secondary Hs and Ls, whereas for Inkelas, the two tiers can spread independently.

Inkelas (1987) does not address the issue of contour tones explicitly. Yip (1980) differentiates the Register feature from the Tone feature, and a contour tone is represented by the branching structure of the Tone feature [raised]. Since Inkelas (1987) does not differentiate the two tone tiers, it is not clear how the two-tiered model can accommodate tonal contours internal to the tonal node tier. Certainly, a cluster analysis is possible, in which two or more tonal nodes are associated with a single tone-bearing unit. The high falling tone, for example, would have the structure below.

(29)
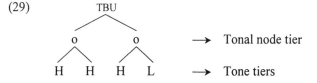

HH defines an H, and HL defines a possible M tone. This representation of the fall contour is quite cumbersome, however, and it will run into difficulty in dealing with languages with rich tonal contours.

2.12   Hyman (1993)

The theory proposed in Hyman (1993) differs markedly from that of his 1986 study discussed in section 2.9. Hyman (1993:2) proposes the two tone features defined below:

(30)   Tone features
         H = at or above a neutral tone height
         L = at or below a neutral tone height

The neutral reference tone height is the Mid (M) pitch. The features are related to one another in the tone geometry shown in (31).

(31)   TBU

         Tonal root node (TRN)

         Tonal node (TN)

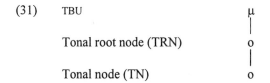

The features H and L are linked to the TN, which is optionally branching. The sequences LH and HL merge to define M. The system therefore generates three level tones, as illustrated in (32).

(32)   a.   b.   c.

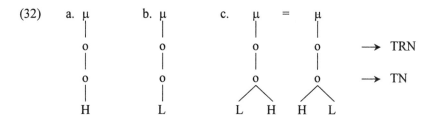

Contour tones are represented as concatenations of level tones. The rising and falling tones have the structures shown in (33).

(33)   a.   b.

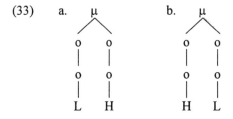

The tonal geometry in (31) is augmented further by what Hyman calls the "R-plane" (the register plane). The features that link to the TNs form the "T-plane" (the tonal plane). The register plane is specified by the two tone features H and L, plus a zero value. In all, a total of nine levels can be generated, as (34) shows.

(34) T-plane: H L LH H L LH H L LH

R-plane: 0 0 0 H L LH H L LH

Tone: H L M ᴴ ᴸ ᴹ ꜛH ꜛL ꜛM

Within the tonal geometry, the register-plane features are linked to the TRNs. The model thus allows three types of structure, shown in (35).

(35) a. b. c.

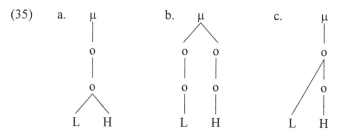

(35a) defines an M tone; (35b), a rising tone; and (35c), a downstep. Since the register feature links to the TRN, Hyman's model differs from that of Yip (1989), in which the register *is* the TRN (see section 2.13). But the notion of register in Hyman's work differs from that in Yip's in two respects. First, in Yip's model, the register feature is binary, and therefore there are only two registers: high ([+upper]) or low ([-upper]). A zero-valued register is not permissible featurally and geometrically: the structure in which a sequence of [raised] specifications ([+raised] or [-raised]) is dominated by 0 register is not interpretable.

Second, in Yip's model, the high register, which is dominant over the sequence [-raised] [+raised], defines a high rising tone. In other words, the register is a relevant geometrical property not only of level tones but also of contour tones. For instance, Yip's model captures the alternation of 53/31 in Songjiang (cf. (2)) as follows:

(36) a. High fall 53

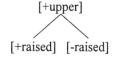

b. Low fall 31

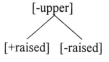

The two falling tones, 53 and 31, alternate on their registers. In Hyman's model, however, contour tones cannot in principle alternate on the register, as the structures in (37) show.

(37)   a.   b.

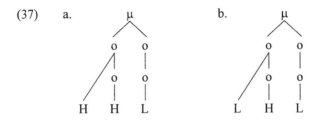

(37a) is the structure of an upstepped H followed by an L; (37b) is the structure of a downstepped H followed by an L. The register does not affect the second TRN in either structure. The tones 53 and 31 may best be represented in Hyman's model as HM and ML respectively. But these representations do not reflect the fact that 53 and 31 alternate on the register conditioned by syllable-initial voicing, nor the fact that the differential between the start and end points of the tones—the tone's slope over time—remains constant while the register changes. This difficulty is not unique to Hyman's theory; any cluster model of contour tones will have difficulty accounting for the interaction between syllable-initial consonants and tones on the following vowels (see section 2.5).

2.13 Yip (1989)

The model that Yip (1989) proposes for contour tones parallels the structure of affricates argued for by Sagey (1986). Sagey's representation of affricates makes use of a sequence of the manner-of-articulation feature [continuant] ([cont]) associated with a single root node, as in (38).

(38)   root

           [-cont]   [+cont]

The branching [cont] feature is interpreted linearly along the temporal dimension. This model captures the intuition that affricates involve a change in the state of continuancy: they start as stops ([-cont]) and end as fricatives ([+cont]). Similarly, contour tones can be seen as resulting from a change in pitch during the temporal span of the tone-bearing units on which the tones are realized. Using the two features [upper] and [raised] of Yip (1980) and Pulleyblank (1986), Yip proposes that the register feature [upper] be the tonal root node, which dominates a possibly branching [raised]. The structure of tone is shown in (39a), and the structure of the high falling tone in (39b).

(39)   a.   σ   b.   σ   ⟶   Tone-bearing unit

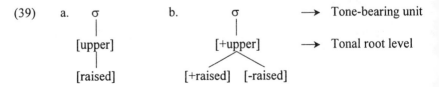

This use of the feature [upper], however, differs from that of Sagey (1986) and Halle (1989), among others. In the works cited, terminal nodes are features. Non-terminal nodes such as Place are articulators. Articulator nodes dominate features that represent the articulatory behavior of the articulators. Features, therefore, do not dominate other features. In this regard, Yip's model is similar to Hyman's model shown in (23), in which the terminal node of T on the primary tier dominates another terminal node on the secondary tier. In terms of the representation of tones, (39) differs from Yip's earlier treatment of contour tones in that the register feature [upper] and the Tone feature [raised] now form a single melodic unit, which is associated with a TBU. In Yip (1980), the register and Tone are considered two distinct autosegments associated with a single TBU; see section 2.7.

Although the diagrams of Yip's model and Inkelas's (1987) model look deceptively similar, there is an important difference between the two. This has to do with the representation of tonal contour. In Yip's model, tonal contour is represented through the branching of the [raised] tiers. The two tiers are nevertheless "inside" the tonal root node. In Inkelas's model, as we have seen in section 2.11, tonal contour can be represented only through the concatenation of two tonal root nodes on the same tone-bearing unit, "external" to the overall structure of tone. We will see the empirical consequences of this difference throughout the present work, and we will show that it is crucial that contour be an integral part of tone.

2.14   Duanmu (1990, 1994)

Duanmu (1990) covers a wide range of topics, including discussions of tone and tone-bearing units in Chinese. An expanded treatment of tonal contour is found in Duanmu (1994).

The structure of tone Duanmu (1990:98) proposes is shown below, where V/R stands for voicing/register.

(40)

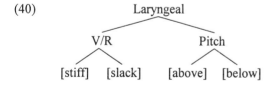

The V/R node specifies the register in tones, and voicing in consonants. The Pitch node modifies the pitch of a tone within each of the three registers that are made possible by the two features [stiff] and [slack]. The model allows a total of nine distinct levels of pitch contrast. In this respect, it differs from the tonal models proposed by Yip (1980, 1989), Inkelas (1987), and Bao (1990b).

Duanmu (1990) makes two related claims, which are further defended in Duanmu (1994). One claim is that the syllable in all Chinese dialects has three x-slots, as shown in (41).

(41)

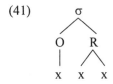

Furthermore, each x-slot dominated by the rime node R corresponds to one mora. So, in effect, all Chinese syllables are bimoraic. The facts Duanmu (1990) adduces to support the claim include rime inventories, rime changes, language games, and co-occurrence restrictions. However, these types of data do not provide conclusive evidence. For example, rime inventories presented in Chinese linguistics do not shed light on the internal structure of the syllable at all. In fact, many studies, including Luo and Wang (1981), Y.-H. Lin (1988, 1989), and Bao (1990a, 1995), show quite convincingly that Chinese dialects do not share the same syllable structure. Moreover, no attested phonological process in Chinese is sensitive to syllabic weight.

The second claim Duanmu (1990, 1994) makes has to do with the formal representation of complex segments, among them affricates and contour tones. Recall that in Sagey's geometry of features, affricates are represented with a branching structure of [continuant], and in Yip's (1980, 1989) theory of tone, contour tones are represented with a branching structure of [raised]. Duanmu argues against such representations. He stipulates the *No Contour Principle*, stated below (Duanmu 1990:14).

(42)   *The No Contour Principle*

This stipulation is defended at length in Duanmu (1990, 1994). Because of this stipulation, Duanmu is forced to represent contour tones as concatenations of level tones. The same set of problems that were encountered with Woo's (1969) theory (see section 2.5) challenge Duanmu's with equal force.

The two claims are related. In Chinese, since each syllable is exactly two moras in length, a fall or rise is created if different tones are mapped onto the moras of the same syllable. Even, falling, and rising tones have the structures shown below.

(43)   a. Even   σ   b. Rise   σ   b. Fall   σ

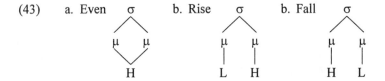

The elements H and L are defined in terms of the features shown in (40). In other words, in Chinese, moras—not syllables—are the tone-bearing units, and tone

mapping is strictly one-to-one: there can be no more than one tone mapped onto one mora.

There are many technical problems with Duanmu's approach; we will mention only two here. The first problem is the treatment of *ru* tones. The *ru* syllables end in voiceless stops and are shorter than other, non-*ru* syllables. Consequently, many of the *ru* tones are short, and their contour tends to be even. Duanmu stipulates that the voiceless stops in coda position, though they carry one mora, cannot bear tone. This means that *ru* syllables cannot have contour tones. This prediction is false, as we have seen in our discussion of Woo (1969) in section 2.5.

The second problem has to do with concave and convex tones, which have the forms HLH and LHL respectively (or other combinations of tones with different pitch levels, such as HMH or LML). If we stipulate that a syllable has only two moras, concave and convex tones are not possible. Duanmu (1990:154) says that syllables with concave and convex tones are extra long; in other words, they are tri-moraic. This treatment is ad hoc. Empirically, it is also false. Across Chinese dialects, not only do concave and convex tones occur as freely as other tones within phrases, they can also occur on *ru* syllables, as in the Mandarin dialect of Pingyao, which we first saw in section 2.5. Even in Beijing Mandarin, the concave 214 (the third tone) occurs freely, contrary to the claims of Duanmu (1990:154). In Wu's (1984) study of tri-syllabic tone patterns of Beijing Mandarin, 214 occurs phrase-initially (44a), phrase-medially (44b), and phrase-finally (44c).

(44) a. tu-di miao   "temple of Earth"
         earth temple
         214-51 51 → 214-LT 51
      b. xun   nu-xu   "to look for son-in-law"
         look-for son-in-law
         35 214-51 → 35 214-LT
      c. sheng   mei-zhan   "provincial arts exhibition"
         province arts-exhibition
         214 214-214 → 21 35-214

In the data, LT marks the light tone, which many scholars consider to be toneless. It is true that in Beijing Mandarin, owing to the well-known sandhi rule that affects the concave 214 in phrase-initial position, 214 occurs more frequently in phrase-final position; however, this does not warrant the sweeping generalization that 214 occurs only phrase-finally. In the examples above, the condition for the sandhi rule no longer obtains, and we find 214 in non-phrase-final positions.

2.15 Snider (1990)

The model of tone that Snider (1990) proposes is structurally similar to those proposed by Yip (1980), Inkelas (1987), and Hyman (1989). The same model is also argued for in Snider (1988). The model makes use of two distinct features, or tiers. For Snider (1990), a tone is represented by the Tonal Node Tier, which is linked to two tonal tiers labeled Register Tier and Modal Tier. The Tonal Node Tier is associated with the tone-bearing unit. The structure is shown below.

(45)

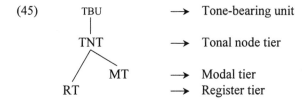

The Modal Tier represents two modes of a tone, the upper mode (H) and the lower mode (L). The Register Tier represents degrees of tonal height—h for a higher step, and l for a lower one. Unlike the Modal Tier, the Register Tier is not binary; the number of tone heights could, in theory, be infinite. Conceptually, Snider's model is in line with the model proposed by Clements (1983), which allows an infinite number of tone heights.

It is worth noting that Snider's notion of register is different from Yip's (1980, 1989). Snider's Modal Tier is functionally equivalent to Yip's register feature [upper]; both are binary, producing two registers in Yip's theory, and two modes in Snider's. Snider's Register Tier is similar to Yip's Tone feature [raised], with one crucial difference: [raised] is binary, whereas the Register Tier is gradient.

The tonological evidence Snider (1988, 1990) adduces to support the two-tier structure of tone comes from various African languages. Downstep is a common sandhi process in many African tone languages. In languages with downstep, a sequence Hi-Lo-Hi may surface as Hi-Lo-ꜜHi, where the phrase-medial Lo causes the following Hi to be realized lower in pitch than normal—that is, a downstepped Hi. Snider (1990) shows that, given the two-tier structure, downstep can be accounted for straightforwardly in terms of register spread. The sequence Hi-Lo-Hi has the structure shown in (46a), and register-spread yields the structure in (46b) (Snider 1990:463).

(46)

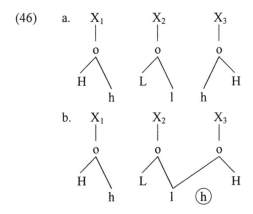

The l register of X_2 spreads to X_3, delinking the original register h in the process. The "floating" tone, now no longer linked to a tone-bearing unit, is circled in (46b). H,l is the representation for the downstepped Hi; the "normal" Hi would have the structure H,h (cf. X_1). The phenomenon of upstep can be handled in analogous fashion.

Snider's (1990) preoccupation appears to be with the tonal phenomena of African languages, in which terraced-tone systems are prevalent. It is not clear how Snider (1988, 1990) would represent contour tones. Since the Register Tier and Modal Tier perform conceptual roles that preclude the possibility of a branching structure dominated by the Tonal Node Tier, a contour tone can be represented only through the concatenation of Tonal Node Tiers: a high fall, for example, could have the structure shown below.

(47)

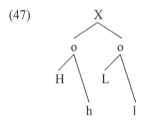

In other words, a contour tone arises when two Tonal Nodes are associated with the same tone-bearing unit, which is the position of early autosegmental phonology. If this is the correct interpretation, the two tonal tiers of Snider (1988, 1990) are conceptually different from the two features, or tiers, proposed by Yip (1980), even though structurally they may have the same explanatory power. In fact, the downstep case shown in (46) can be handled in the same fashion in any theory that admits multi-tier structure for tone, such as Yip (1980), Clements (1983), Inkelas (1987), and Hyman (1989).

Snider's theory has its limitations. The spreading account of downstep in a two-tone system cannot be extended to a system with four underlying tonal contrasts. This is because, in a four-tone system, all possible combinations of H/L and h/l are used to specify the tonal contrasts, as shown below (Snider 1990:462).

(48) a. Hi: H and h
      b. Mi-Hi: H and l
      c. Mi-Lo: L and h
      d. Lo: L and l

We cannot say that H,l is the representation of a downstepped Hi, if we are to keep the representation of a downstepped Hi distinct from the representation of an underlying Mi-Hi, even though they may be realized with the same pitch value. This problem can be solved by the introduction of an additional tier, as in Clements (1983) and Hyman (1989), which increases the number of formally distinct representations (see sections 2.8 and 2.12; note that Hyman does not use the term "register" in the same sense as Snider). Alternatively, we can increase the number of registers, an option allowed in Snider's (1990) theory. This option is not an easy one. To see this, let us introduce a new register, m, to the four-tone language with downstep. With the two modes H and L, and three registers, h, m, and l, the system can yield six formally distinct tones. For maximum differentiation among the tones, the four underlying tones are assigned the structures shown in (48). The structure H,m could be considered the representation of a down-stepped Hi. We are immediately faced with a technical problem: how do we derive H,m from the underlying tones that do not have m? In other words, the additional register cannot be introduced by register-spreading rules. Register-insertion rules must be formulated to account for the effects of downstep—or of upstep, for that matter. The gradient nature of the Register Tier, though capable of specifying more tonal contrasts, nevertheless complicates matters enormously. Downstep or upstep cannot be analyzed as a simple case of assimilatory spread.

2.16 Chang (1992)

M.-C. L. Chang's (1992) work builds on the previous models of tone proposed in Yip (1980, 1989), Bao (1989, 1990b), and Duanmu (1990, 1994), among others. The prosodic model, as Chang (1992) calls it, consists of two "tiers" that are relevant for tone—tonal register and tonal pitch. The innovative aspect of Chang's work lies in the way the two tiers relate to each other and to the tone-bearing unit. The two tonal tiers are separate and do not link to a common tier; nor do they link to a common tone-bearing unit, as is the case with the work of early autosegmental phonology, notably Yip (1980). The two tonal tiers are anchored on different nodes (or tiers) within the prosodic structure of a word. Specifically, the tonal register is associated with the syllable, whereas the tonal pitch is associated with the mora. In effect, there are two tone-bearing units, one for each tonal feature. The position of the tonal features is shown in the prosodic hierarchy below (adapted from Chang 1992:85).

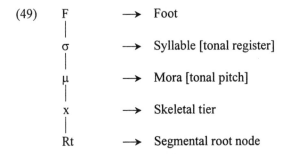

(49)   F   ⟶   Foot

         σ   ⟶   Syllable [tonal register]

         μ   ⟶   Mora [tonal pitch]

         x   ⟶   Skeletal tier

         Rt   ⟶   Segmental root node

The register tier is specified by the laryngeal feature [stiff vocal cords], and the pitch tier by the laryngeal feature [spread glottis] (Halle and Stevens 1971). These two features define two registers and two pitches, yielding a total of four distinct tones.

At the level of underlying representation, therefore, the features are part of the prosodic structure shown in (49). They percolate down the prosodic hierarchy to the segment that realizes the tone phonetically, and they become part of the geometry of that segment's laryngeal features. At the underlying level, however, it is of no consequence exactly what features characterize the register and pitch tiers. We can use Yip's [upper] to define two registers and [raised] to define two pitches for each register.

One property of Chang's (1992) prosodic model that must be made explicit is the mapping relationship between the syllable and mora on the one hand, and the tonal tiers on the other. It appears that the mapping between the tonal register and the syllable is strictly one-to-one, whereas the mapping between the tonal pitch and the mora could be either one-to-one or many-to-one. The mapping relations do not matter much in the representation of level tones; however, in the representation of contour tones, the mapping relation becomes crucial. Given the assumption that there is only one tonal register per syllable, contour tones can be represented in two ways. First, if the mora-pitch mapping is one-to-one, contour tones are possible only in heavy syllables—a position that is empirically inadequate, despite the arguments provided in Duanmu (1990, 1994). Second, if the mora-pitch mapping is one-to-many, tonal contour is represented by the concatenation of different pitches on the same mora. The two possible structures are illustrated below.

(50)   a. One-to-one mora-pitch mapping

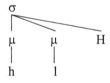

     b. One-to-many mora-pitch mapping

These two structures could be representations of high falling tone. Chang (1992) is not explicit about the mapping relationship that can hold between tonal pitch and mora. Most likely the question is of no theoretical significance, since the two structures have practically the same empirical consequence.

2.17 Tsay (1994)

Most theories of tone we have surveyed so far have, implicitly and explicitly, adopted a binary approach to tonal features. Although Clements's and Snider's theories are notable exceptions, the gradient nature of their models, particularly that of Clements (1983), is more a result of the geometry of the tonal features than of the features themselves. This is particularly true of Clements's (1983) work, in which the row geometry of the tonal elements h and l, which can be defined with a single binary feature, yields a potentially infinite number of tone heights. Snider's theory is really a hybrid: the Modal Tier is binary, and the Register Tier is gradient. The preference for binary features is indeed common among researchers of tonal phenomena.

Tsay (1994) adopts a gradient approach to the study of tone. Only one feature is postulated. [Pitch], [P] for short, defines an infinite number of pitch levels and is constrained only by extra-linguistic factors. In a language that contains two tones, we have [1P] and [2P]; in a language with three tone levels, we have [1P], [2P], and [3P]; and so on. The number 1 represents the lowest pitch; the larger the number, the higher the pitch. A tonal inventory can only consist of tone levels specified by contiguous digits: {1P, 2P, 3P} is a possible inventory, but not {1P, 3P, 4P}.

The pitch levels are associated with moras, which are assumed to be the tone-bearing units. This association need not be one-to-one. Contour tones are represented as concatenations of level tones associated with a single mora (cf. (51b)), or as multiple moras, each associated with one level tone (cf. (51c)). The structures of a low tone and a rising tone are shown below.

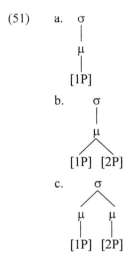

(51)   a.   σ
              |
              μ
              |
             [1P]

        b.   σ
              |
              μ
             /\
          [1P] [2P]

        c.   σ
             /\
            μ μ
            | |
          [1P] [2P]

There is little empirical difference between the two structures of the rising tone in (51b) and (51c).

Although there is nothing wrong *a priori* with the gradient representation of tone, its inability to express assimilation as spreading is a serious drawback from the theoretical perspective of nonlinear phonology. Tone lowering and raising are two classical examples of assimilation; they are accounted for straightforwardly as feature spread within a theory that makes use of binary features. With a single gradient feature, Tsay (1994) is able to account for tone raising or lowering only with the help of additional stipulations. A brief examination of the raising and lowering data from Yala, a language spoken in Nigeria, helps make this point clear.

Yala has three underlying level tones. The high tone becomes mid when it follows a mid or low tone, and the low tone becomes mid when it precedes a high or mid tone. Relevant facts are shown in (52) (Tsay 1994:70-71).

(52) a. High → Mid / Mid, Low _
/á wa ní/ → [á wa ni] "you did not come"
/ó-fú-à-má/ → [ó-fú-à-ma] "therefore"
b. Low → Mid / _ High, Mid
/òyí yɔŋr̄ɔ̀/ → [oyí yɔŋr̄ɔ̀] "boy"
/ìjenù/ → [ijenù] "jaw"

In the data, the grave accent marks the low tone and the acute accent the high tone; the mid tone is unmarked. For clarity, the tone undergoing the tone sandhi is underlined. Note that both lowering and raising produce the mid tone.

In a theory with binary features, the account of the sandhi facts is quite straightforward. Since Yala has three underlying tones, two features are sufficient. We can use the features [upper] and [raised] of Yip (1980, 1989), and define the three tones as follows:

(53) a. High [+upper, +raised]
b. Mid [+upper, -raised]
c. Low [-upper, -raised]

There is another specification for the mid tone, namely [-upper, +raised], which we will not consider for reasons that will become clear in due course. Since Mid and Low share the specification [-raised], and High and Mid share the feature specification [+upper], the former pair forms the natural class that triggers lowering, and the latter pair forms the natural class that triggers raising. The two sandhi processes can be expressed as feature spread.

(54) a. Lowering

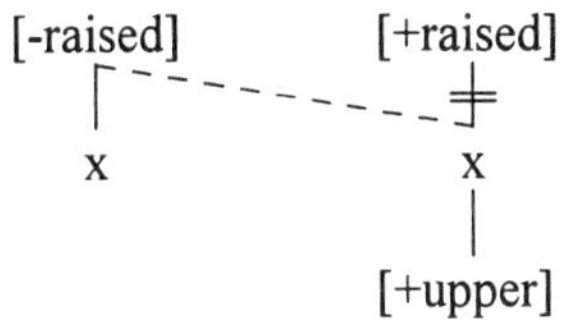

b. Raising

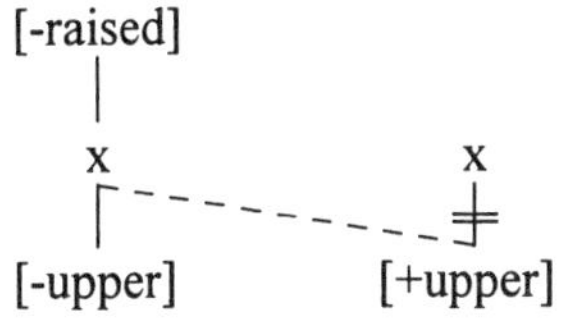

The two rules yield [+upper, -raised]. It is not surprising, therefore, that both raising and lowering produce the mid tone with the same feature specification.

It is possible, of course, to account for the facts within the theory proposed in Tsay (1994). Tsay's analysis is quite interesting. Two rules are proposed, as follows.

(55)   a. Lowering

         [3P] → [2P] / [1-2P] _

         b. Raising

         [1P] → [2P] / _ [2-3P]

[1-2P] is short for the set of the tones {[1P], [2P]}, and [2-3P] for the set {[2P], [3P]}. These are the so-called "tone classes," which are defined as sets of contiguous tones. Tsay (1994:69) stipulates that targets and triggers must be tone classes, which is amply exemplified in the above two rules. We also need another stipulation: the input and output of the rules must form a tone class—a [nP] can lower to [n–P], but not to, say, [n–2P]. Similarly, a tone can raise to the next tone, but no higher. In other words, [3P] can lower to [2P], but not to [1P]; while [1P] can raise to [2P], but not to [3P]. The two stipulations ensure that the high tone lowers, and the low tone raises, to the mid tone. Although technically adequate, this account fails to highlight the nature of assimilation, and the common phonological characteristic of the high and mid tones on the one hand, and the mid and low tones on the other. In this respect, a theory based on binary features is superior to a theory based on a single, multi-valued feature.

3

The Representation of Tone

3.1   The Geometry of Tone

The tone model that I will propose makes use of the two binary features of Halle and Stevens (1971), [stiff] and [slack]. As I have pointed out in section 2.6, the advantage of the Halle-Stevens feature system is its ability to express the pitch of vowels and voicing of consonants as featurally the same phenomenon. Thus, [+stiff] specifies voicelessness in consonants and relatively high pitch in vowels, and [-stiff] specifies voicing in consonants and relatively low pitch in vowels. This captures directly the well-known correlation between tone registers (the *yin-yang* registers in traditional Chinese philology) and the voice qualities of consonants. Under the interpretation of Halle and Stevens (1971), the feature [stiff] provides the articulatory instruction to raise the degree of stiffness of the vocal cords, while the feature [slack] gives the opposite instruction. The two features combine to determine three states of vocal cord tension, which produces three distinct pitches:

(1)   H   M   L
     stiff   +   -   -
     slack   -   -   +

This view holds that [+stiff] and [+slack] are mutually exclusive on logical grounds.

By Halle and Stevens's account, the two features are not identified with any laryngeal muscle, either intrinsic or extrinsic. Unlike the feature [nasal], which provides the articulatory instructions to the soft palate (Sagey 1986), the features [stiff] and [slack] must rely for their phonetic execution on muscle complexes whose activities affect, in one way or another, the tension of the vocal cords. To rule out [+stiff, +slack] on logical and physiological grounds, one must assume that [stiff] and [slack] are executed by the same set of muscles—[+stiff] stiffens the vocal cords, while [+slack] slackens them. This assumption is no better supported experimentally than is the assumption that the two laryngeal features are articulatorily executed by different sets of muscles. The latter assumption leads to a different interpretation of the two features. In feature-theoretic terms, the muscular activities of the feature [stiff] can be interpreted as determining the overall tension of the vocal cords, which is subject to modification by the muscular activities regulated by the feature [slack]. Instead of three states, the two features combine to produce four states of vocal cord tension. The two features have different functions. Their interaction gives rise to four distinct pitch levels.

(2)

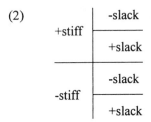

The features [stiff] and [slack] are functionally equivalent to [upper] and [raised] of Yip (1980) and Pulleyblank (1986); indeed, they are functionally equivalent to the components of any two-feature theory that assigns different roles to the two features. The feature [stiff] specifies two registers, each of which is divided by the feature [slack] into two sub-registers. Following Yip (1980, 1989), I assume that two specifications of the feature [slack] can occur in sequence under the same tonal node. The sequence is temporally significant and is directly dominated by what I call the "c node." The c node specifies the contour of the tone. The register and contour nodes are dominated by the tonal root node, denoted by t. The geometry of tone is then as shown in (3).

(3)   t
          ⟋ ⟍
        r   c

The register node, r, is specified by either [+stiff] or [-stiff]. The contour node, c, may optionally branch. When it branches, it has the structure shown in (4).

(4)   c
            ⟋ ⟍
    [αslack] [-αslack]   where α = + or -

For ease of exposition I will use H and L for the r node, and h and l for the c node. Featurally, H is defined as [+stiff], L as [-stiff], h as [-slack] and l as [+slack].

   A tone consists of two components, the register and the contour, represented by the r node and the c node respectively. The register specifies the relative pitch height for the tone, while the c node specifies how the tone behaves over the duration of the tone-bearing unit. The two notions register and contour are familiar ones in the literature. The r node is functionally equivalent to the traditional notion of the *yin-yang* registers (cf. sections 2.1, 2.3); to the Register autosegment of Yip (1980) (cf. section 2.7); to row 1 of Clements (1983, 1989) (cf. sections 2.8); to the primary tier or register of Hyman (1986, 1993) (cf.

sections 2.9 and 2.12); and to the tonal root node of Yip (1989) (cf. section 2.13).[1]

The novel feature of the tone model in (3) lies in the conception of register and contour, and in the structural relationship between these two notions. Structurally, the r node and the c node are sister nodes dominated by the tonal root node t. The relation of temporal precedence is irrelevant between the two sister nodes. The two structures below are formally equivalent.

(5)   a.   t   b.   t
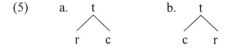
             r   c   c   r

Conceptually, however, they are distinct. The r node is static in the sense that it provides the overall pitch register, which is relatively stable throughout the duration of the tone-bearing unit. Since it specifies the pitch register in which the tone is to be realized, the r node must be either L or H. The c node is dynamic and is interpreted over time. A branching c node is temporally significant: the sequence h followed by l involves a change from the high end to the low end of the register specified by the r node, creating a falling contour. A rising contour involves a change from l to h. A non-branching c node (an even contour) maintains the same pitch level over the temporal span of the tone-bearing unit. I make the following stipulation:

(6)   Underlyingly, the contour node may have at most two branches.

This stipulation constrains the number of tones that the model in (3) can generate. It is necessary because no lexical tone has the contour rise-fall-rise—the sequence l-h-l-h—or the contour fall-rise-fall, the sequence h-l-h-l. If the c node is not so constrained, such non-occurring tonal contours would be expected to occur. As for concave and convex contours—h-l-h and l-h-l—they do occur in certain languages, but their occurrence is severely limited, at least among Chinese dialects. C.-C. Cheng (1973b:103) studied the distribution of tonal contours among tones collected from Chinese dialects, with the following results.

(7)   Contour   Number of tones with contour
       Falling   1125
       Level   1086
       Rising   790
       Concave   352
       Convex   80

The figures are quite revealing. Complex contours do not occur in languages as widely as less complex contours.

The stipulation (6) implies the proposition in (8).

(8)   Concave/convex contours are surface phenomena.

In section 3.4.2, I will show that at least two dialects that exhibit surface complex contours can be analyzed without postulating the complex contours as underlying. The stipulation in (3) not only puts a constraint on the formal possibilities of tonal representation; it also has empirical support.

The tonal geometry proposed in (3) generates two registers and three contours, for a possible inventory of eight underlying tones.

(9)   a. Even tones

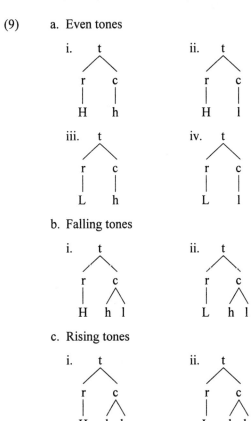

b. Falling tones

c. Rising tones

In (9a) I use the word "even" to denote the pitch contour resulting from a non-branching c node. The word "level" is used to refer to points on the pitch scale. The even, falling, and rising contours are the three possible underlying contours that the model allows. The structures in (10) are equivalent to those in (9).

(10)   a. Even tones
            i.   [H, h]   ii.   [H, l]
            iii. [L, h]   iv.   [L, l]
        b. Falling tones
            i.   [H, hl]   ii.   [L, hl]
        c. Rising tones
            i.   [H, lh]   ii.   [L, lh]

It has often been observed that the voicing of obstruents and the pitch of following vowels are related (see, for example, Haudricourt 1954, Halle and Stevens 1971, Ladefoged 1973, and Matisoff 1973). The correlation between voicing and tone height can be seen clearly in the tonal inventory of Songjiang (Jiangsu 1960).

(11)   Tonal inventory of Songjiang

     Yin-register

a. *ping*	53	ti	"low"
		t'i	"ladder"
b. *shang*	44	ti	"bottom"
		t'i	"body"
c. *qu*	35	ti	"emperor"
		t'i	"tear"
d. *ru*	5	paʔ	"hundred"
		p'aʔ	"tap"

     Yang-register

A. *ping*	31	di	"lift"
B. *shang*	22	di	"brother"
C *qu*	13	di	"field"
D. *ru*	3	baʔ	"white"

(5 and 3 are short tones realized only on syllables ending in the glottal stop.) In the data in (11), both aspirated and unaspirated voiceless obstruents occur only with high tones (the *yin*-register tones), and voiced obstruents only with low tones (the *yang*-register tones).[2] Songjiang's tonal inventory is a paradigmatic case of the direct correlation between the voicing qualities of syllable-initial obstruents and the tonal registers. If the syllable-initial obstruent is voiced, the register of the tone on the following vowel is low; if the initial obstruent is voiceless, the register is high. The tones of Songjiang can be represented as in (12).

(12)   Tone inventory of Songjiang

    Falling tones

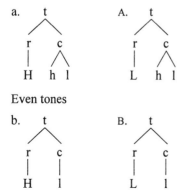

    Even tones

Rising tones

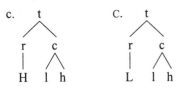

In the structures in (12), the r nodes need not be specified, since they are predictable from the syllable-initial obstruents. I include the registers for clarity. The short tones 5 and 3 are not distinctive and are derivable from the falling tones (12a,A). The tone inventory of Songjiang makes full use of the contours that the proposed theory provides: the falling contour, the even contour, and the rising contour.

The geometry of tone features proposed here makes several claims about possible tone sandhi processes. Specifically, it predicts the four kinds of assimilation by spreading shown in (13) (asterisks are tone-bearing units).

(13)   a. Tone spread

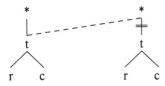

b. Register spread

c. Contour spread

d. Contour feature spread

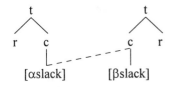

In (13a), the entire tone structure spreads as a melodic unit, whether it is an even tone or a contour tone. This is not expressible in theories such as those of Woo (1967), Yip (1980), Hyman (1993), Duanmu (1990, 1994), and Tsay (1994), all of which treat contour tones as clusters of level tones, albeit at different levels of representation. To the extent that the r node and the c node spread together, the tone spread phenomena support the geometry of tone in which the r node and the c node are sister nodes dominated by the tonal root node. In (13b), the register node spreads without the contour being affected. This phenomenon cannot be explained in Yip's (1989) theory, in which the register dominates the sequence of the feature [raised], which is functionally equivalent to [slack] (i.e. the c node). In Yip's theory, spreading the register automatically takes the contour along. In (13c), the contour node spreads without affecting the register, which justifies representing the sequence of the feature [slack] as a separate node—the c node. In other words, a structure in which the features [stiff] and [slack] are sister nodes, as shown in (14), will fail to account for the phenomenon of contour spreading.

(14)

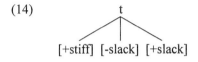

[+stiff] [-slack] [+slack]

The fourth possibility of assimilatory spreading is illustrated in (13d), in which a single feature spreads. This kind of spreading involves a terminal node dominated by the c node, and it differs from contour spreading, which involves the non-terminal c node. The target c node [βslack] need not delink as a result of the spreading.

We will show that these theoretical predictions are borne out empirically in section 3.3. First, however, let us consider some tonal phenomena that motivate the postulation of underlying contour.

3.2 Motivation of Underlying Contour

It is not obvious that contour must be present in the underlying representation. Intuitively, a contour is created if two tones of different pitch are placed next to each other on the same tone-bearing unit. The default assumption is that the abstract notion of contour (as represented by the c node in (3)) does not exist at the underlying level. This is the position held by most linguists working on African tone languages (cf. Leben 1973, Williams 1976, Pulleyblank 1986, Goldsmith 1990, Kenstowicz 1993, and Odden 1995), with the notable exception of Newman (1986, 1995). Among linguists who work on Asian tone languages, mainly Chinese, many hold this position as well—among them are Woo (1969), Duanmu (1990, 1994), and Tsay (1994). Any postulation of underlying contour in the representation of tone must be empirically motivated.

Strong empirical evidence in support of the tone model comes from tonal assimilation, which we will investigate in section 3.3. In the present section I will consider tonal inventory, natural class, and OCP-effect with regard to tone, showing that tonal contour must be available at the level of underlying representation.

3.2.1   Tone Inventory and Tonal Contour

One motivation for underlying tonal contour comes from the consideration of the tonal inventory of a tone language. Given the two features [stiff] and [slack], we can account for four distinct level tones at the underlying level. The system fails if there exists a language that has more than four distinctive tones in its tonal inventory. When we consider such tone inventories, we must pay attention to factors such as voicing of the syllable-initial obstruents, vowel height, and the structure of the syllable on which tones are realized. Consideration of the tone inventories of languages that do not show a correlation between consonant voicing and tone leads to the conclusion that contours must be represented at the underlying level. Weining Miao, a dialect of Miao spoken in Weining, Guizhou Province, is a language with such a tone inventory, possessing seven tones, as shown in (15) (F.-S. Wang 1957).[3]

(15)   a. 55   ku   "I"
        b. 33   ko   "root"
        c. 11   ku   "be"
        d. 53   ly   "willow"
        e. 31   la   "friend"
        f. 35   v'ae   "that"
        g. 13   v'ae   "grab"

As the data in (15) show, the number of tones cannot be reduced on the basis of syllable-initial consonants, since there is no correlation between consonant voicing and tone pitch. The voiceless consonant /k/ occurs with high even 55, mid even 33, and low even 11 (cf. (15a,b,c)); and the voiced aspirated consonant /v'/ occurs with both high rising 35 and low rising 13 (cf. (15f,g)). The same is true of the two falling tones (cf. (15d,e)).

The distribution of tones in the inventory of Weining Miao furnishes evidence that the falling and rising contours that we see in the citation tones cannot be reduced to underlying level tones, unless we introduce more features to supplement [stiff] and [slack]. Supplemental features are not necessary, however, if we allow the [slack] feature to occur in sequence, as suggested by Yip (1980, 1989). Any system that employs two binary features must allow contour to be represented underlyingly.

3.2.2   Natural Class and Tonal Contour

It is a fundamental assumption in phonological theorizing that phonological processes involve natural classes, which can be defined in terms of distinctive features. In tonological work, it has been amply demonstrated that tones form natural classes on the basis of their features. In this section, I will document natural classes that are defined by tonal contour. To the extent that such natural classes are found to participate in phonological processes, an adequate theory must admit tonal contour in the representation of tone.

3.2.2.1 Changzhi

The first case we will consider is the Mandarin dialect of Changzhi. Here we will examine the phonological environment of a rule that deletes the glottal stop. All Changzhi facts are cited from Hou (1983).

Changzhi has six tones, two of which are concave, transcribed as 213 and 535 respectively. The diminutive suffix, *tə?*, has the high concave tone 535 in citation, but it acquires the tone of the stem to which it is attached. Relevant facts are shown in (16).

(16)   a. ts'ə 213 tə 213   "cart"
        b. paŋ 535 tə 535   "board"
        c. xæ 24 tə? 24   "child"
        d. çiaŋ 53 tə? 53   "fillings"

The detailed analysis of the tonological phenomenon exhibited in the above data is given in section 3.3.1.2. Note that the glottal stop is deleted when the newly acquired tone has concave contour. In other words, tonal contour defines the natural class of {213, 535}, which triggers the deletion of the glottal stop. In section 3.4.2.1 I will show that the surface concave contour is derived from the falling contour, which is postulated at the underlying level. Regardless of levels of representation, tonal contour plays an indispensable role in glottal deletion.

3.2.2.2 Lingxi and Luoyang

Total reduplication data found in Lingxi and Luoyang furnish unequivocal evidence in support of the view that tonal contour defines natural classes. We will consider the Lingxi facts first. Lingxi, a Southern Min dialect spoken in coastal areas of Zhejiang Province, has five tones in citation form (all Lingxi data are cited from Wen 1991).

(17)   a. 44   [H,h]   A. 24   [L,lh]
        b. 53   [H,hl]   B. 31   [L,hl]
        c. 11   [L,l]

The structures we assign to the tones are given in square brackets.

In reduplication, the first tone undergoes change. Relevant data are presented below.

(18)   a. t'ian 44 (31) t'ian 44   "everyday"
           ti 44 (31) ti 44   "low"
        b. si 21 (11) si 24   "continually"
           tuan 21 (11) tuan 24   "short"
        c. tuan 53 (33) tuan 53   "short"
           suɐ 53 (33) suɐ 53   "to explain"

d. hou 31 (11) hou 31   "thick"
   kian 31 (11) kian 31   "every piece"
e. se 11 (53) se 11   "every generation"
   sia 11 (53) sia 11   "thanks"

The tones in parentheses are sandhi tones. For the sake of clarity, I arrange the reduplication sandhi patterns in (19).

(19)   a. 44-44 → 31-44
        b. 24-24 → 11-24
        c. 53-53 → 33-53
        d. 31-31 → 11-31
        e. 11-11 → 53-11

We can make three interesting observations about the patterns in (19). First, if the original tone is even-contoured, the sandhi tone is falling; and if the original tone is rise or fall, the sandhi tone is even—compare (19a,e) and (19b,c,d). Second, among the even tones, if the original tone is H-registered, the sandhi tone is L-registered, and vice versa—compare (19a) and (19e). Third, among the contour tones, if the original tone is H-registered, the sandhi tone is H-registered as well—we consider 33 to be [H,l]; and if the original tone is L-registered, the sandhi tone is also L-registered—compare (19c) and (19b,d). The first observation has to do with contour; the second and third observations have to do with register. Clearly the post-sandhi representations are OCP-optimal: the reduplicated words do not consist of tones with identical contours. We will see more OCP-related evidence in section 3.2.3.

These observations serve as the basis for the proposed analysis. The derivation of the sandhi facts requires a few steps. Assuming that the structures of the tones in (17), we need the following rules.

(20)   a. c   →   c
           | /\
           h   l

        b. [αstiff] → [-αstiff] / _   c
                                          |

        c. c   →   c
           /\ |
                     l

Graphically, I use a single line to indicate an even contour, and branching lines to indicate the fall or rise contour. Rule (20a) turns an even contour into a fall, and (20b) changes the register—from H to L, or from L to H—just in case it precedes an even-contoured tone. These two rules therefore derive the patterns shown in (19a,e). Rule (20c) turns a falling or rising contour into an even one, yielding the patterns shown in (19b,c,d). The derivation of (19a,b) in (21) illustrates how the rules work.

(21)

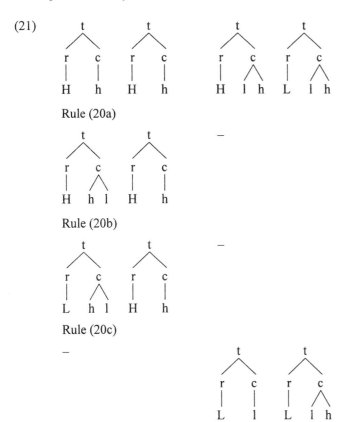

Rule (20a)

Rule (20b)

Rule (20c)

Luoyang, a Mandarin dialect, furnishes further evidence of natural classes defined on the basis of tonal contour. This dialect has four tones in citation form (He 1993).

(22)   a. 33
         A. 31
         b. 53
         c. 412

In addition, Luoyang has the so-called "light tone," which has a pitch of 3. In reduplication, the two falling tones become 33, while the remaining two tones are reduced to the light tone. Relevant data are presented in (23).

(23)   a. gong 33 gong 3   "grandpa"
         b. yi 31 yi 33   "to move"
         c. nai 53 nai 33   "grandma"
         d. kan 412 kan 3   "to take a look"

The light tone can be considered toneless phonologically. The tones 31 and 53 are not reduced on account of their contour.

3.2.2.3 Lü

Lü, a Tai language spoken in southern Yunnan Province, China, and parts of
Thailand, furnishes evidence for the need of tonal contour. The description on
the grammar of Lü is rather sketchy. Our knowledge comes mainly from F.-K. Li
(1964) and Gandour (1975), two rather short articles on the language. Lü has six
tones, T1 through T6, as follows.

(24)   T1   55   ma   "dog"
         T2   31   na   "rice"
         T3   25   pɛt   "eight"
         T4   33   nok   "bird"
         T5   13   xa   "kill"
         T6   22   caŋ   "elephant"

The data are cited from F.-K. Li's (1964) brief account of the language. We will
be concerned here with the sandhi behavior of T5. According to Li, T5 is
realized as 13 before pauses, and before T1, T4, and T6; otherwise, it is realized
as 11. In other words, the tone has the following sandhi pattern.

(25)
$$T5 \rightarrow \begin{cases} 13 \ / \ \_ 55, 33, 22 & \text{a.} \\ 11 \ / \ \_ 31, 25, 13 & \text{b.} \end{cases}$$

The T5 sandhi is sensitive not to the pitch height of the following tone, but rather
to its contour: T5 is a low rise if the following tone has the even contour, and a
low even if the following tone has either the falling or rising contour. Based on
the sandhi pattern, Gandour (1975) argues that the feature [contour] proposed by
Wang (1967) must be permitted by phonological theories, since the tones in
(25a) are all [-contour] and those in (25b) are [+contour]. Translated into our
terms, the c node of T5 branches if the following tone does not, and vice versa.
The branchingness of the c node defines the natural classes of {55, 33, 22} and
{31, 25, 13}.

3.2.3   The OCP and Tonal Contour

The *Obligatory Contour Principle* (OCP) is an important principle in phonological representation, and much research has been devoted to it (see, for
example, McCarthy 1986; Odden 1986, 1988; Yip 1988; Goldsmith 1990; and
references cited therein). The OCP prohibits two identical elements from being
adjacent at some level of representation. It has been found to play a decisive role
in many phonological processes, among them metathesis, deletion, insertion, and
gemination. In this section I will examine a few examples of tone sandhi that can
be seen as motivated by the OCP.

3.2.3.1 Danyang and Pingyao

In many Chinese dialects, contour change is commonplace. I will use the term "contour metathesis" to refer to change from a rise to a fall, or from a fall to a rise. Although some of the contour changes take place regardless of the contour of the following tone, there are examples of contour metathesis taking place in the environment of an adjacent tone of the same contour. Here we will consider two such cases, from Danyang and Pingyao. Since the phenomenon is part of a complete tone sandhi pattern, I will only highlight the OCP effect here, and will defer the detailed analysis of the whole pattern to section 3.3.1.1 (Danyang) and section 3.3.2.1 (Pingyao). Justification for the analysis presented here can also be found in those sections.

The first case we consider is from Danyang. This dialect has a set of six so-called "word melodies," which are the tone patterns for phrases with two, three, or four syllables. Detailed analyses of the Danyang data are presented in section 3.3.1.1; here we will focus on the word melodies that are derived from the base tone 24. For phrases with two, three, or four syllables, the base tone gives the following patterns.

(26) Base   24
      Bisyllabic   42-24
      Trisyllabic   42-42-24
      Quadrisyllabic   42-42-42-24

According to Lü (1980), the tone sequence 24-24 is disallowed; when such a sequence is generated through word formation, the first tone becomes 42. In other words, the falling contour metathesizes to the rising contour when followed by another falling tone. We can attribute this phenomenon to the OCP operating on the c node. Tones with identical c nodes are not preferred.

A similar case is found in Pingyao, which is treated in sections 2.5 and 3.3.2.1. This dialect has five tones, shown below (Hou 1980).

(27)   a. 13   b. 35   c. 53
       d. 23   e. 54

In bisyllabic phrases, the two rising tones, 13 and 35, become 31 when followed by 35, and the falling tone 53 becomes 35 when followed by 53. Informally, we express the tone sandhi as follows.

(28)   a. 13-35 → 35-35
          35-35 → 35-35
       b. 53-53 → 35-53

Although the analysis would involve more than contour metathesis (see section 3.3.2.1), the facts make it amply clear that two adjacent tones with identical contours are not preferred, in accordance with the content of the OCP. Crucially, the identity is calculated on the basis of tonal contour.

3.2.3.2 Yantai

Yantai, a Mandarin dialect spoken in Shandong Province, furnishes sandhi evidence that can be attributed to the OCP prohibition against adjacent identical tones. Yantai has only three tones, as follows.

(29)   a. 31   fu   "man"
         b. 214   fa   "method"
         c. 55   t'u   "picture"

All Yantai data are cited from Qian et al. (1982). In a bisyllabic phrase consisting of two identical tones, the phrase-initial tone undergoes tone sandhi. Relevant data are shown below.

(30)   a. 31-31 → 35-31
            san p'o   "hill slope"
            tçy tsuŋ   "pig's bristles"
         b. 214-214 → 55-214
            çiao mo   "wheat"
            y sui   "rain water"
         c. 55-55 → 31-55
            çy p'i   "tree bark"
            tç'iaŋ çI   "to stage performance"

In addition, 214 changes to 35 when followed by 31:

(30)   d. 214-31 → 35-31
            çiu çin   "palm"
            çiao san   "small hill"

All other combinations do not exhibit tone sandhi at all. The sandhi facts are summarized in the table below, where the sandhi combinations are boxed.

(31)   Post-sandhi bisyllabic tone patterns in Yantai

	31	214	55
31	35-31	31-214	31-55
214	35-31	55-214	214-55
55	55-31	55-214	31-55

The derivation of the sandhi patterns from the underlying lexical tones would require a few rules, which we will not attempt to formulate here. The tones may be assigned the following structures.

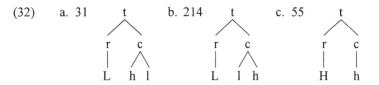

(32) a. 31   b. 214   c. 55

We can make two observations about the post-sandhi bisyllabic tone patterns. First, adjacent tones have different contours; second, with the exception of 31-214, adjacent tones have different registers as well. A quick inspection of (31) confirms these two observations.

The Yantai tone sandhi can be attributed to the OCP operating either on the c node or on the t node. In any event, tonal contour must be represented at the underlying level. As for 214-31, which surfaces as 35-31, we note that the tones preceding 31 are 35 and 55, which are H-registered. We can propose a rule that raises the register of a pre-31 tone, as follows.

(33)   r →   r / _ 31
                   |
                   H

The 214-31 sandhi does not weaken the OCP effect evident in the Yantai data.

3.2.3.3 Tianjin

Similar facts can be found in Tianjin, another Mandarin dialect. The Tianjin data have been the subject of intense study by Chen (1986a, 1987a), Hung (1987), Tan (1987), Z.-S. Zhang (1987), and Milliken et al. (1997), each of whom approaches the data for different theoretical purposes. Here, I will focus on the tonal combinations that undergo tone sandhi, arguing that the Tianjin sandhi shows the OCP effect.

Tianjin has four citation tones, as follows (Li and Liu 1985).

(34)   a. 21   kɑu   "high"
          b. 45   fəŋ   "to sew"
          c. 213   çi   "to wash"
          d. 53   xuei   "meeting"

There are various ways to interpret these numbers; for our purpose, we consider 21 a low fall, 53 a high fall, 213 a low rise, and 45 a high rise. Only four bisyllabic tonal combinations exhibit tone sandhi; these are exemplified below (Li and Liu 1985:76-77).

(35)   a. 21-21 → 213-21
             kɑu ṣɑn   "high mountain"
             tṣ'u fɑ   "to set out"

b. 213-213 → 45-213
   çyɑn tṣuŋ   "to select seeds"
   pɑu kuɑn   "to safe-keep"
c. 53-53 → 31-53
   tçiɑn tṣu   "architecture"
   xuei I   "meeting"
d. 53-21 → 45-21
   tɑ ku   "aunt"
   fɑŋ çin   "at ease"

For the sake of clarity, I summarize Tianjin tone sandhi in tabular form, with sandhi combinations in boxes.

(36)   Post-sandhi bisyllabic tone patterns in Tianjin

	21	45	213	53
21	213-21	21-45	21-213	21-53
45	45-21	45-45	45-213	45-53
213	213-21	213-45	45-213	213-53
53	45-21	53-45	53-213	21-53

Like Yantai, Tianjin avoids bisyllabic phrases with the same tones. Of the sixteen post-sandhi types, only 45-45 is an exception.

The derivation of the sandhi patterns requires a few steps. We observe that in 21-21 and 53-21, the phrase-initial tones change their contour from fall to rise, and their register remains the same; but in 213-213 and 53-53, the register changes, but not the contour. We assume that the four tones of Tianjin have the following structures.

(37)   a. 21   b. 45   c. 213   d. 53

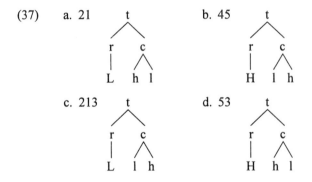

We formulate the two rules informally in (38).

(38)   a. *Contour Metathesis*

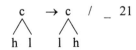

b. *Register Dissimilation*

[αstiff] → [-αstiff] / r₁   r₂

                _   [αstiff]

Register Dissimilation needs to be restricted to 213-213 and 53-53 only, so that it does not apply to 45-45 to yield the ill-formed *13-45. The following derivations show how the two rules work.

(39)   Underlying   21-21   53-21   213-213 53-53

             Contour Metathesis (38a)   213-21 45-21   –   –

             Register Dissimilation (38b) –   –   45-213 21-53

Note that 213 is the shorthand for the low rising tone, and 45 for the high rising tone. The two rules must be applied in the order given, since *Register Dissimilation* also applies to 21-21. From our informal analysis, we can see that Tianjin, like Yantai, avoids identical tones in bisyllabic phrases—an avoidance we attribute to the OCP. Since the OCP requires contour in the representation of tone for the purpose of identity calculation, we conclude that tonal contour must be available at some level of phonological representation. In addition, the Tianjin data clearly demonstrate the formal separation of register and contour, a point that will be the focus of the next section.

3.3 Assimilation in Tone Sandhi

Assimilation is a common process not only in segmental phonology, but also in tonal phonology. In autosegmental theories, assimilation is formally expressed as spreading. Indeed, spreading facts are used as positive evidence of constituency: if two features are found to spread together, they form a constituent. This line of work has been quite successful in establishing the geometry of distinctive features (cf. Clements 1985, Sagey 1986, and Halle 1995). In this section, I will use spreading as a constituency test in examining tonal assimilation, and show that assimilatory spreading affects register, contour, and tone as a melodic unit— exactly the kinds of assimilation predicted in (13). In other words, in order to express tonal assimilation as spreading of tonal constituents, we need a well-articulated model of tone.

3.3.1 Tone Assimilation

Pike (1948) recognizes two distinct tonal systems: the level tone system of African languages, and the contour tone system of Chinese. I will return to Pike's dichotomy in Chapter 7. Here, it is sufficient to point out that tone spreading has different properties in the two systems. Although tone spreading is commonplace in both systems, contour tone spreading is nevertheless not attested in level tone systems. In autosegmental phonology, this fact can be readily explained: contour tones are concatenations of level tones, so they are not formal constituents capable of assimilatory spreading. To argue that tone consists of register and contour, we need to show that tones, especially contour tones, spread as single melodic units. In other words, contour tones are not concatenations of level tones. We find precisely this type of tone spreading in Danyang and Changzhi.

3.3.1.1 Danyang

Danyang, a Wu dialect spoken in the province of Jiangsu, has been discussed by Chen (1986b), Yip (1989), Chan (1989), Duanmu (1990, 1994), and Yip (1995). These works are based on the original paper of Lü (1980), from which I draw my data. In citation form, Danyang has six surface tones, shown in (40). (The original data are given in characters, which are transcribed in *pinyin*, the official romanization scheme, in accordance with Mandarin pronunciation, except for the glottal stop, which is set in square brackets.)

(40)   a. 11   lan   "rotten"
        b. 33   wang   "net"
                     gao   "high"
        c. 24   fang   "house"
                     dao   "arrive"
        d. 55   tu   "earth"
        e. 3   yi[?]   "one"
        f. 4   fu[?]   "coat"

Unlike most Wu dialects, Danyang does not have the contrast voiced versus voiceless, except among fricatives. The tones in (40) do not show the effect of syllable-initial voicing, as is often the case with Wu dialects that maintain the voiced/voiceless contrast among obstruents. (40e,f) are short tones, realized on syllables ending in glottal stop.

There are six bisyllabic tone melodies in this dialect, which are enumerated in (41).

(41)   a. 11-11   shi zi   "persimmon"
                     di yu   "hell"
                     jiu jiu   "uncle"
        b. 42-11   ji dan   "chicken egg"
                     ming ci   "noun"
        c. 42-24   nu er   "daughter"
                     jie mei   "sister"
                     zhi tou   "finger"
        d. 33-33   lao hu   "tiger"
                     mo li   "jasmine"

e. 24-55   peng you   "friend"
              pi xie   "leather shoe"
              niang jiu   "uncle"
f. 55-55   nan men   "south gate"
              che zhan   "station"
              yi niang   "aunt"

We will not be concerned with the relationship between the lexical tones and the phrasal bisyllabic tone patterns. Suffice it to say that the tone melody of a phrase depends on the historical origin of the initial syllable of the phrase, rather than on its tone. It is not possible to derive the phrasal tone melodies from the lexical tones of the component syllables. Chen (1986b) calls the phrasal tone melodies "word melodies," a practice I will follow here. Consider now the word melodies of trisyllabic phrases in (42).

(42)   a. 11-11-11
           lan   [shi zi]   "rotten persimmon"   [11-11]
           rotten persimmon
           huo   [di yu]   "living hell"   [11-11]
           living hell
        b. 42-11-11
           sheng [ji dan]   "raw chicken egg"   [42-11]
           raw   chicken egg
           san   [nu er]   "third daughter"   [42-24]
           three daughter
           xin   [ming ci]   "new noun"   [42-11]
           new noun
        c. 42-42-24
           hao   [peng you]   "good friends"   [24-55]
           good friend
           qi   [jie mei]   "seven sisters"   [44-24]
           seven sister
           qi   [yi niang]   "seventh aunt"   [55-55]
           seven aunt
           qi   [jiu jiu]   "seventh uncle"   [11-11]
           seven uncle
        d. 33-33-33
           pi   [lao hu]   "leather tiger"   [33-33]
           leather tiger
           si   [nu er]   "fourth daughter"   [42-24]
           four daughter
        e. 24-55-55
           nan   [peng you]   "boyfriend"   [24-55]
           male   friend
           huang [pi xie]   "yellow leather shoe"   [24-55]
           yellow leather shoe

f. 55-55-55

xin [nan men]	"new south gate"	[55-55]
new south gate		
dong [che zhan]	"east station"	[55-55]
east station		

Syntactically, trisyllabic phrases that exhibit the tone patterns in (42) are of the form [x [y z]], as the data indicate. Phrases with syntactic structure of the form [[x y] z] have their own tone patterns, which we will not discuss here. The tone patterns in square brackets to the right of the glosses are those of the bisyllabic phrases when they are not part of a trisyllabic phrase. Note that the bisyllabic phrase *peng you* "friend" has the tone pattern 24 55 (cf. (41e)), but *nan* [*peng you*] "boyfriend" surfaces as 24 [55 55], and *hao* [*peng you*] "good friend" as 42 [42 24] (cf. (41c,e)). Similarly, *qi* [*yi niang*] "seventh aunt," *qi* [*jie jiu*] "seventh uncle," and *qi* [*jie mei*] "seven sisters" all surface as 42 [42 24] (cf. (42c)), even though, as bisyllabic phrases, [*yi niang*] "aunt" surfaces as 55 55, [*jiu jiu*] "uncle" as 11 11 and [*jie mei*] "sister" as 42 24. Like bisyllabic word melodies, the trisyllabic word melodies are determined solely by the initial syllables of the phrases. The word melodies of the bisyllabic constituents do not affect the word melodies of the trisyllabic phrases at all.

Phrases with four syllables display the same tone patterns, as shown in (43).

(43)   a. 11-11-11-11

jiu [yang mao shan]	"old woolen sweater"	[55-55-55]
old sheep hair shirt		
da [shou yin ji]	"big radio"	[55-55-33]
big receive sound machine		

b. 42-11-11-11

xin [yang san yu]	"new sweet potato"	[24-55-55]
new foreign potato		
zhen [jin jie-zhi]	"real gold ring"	[42-11-11]
real gold ring		

c. 42-42-42-24

[ke ke qi qi]	"polite"
(reduplicated from ke qi, "polite")	

d. 33-33-33-33

ye [bai ju-hua]	"wild white mum"	[11-11-11]
wild white mum		
fu [zhong zhi-hui]	"deputy chief"	[33-33-33]
deputy chief commander		

e. 24-55-55-55

[ming ming bai bai]	"clear"
(reduplicated from ming bai, "clear")	

f. 55-55-55-55

xian [mi xian zhou]	"salty rice gruel"	[33-33-33]
salty rice flour gruel		

Like their bisyllabic and trisyllabic counterparts, quadrisyllabic tone patterns are determined by the historical origin of the initial syllable, and their trisyllabic components play no role.
In (44), the patterns are juxtaposed for easy inspection.

(44)   Bisyllabic Trisyllabic   Quadrisyllabic
   a. 11-11   11-11-11   11-11-11-11
   b. 42-11   42-11-11   42-11-11-11
   c. 42-24   42-42-24   42-42-42-24
   d. 33-33   33-33-33   33-33-33-33
   e. 24-55   24-55-55   24-55-55-55
   f. 55-55   55-55-55   55-55-55-55

Descriptively, the polysyllabic tone patterns in (44a,b,d,e,f) can be seen as derived from the corresponding bisyllabic patterns by left-to-right association and the spreading of the second tone. (44c), however, cannot be derived in this fashion. Instead, it can be derived by right-to-left association and the spreading of the first tone, as illustrated by the derivations of the quadrisyllabic patterns from (44b,c) below.

(45)   a. Derivation of pattern (44b) with base melody 42 11

         Left-to-right association
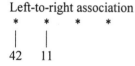

         Left-to-right spreading

         *   *   *   *
         | | | |
         42   11   11   11

         b. Derivation of pattern (44c) with base melody 42 24

         Right-to-left association

         Right-to-left spreading

The pattern in (44c) has generated a great deal of interest among scholars. A number of analyses have been proposed to account for it, which I will sketch briefly. Chen (1986b:12) takes the Danyang data as suggesting that "the directionality of tone mapping may be lexically marked." Yip's (1989) analysis leads to the same conclusion. In her analysis, the bisyllabic pattern [42-24] is the base melody from which the polysyllabic tone patterns in (44c) are derived by means of edge-in association and left-to-right spreading. Her derivation of the quadrisyllabic pattern in (44c) is as follows.

(46)   Edge-in association

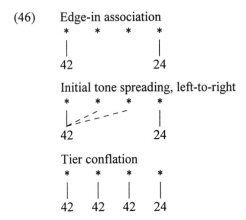

Although Yip (1989) does not address the issue, the question of directionality of spreading arises in her analysis. Only (44c) is derivable by left-to-right spreading of the initial tone of the base melody. The rest of the polysyllabic patterns in (44) can be derived only by right-to-left spreading of the final tone, as illustrated by the following derivation of the quadrisyllabic pattern in (44b).

(47)   Base melody 42 11

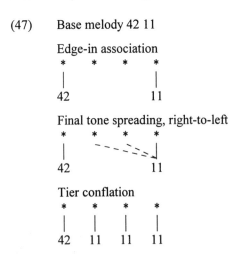

Chan's (1989) analysis circumvents the problem of directionality of association. Following an observation made by Lü (1980:88) to the effect that in strings with two consecutive 24s, the first 24 becomes 42, Chan assumes that the base melody of the patterns in (44c) is LH, which spreads as a unit across a polysyllabic phrase. The quadrisyllabic pattern is derived as follows (o is the tonal root node of Yip 1989; cf. section 2.13):

(48)   Association and tone spreading, left-to-right

Tier conflation, contour formation

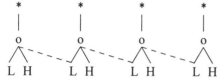

Simplification (delinked L does not surface)

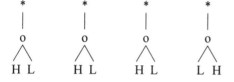

The rule of contour formation creates a tonal root node that dominates LHL, to which the rule of simplification applies to delink the leftmost branch—the L branch of all non-phrase-final tones. Other patterns in (44) can be derived by left-to-right association and spreading. Thus, the issue of the directionality of association and spreading does not arise.

So far in this section I have summarized in general terms three analyses of the Danyang data. The analysis I give below follows Lü (1980) and Chan (1989). According to Lü (1980), the tone patterns of trisyllabic and quadrisyllabic phrases are extensions of their corresponding bisyllabic tone patterns. In the terminology of nonlinear phonology, polysyllabic tone patterns are derived by the left-to-right spreading of the rightmost tone of a base melody. This is true of all cases except (44c). But the patterns in (44c) turn out to be the surface manifestation of under-lying patterns that can be derived in the same way as the rest of the patterns. As noted earlier, in strings of two consecutive 24s, the first 24 dissimilates to 42 (Lü 1980:88). Recall that the tone 42 does not occur in citation form. To formally characterize the dissimilatory process, I assume that 24 and 42 are both H-registered, and that they have the following structures.

(49)   a.   t   b.   t

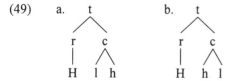

        Contour dissimilation can be viewed as metathesis of the c node. The meta-thesis rule is given in (50).

(50)   *Contour Metathesis*

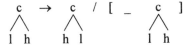

Contour Metathesis (50) applies to strings of the form 24-24, yielding 42-24. The intermediate representations of the tone patterns in (44c) are therefore [24-24], [24-24-24], and [24-24-24-24], respectively. The contour dissimilation rule (50) applies from left to right, deriving the surface tone patterns of [42-24], [42-42-24], and [42-42-42-24].

As we have noted earlier, the phrasal tone patterns in (44) are completely determined by the phrase-initial syllable. It is thus reasonable to assume six basic word melodies from which the polysyllabic tone patterns are derived. The word melodies are given in (51) (the numerical notation is in square brackets).

(51)   a.   t   [11]

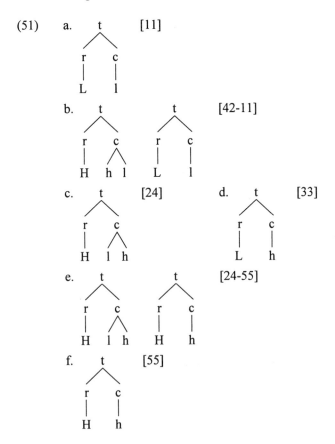

Phrases select their tone melodies from the inventory displayed in (51) on the basis of the historical origin of their initial syllables. Once the base tone melodies are selected, the polysyllabic tone patterns can be derived in the following steps.

(52)   a. Delete lexical tones.
     b. Associate from left to right base melodies to tone-bearing units.
     c. Spread last tone rightward to tone-bearing units.
     d. Apply *Contour Metathesis* (50).

The following derivations of the quadrisyllabic patterns of (44b,c) illustrate how (52) works (t_1 through t_4 are lexical tones).

(53)   a. Phrases with base tone melody [42 11] (cf. (51b))

Delete lexical tones/Associate base tone melody

[H,hl] [L,l]

Spread tone rightward

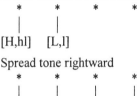

[H,hl] [L,l] [L,l] [L,l]

     b. Phrase with base tone melody [24] (cf. (51c))

Delete lexical tones/Associate tone melody

[H,lh]

Spread tone rightward

[H,lh] [H,lh] [H,lh] [H,lh]

Contour Metathesis (52e)

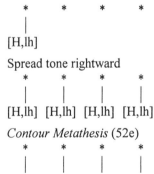

[H,hl] [H,hl] [H,hl] [H,lh]

Other tone patterns in (44) can be derived in the same way.

The derivation of the melodies in (53b) embodies an important property concerning contour tones: the register and contour spread together as a unit. In addition, as pointed out by Chen (1986b:12), the Danyang data of phrasal tone patterns, particularly (44c), indicate that contour tones are referred to as indivisible units by certain rules, which poses great difficulty for any theory that treats contour tones as concatenations of level tones with no internal structure.

The analysis presented above has been challenged by Duanmu (1990, 1994). Duanmu adopts the Africanist position that contour tones are concatenations of level tones. The melodies [42-24], [42-42-24], and [42-42-42-24], which are, in our analysis, derived from the base melody [24] (cf. (51c)), present a serious problem for that position: the derivation of the melodies crucially depends on the spreading of a contour tone, namely 24. It must be acknowledged that out of the six base melodies in (51), only [24] presents a theoretically interesting challenge. The other melodies can be accommodated within a theory that does not admit tonal contour. For example, the melody [24-55] in (51e) can be represented as [LH]; the rightward spread of H yields the bisyllabic, trisyllabic, and quadrisyllabic patterns of [24-55], [24-55-55], and [24-55-55-55]. (The difference between 4 and 5 is inconsequential.) However, the patterns [42-24], [42-42-24], and [42-42-42-24] cannot be derived in this manner. (Henceforth, these patterns will be referred collectively as [42...24].) The heart of the matter is whether the patterns [42...24] are derived through the spreading of 24, which Duanmu represents as a concatenation of two level tones (e.g. 2 and 4). If they are, as we have argued, the data are damaging to any theory that does not admit contour tones as unitary tones.

Duanmu's argument is negative in character. It attempts to show that, at least in the bisyllabic pattern [42-24], the second tone is not derived from the base melody [24]. The main claim is that most bisyllabic phrases that surface as [42-24] in fact contain the lexical tone 24 in the second position. It is not derived from the base melody at all. The claim is based on the following table, which shows the source tones for the word melody [42-24] (Duanmu 1994:593).

(54)   Input combinations that give rise to surface [42 24]

Pattern	Tokens	Percent
[24 24]	40	55.5
[55 24]	20	28
[24 55]	8	11
[55 55]	4	5.5

Essentially the same line of reasoning is presented to support the claim that the trisyllabic and quadrisyllabic patterns, like their bisyllabic counterpart, are not derived from the base melody [24] through spreading. Based on the figures in table (54), Duanmu (1994) argues that the non-initial 24s in the surface word melodies [42...24] come from underlying sources, rather than from the initial tone of the base melody [24]. Cases derived from the input combinations [24 55] and [55 55] are treated as exceptions.

The claim, however, is based on questionable statistical tabulation. The statistical profile is obtained from a count of the examples in Lü (1980), rather than from an exhaustive combing of the vocabulary of Danyang. The figures are therefore not reliable. Even if we accept this method of tabulation, the imbalance in the input combinations is hardly surprising. In modern Danyang, a character typically has two readings—the literary reading and the colloquial reading. The two readings of any given character need not have the same tone. The phonetic realization of the eight traditional tonal categories in the two readings is shown below (Lü 1993:8).

(55)	Tonal Category	Literary	Colloquial
a.	*yin ping*	33	33
A.	*yang ping*	33	24
b.	*yin shang*	55	55
B.	*yang shang*	55	24
c.	*yin qu*	24	24
C.	*yang qu*	24	11
d.	*yin ru*	4	3
D.	*yang ru*	4	4

In (55), the tonal categories refer to the tones in classical Chinese. Note that the *yin-yang* distinction in the four tones of classical Chinese is lost in the literary readings of modern Danyang, but in the colloquial readings, the historical *yin-yang* distinction is preserved. Interestingly, in modern Danyang, the historical *yang ping* (55A), *yang shang* (55C), and *yin qu* (55d) are all realized as 24 in colloquial reading, and the *yin qu* (55c)and *yang qu* (55C) are both realized as 24 in literary reading. Since Duanmu counts tokens of 24 regardless of readings, we naturally expect to find far more characters with 24 than with any other surface tone. It is therefore not surprising that many phrases with the word melodies [42...24] contain characters with their lexical tones realized as 24, in either literary or colloquial reading. The statistical profile in (54), if valid, is a lexical accident of colloquial Danyang. It has nothing to do with the structure of tone, and it sheds no light on how the surface word melodies [42...24] are derived. What Duanmu considers exceptional is in fact the rule. Non-initial underlying tones do not play a role in determining the word melody of a phrase in Danyang. See Yip (1995) for a similar conclusion against Duanmu's (1990, 1994) analysis of the Danyang data.

3.3.1.2 Changzhi

Another dialect of Chinese that exhibits the phenomenon of tone spreading is Changzhi, spoken in the province of Shaanxi in central China. Changzhi has six tones in citation form, as shown in (56). All Changzhi data are cited from Hou (1983).

(56)	a. 213	ts'əu	"suck"
		paŋ	"spotted"
	A. 24	ts'əu	"thick"
		p'aŋ	"plate"
	b. 535	ts'ɔ	"weed"
		pu	"cloth"

c. 44	ts'əu	"stinky"
	paŋ	"half"
C. 53	tsu	"column"
	paŋ	"stick"
d. <u>54</u>	tsə?	"choose"
	pa?	"pull"

The underlined tone <u>54</u> is a short tone realized in syllables ending in glottal stop. Changzhi does not have voiced obstruents; the pairs (56a,A) and (56c,C) are distinctive, as can be seen from the onset obstruents in the forms given.

Changzhi has two suffixes, *tə?* and *ti*, represented by two characters which have the lexical tone 535 when read in isolation. Syntactically, *tə?* is suffixed to a nominal stem, producing a bisyllabic noun. The suffix *ti* is attached to an adjectival stem. Judging from the glosses given by Hou (1983), the suffixes do not appear to contribute much to the meaning of their respective stems. Relevant data are given in (57) (in the tone patterns the first tone is that of the stem, and the second tone is that of the suffixes).[4]

(57)   a. 213 535 → 213 213
        ts'ə tə   "cart"
        çiaŋ tə   "trunk"
        suaŋ ti   "sour"
        tç'iŋ ti   "green"
       b. 24-535 → 24-24
        xæ tə?   "child"
        luŋ tə?   "wheel"
        xuaŋ ti   "yellow"
        ts'əu ti   "thick"
       c. 535-535 → 535-535
        paŋ tə   "board"
        i tə   "chair"
        ləŋ ti   "cold"
        yaŋ ti   "soft"
       d. 44-535 → 44-535
        tçiɔ tə   "shoulder carriage"
        tçiŋ tə   rice pastry
        aŋ ti   "dark"
        ts'əu ti   "stink"
       e. 53-535 → 53-53
        çiaŋ tə?   "fillings"
        təu tə?   "bean"
        laŋ ti   "rotten"
        iŋ ti   "hard"

Note that the nominal suffix *tə?* loses its glottal stop when the tone of the nominal stem is either 213 or 535, as shown in (57a,c), suggesting that 213 and

535 form a natural class on account of their contour. (The suffix *tə?* also loses its glottal stop when the tone of the stem is 44, as shown in (57d).) Phrases with the two suffixes have exactly the same tone patterns, which are summarized below.

(58) Stem tones   Phrasal tone patterns
      213   213-213
      24   24-24
      535   535-535
      44   44-535
      53   53-53

With the exception of 44 (57d), all the phrasal tone patterns can be derived from the stems by spreading their tones; hence the data clearly demonstrate the spreading of tones as melodic units. The tone 44 does not present any problem if we assume that its c and r nodes are unspecified, as in (59),

(59)   t
         ╱ ╲
        r   c

and that the following default rules supply the unspecified values.[5]

(60) *Default Rules*
      a. [ ] → [-stiff]
      b. [ ] → [slack]

The spreading process involves a fully specified tone. Underspecified tones do not spread. I will defer the discussion of the underlying structures of Changzhi tones until section 3.4.2.1; for the present I will continue to use the numerical notation. The derivation of the bisyllabic phrasal tone patterns is illustrated in (61).

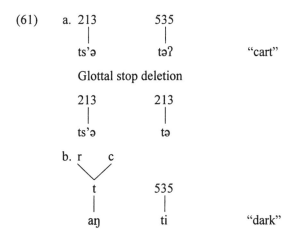

(61)   a. 213   535
           | |
           ts'ə   tə?   "cart"

        Glottal stop deletion

           213   213
           | |
           ts'ə   tə

        b. r   c
            ╲   ╱
             t   535
             | |
             aŋ   ti   "dark"

Default Rules (60)

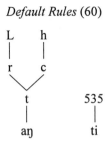

In (61a), the tone of the first syllable spreads to the second syllable, displacing the latter's lexical tone. Spreading does not take place in (61b), because the tone 44 is by assumption unspecified. The default rules (60) apply to derive the surface phrasal pattern 44-535. The rule deleting the glottal stop is not formulated here because it is of marginal interest for our purpose.

The Changzhi facts cannot be derived in a theory that represents contour tones as clusters of level tones. Take the tone 24 as an example. In a cluster representation, the rising tone can be represented as LH. When the stem is suffixed, H is able to spread, but not L.

(62)

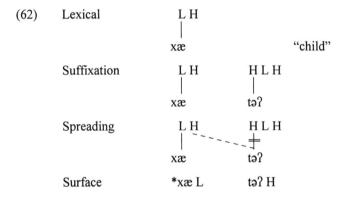

Whether or not HLH is associated with the suffix *təʔ*, we cannot derive the phrasal pattern through a single iteration of spreading. The tone spreading facts of Changzhi support the view that contour tones must be represented as melodic units.

Duanmu (1990, 1994) proposes an alternative analysis of the Changzhi data that attempts to avoid the theoretical consequence of whole tone spreading. The analysis consists of two processes: the stem tone is copied, and the copied tone replaces the lexical tone of the suffix. This is illustrated below.

(63)   24   24   24   24   24
           | | | | |
    xæ   təʔ   →   xæ   təʔ   →   xæ   təʔ
           | |
          535   535   (535)

The replaced tone is in parentheses. This copy-and-replace analysis is not only technically complicated, but the copying and replacing processes target the tones as melodic units, a conclusion Duanmu wants to avoid in the first place. In addition, Changzhi has a separate sandhi pattern for reduplication, which cannot be analyzed in the same way. On the basis of the data discussed in this section, and the reduplication data to be discussed in section 3.4.2.1, Yip (1995) concludes that the copy-and-replace analysis is not tenable. Whole tone spreading is the only viable analysis of the facts.

3.3.2   Register Assimilation

Register-related tone sandhi processes are quite common in Chinese, especially those that involve syllable-initial consonants. For register assimilation data, we turn to Pingyao, a Mandarin dialect, and Chaozhou, a Southern Min dialect known as Teochow in the local vernacular.[6] We will show that these dialects furnish compelling evidence for the separation of contour and register.

3.3.2.1 Pingyao

Pingyao has five tones in citation form (Hou 1980).

(64)   a. 13   ti   "animal's foot"
         b. 35   ti   "field"
         c. 53   ti   "top"
         d. 23   xuʌʔ   "hair"
         e. 54   xuʌʔ   "live"

I assume that the two short tones are derived—23 from 13, and 54 from 53. Thus Pingyao has three underlying tones, which can be represented as in (65).[7]

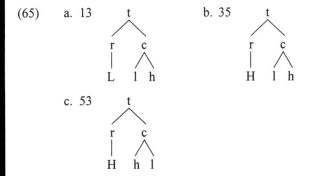

(65)   a. 13   b. 35

        c. 53

Bisyllabic phrases of verb-object and subject-verb constructions show tone sandhi effects. Relevant data are as follows.[8]

(66)   a. 13-13 → 13-13
           t'aŋ u   "embezzle"
           ts'əu tɕ'iɛ   "draw lottery"
           kuaŋ məŋ   "close the door"
           tɕ'iɛ ɕiŋ   "care"
        b. 13-35 → 31-35
           tsəu ti   "rent land"
           pu taŋ   "hatch an egg"
           t'aŋ xua   "talk"
           tei t'aŋ   "carry charcoal"
        c. 13-53 → 35-423
           ts'uŋ mi   "grind rice"
           tɕi ma   "ride a horse"
           xei tsuə   "river flood"
           tsəŋ ts'aŋ   "raise production"
        d. 35-13 → 13-13
           t'uæ paŋ   "quit class"
           xa kuei   "start cooking"
           nia tɕ'iŋ   "play musical instrument"
           yɛ səŋ   "courtyard (is) deep"
        e. 35-35 → 31-35
           pæ ɕiŋ   "upset"
           ts'i ts'æ   "cut vegetables"
           ʂəu tʂi   "get wronged"
           kuei tʂ'aŋ   "harvest celebration"
        f. 35-53 → 35-423
           xa y   "rain"
           tuŋ xuei   "get angry"
           ɕi niaŋ   "hard to see"
           suə ʑiɛ   "greeting by gesture"
        g. 53-13 → 53-13
           tsaŋ iɔ   "stretch waist"
           tsəu sei   "meteorite"
           niɛ ʑəŋ   "distribute work"
           k'əu tiɛ   "sweet-mouthed"
        h. 53-35 → 53-35
           suaŋ tɕ'i   "breathe heavily"
           ti si   "useful"
           tsuə tɕia   "increase prices"
           k'aŋ ti   "plow a field"
        i. 53-53 → 35-423
           ta tiŋ   "take a nap"
           mæ ɕi   "curry favor"
           tɕ'i ts'ɔ   "in heat"
           ər nzuaŋ   "ear soft, gullible"

The short tones 23 and 54 are omitted because they exhibit exactly the same sandhi as their respective underlying tones. The bisyllabic tone patterns are summarized in (67). The vertical axis is the first tone of a bisyllabic phrase; the horizontal axis is the second tone.

(67)   I   II   III
            13   35   53
    13   13-13   31-35   35-423
    35   13-13   31-35   35-423
    53   53-13   53-35   35-423

We make the following observations:

(68)   Contour dissimilation
        a. 13 and 35 become 31 before 35 (Column II).
        b. 53 becomes 35 before another 53 (Column III).

        Register assimilation
        c. 13 raises to 35 before 53 (Column III).
        d. 35 lowers to 13 before 13 (Column I).

        Contour formation
        e. 53 becomes 423 phrase-finally (Column III).

The observations in (68) can be broken down into three types of sandhi effect. First, (68a,b) are cases of contour dissimilation. Second, (68c,d) show register harmony within the bisyllabic phrase; this is the focal point of this section. Finally, (68e) is a contour-changing operation not conditioned by the preceding tone.

Consider first the effect of phrase-final high tones on the preceding tones. The rising tones 13 and 35 become 31 before 35, and the high falling tone 53 becomes 35 before 53 (cf. (68a,b)). In other words, the c node of the first tone metathesizes when followed by a high tone with the same c node. This is a case of contour dissimilation, which can be accounted for in terms of the metathesis rule in (69) (x,y are either [-slack] or [+slack]).

(69)   *Contour Metathesis*

Note that the rising tone 35, which is high-registered, becomes the low falling tone 31, rather than the expected high falling tone 53. This suggests that prior to the application of rule (69), the register of the high rising tone lowers. The lowering rule is given in (70).

(70)   *Register Lowering*

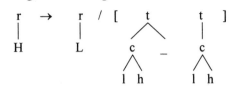

The rules of *Contour Metathesis* (69) and *Register Lowering* (70) derive the tone patterns when the phrase-final tone is 35. The sandhi fact of interest to us is the behavior of the two rising tones 13 and 35 when preceding 13 and 53. The underlying pattern 35-13 surfaces as 13-13, whereas 13-53 surfaces as 35-423. That is, a high tone lowers before a low tone, and a low tone raises before a high tone. Clearly this is a case of register spreading, which is accounted for by the rule in (71).

(71)   *Register Assimilation*

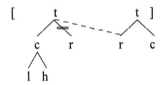

Note that the phrase-initial c node must be specified as rising, because register spreading does not take place when the phrase-initial tone is falling. *Register Assimilation* (71) must order after *Register Lowering* (70) and *Contour Metathesis* (69). The effect of the register assimilation rule (71) is that the register of the phrase-initial rising tone harmonizes with the register of the phrase-final tone.

Finally, we need a feature-inserting rule to derive 423 from 53 in phrase-final position. This rule is *Contour Formation* given in (72).

(72)   *Contour Formation*

```
    c  ]
   / \ - - - -
  h  l      h
```

To illustrate how the rules work, consider the following derivations:

(73)

	I	II	III
Underlying	[L,lh]-[H,hl]	[H,lh]-[L,lh]	[H,lh]-[H,lh]
Rule (70)	–	–	[L,lh]-[H,lh]
Rule (69)	–	–	[L,hl]-[H,lh]
Rule (71)	[H,lh]-[H,hl]	[L,lh]-[L,lh]	–
Rule (72)	[H,lh]-[H,hlh]	–	–
	(35-423)	(13-13)	(31-35)

	IV	V
Underlying	[H,hl]-[H,hl]	[H,lh]-[H,hl]
Rule (70)	–	–
Rule (69)	[H,lh]-[H,hl]	–
Rule (71)	–	–
Rule (72)	[H,lh]-[H,hlh]	[H,lh]-[H,hlh]
	(35-423)	(35-423)

The Pingyao data demonstrate that tonal register spreads independently of tonal contour. This supports the tonal geometry in which the register forms an independent node.

3.3.2.2 Chaozhou

Chaozhou, or Teochow in the vernacular, is a Southern Min dialect of Chinese spoken in the region between Fujian and Guangdong provinces, and by emigrant communities in Southeast Asia. Chaozhou has eight citation tones, as follows.

(74)   a. 33   hung   "divide"
       b. 53   hung   "powder"
       c. 213   hung   "discipline"
       d. 2   huk   "sudden"
       A. 55   hung   "cloud"
       B. 35   hung   "not clear"
       C. 11   hung   "part"
       D. 5   huk   "Buddha"

Unless otherwise noted, all Chaozhou data are cited from Cai (1991). As is typical of Southern Min dialects, the Chaozhou tones, except the two even tones 33 and 11, undergo sandhi in phrase-initial position. The tone sandhi patterns are summarized below. The table is adapted from Cai (1991:5).

(75) | | Citation | Sandhi | Environment |
     |--------|----------|--------|------------------------|
     | a. | 53 | 35 | 53, 55, 5 |
     | | | 24 | 33, 213, 11, 2, 35 |
     | b. | 213 | 53 | 53, 55, 5 |
     | | | 42 | 33, 213, 11, 2, 35 |
     | c. | 2 | 5 | 53, 55, 5 |
     | | | 3 | 33, 213, 11, 2, 35 |
     | d. | 55 | 11 | |
     | e. | 35 | 21 | |
     | f. | 5 | 2 | |

In the table, citation tones change to sandhi tones in phrase-initial position; the tones in the Environment column are phrase-final. A few tones also undergo sandhi in phrase-final position, which is not included in the table. Y.-M. Li (1959) gives 31 as the sandhi tone of 213 (cf. (75b)); I will use Cai's notation but treat it as a low falling tone anyway. It is clear from the data that the checked tones 2 and 5 behave like 213 and 55, respectively (cf. (75b,c,d,f)); the lack of surface contour is obviously due to the short duration of the checked syllables. For this reason, I will treat the pairs 2 and 213, and 5 and 55, as allotones of the same underlying tones, even though they are derived from different historical sources. For the purpose of tone sandhi, natural classes are formed on the basis of actual tonal pitch rather than historical origin.

Only 53 and 213/2 are context-sensitive; other tones undergo sandhi regardless of what follow. We will focus on the sandhi behavior of 53 and 213. Relevant data follow (Cai 1991).

(76) a. hue 53   "fire"
          hue 53 (35) ba 53   "torch"
          hue 53 (35) lou 55   "stove"
          hue 53 (35) tsi? 5   "flame"
          hue 53 (24) suã 33   "volcano"
          hue 53 (24) tsĩ 213   "rocket"
          hue 53 (24) ts'iu 11   a kind of tree
          hue 53 (24) sok 2   "speedy"
          hue 53 (24) kə 35   "torch"
      b. hue 213   "product"
          hue 213 (53) k'uang 53   "money"
          hue 213 (53) lung 55   "freight ship"
          hue 213 (53) mue? 5   "product"
          hue 213 (42) ts'ng 33   "warehouse"
          hue 213 (42) ke 213   "price"
          hue 213 (42) iõ 11   "sample"
          hue 213 (42) sek 2   "product quality"
          hue 213 (42) tsam 35   "freight station"

The sandhi tones are in parentheses. Descriptively, the register of the sandhi tone is determined by the following tone: if it is H-registered, the sandhi tone is also H-registered; and if it is L-registered, the sandhi tone is also L-registered. What is important to note is that the contour of the sandhi tone remains unchanged.

The analysis of the sandhi facts crucially depends on the representation of contour tones. If a contour tone is represented as concatenation of level tones, the Chaozhou data have to be analyzed as simultaneous lowering of the two level tones that make up the contour tones: from HM to ML, and from MH to LM. This can be seen in the derivation of 24-11 from 53-11, shown in (77).

(77)   HM-L $\rightarrow$ MH-L $\rightarrow$ M$\underline{M}$-L $\rightarrow$ $\underline{L}$M-L   (24-11)

The underlined tones are lowered. The second lowering, M$\rightarrow$L, is only triggered by the first lowering, H$\rightarrow$M, which is triggered by the following L on the first iteration. This analysis is *ad hoc*. The domino effect we see here is a direct result of the representational structure. Ordinarily, L does not trigger the lowering of M or H in contour tones such as ML or HL.

Within the tone model proposed in this study, the Chaozhou data can be accounted for as a case of register assimilation. Putting aside the structure of 35 for the moment, I assume that the tones have the following structures (the checked tones are ignored).

(78)   a. 33   A. 55

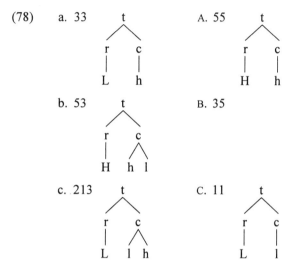

        b. 53   B. 35

        c. 213   C. 11

We need two rules, *Contour Metathesis* and *Register Spread*, given below.

(79)   a. *Contour Metathesis*

        where x, y are h, l

        Condition: applies to contour tones in phrase-initial position

        b. *Register Spread*

Contour Metathesis derives a falling contour from a rising one and a rising contour from a falling one, while *Register Spread* spreads the register of the phrase-final tone leftward, delinking the target's original register node. The derivation follows.

(80)   a. 53-11   b. 53-55

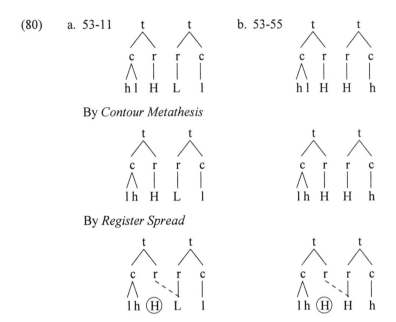

By *Contour Metathesis*

By *Register Spread*

In the derivation, the delinked tones are circled. The Chaozhou tone sandhi is thus a case of register harmony.

In the analysis we assume that citation tones are underlying, from which we derive their sandhi tones. Under this assumption, the behavior of 35 is problematic. It is a high rise, which should be specified as [H,lh]. However, it patterns with L-registered tones in tone sandhi in that the preceding tone is L-registered. This is not surprising if the tone is represented as MH, where M is L-registered. Given the structure [H,lh], the sandhi behavior of 35 is unexpected and needs to be explained.

Ting (1982, 1989) notes that citation tones are not necessarily underlying; quite often it is the sandhi tones that are more basic than the citation tones. Notice that in Chaozhou, *yang ping*, *yang shang*, and *yang ru* (74A,B,D) are high-pitched in citation form, but their sandhi counterparts are low-pitched, as expected of *yang* tones (cf. (75)). Furthermore, *yin qu* and *yin ru* (cf. (74c,d)) are low-pitched in citation form, and their sandhi counterparts are high-pitched, as expected of *yin* tones (cf. (75)). These are cases of tonal flip-flop (Ting 1982, Yue-Hashimoto 1986). To see the effect of flip-flop clearly, I arrange the tones below.

(81)   Tonal Category   Citation   Sandhi   UR
     a. *yin ping*   33   33   L,h
     b. *yin shang*   53   35, 24   H,hl
     c. *yin qu*   213   53, 42   L,lh
     A. *yang ping*   55   11   H,h
     B. *yang shang*   35   21   L,#
     C. *yang qu*   11   11   L,l

For the problem at hand, we can assume that, for *yang shang* (81B), the sandhi tone 21 is underlying, and the citation tone 35 is derived. Under this assumption, it is not surprising that the sandhi tones of (81b,c) are L-registered when they appear before the *yang shang*. We only need to say that *Register Spread* applies before 21 is turned into 35.

There is, however, a technical difficulty. The tone model allows two tones of a given contour, and two even tones of a given register. We are faced with a dilemma in the treatment of 21. If we treat it as falling, we will have three sandhi tones with the falling contour—53, 42, and 21 (cf. (81c,B)). If we treat it as even, however, then we have three L-registered sandhi tones with the even contour— 33, 11, and 21 (cf. (81a,A,B,C)). These facts must be taken into consideration when we determine the underlying tones of Chaozhou.

One formal device we can use is underspecification. We can underspecify 21 and fully specify all other tones. The underlying tones are shown in (81) in the *UR* column. In that column, # stands for the unspecified contour, and [L,#] will eventually surface as 21 in phrase-initial position, and as 35 in phrase-final position and in citation. Given the underlying tones shown in (81), the register of 33, 213, 35, and 11 is L, which spreads to the preceding tone in tone sandhi, keeping the contour of the target intact.

The Chaozhou tone sandhi data support the formal separation of register and contour.

3.3.3 Contour Assimilation

In section 3.2.1, we discussed the tone inventory of Weining Miao and showed that contour must be represented underlyingly as a sequence of the feature [slack]. The tone inventory of Weining Miao does not provide empirical motivation for the existence of the c node. Contour can be represented either as in (82a) or as in (82b).

(82)   a.   b.

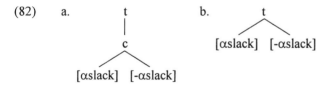

The two structures make different predictions that can be empirically tested. By virtue of the fact that the c node dominates the sequence of [slack], (82a) predicts the existence of sandhi processes that refer to the c node as a unit. Assimilatory spreading of the c node is one such process that is predicted to occur by a theory which adopts the structure (82a). The prediction is not made by a theory which makes use of the structure (82b). To argue that the sequence of [slack] forms the c node in (82a), we need to demonstrate that it behaves phonologically as a unit. I will now present the empirical data that substantiate the claim that contour assimilates.

3.3.3.1 Zhenjiang

One dialect that exhibits the phenomenon of contour spreading is Zhenjiang, a
Mandarin dialect spoken in the province of Jiangsu. Zhenjiang has five tones in
citation form, as shown in (83). All Zhenjiang data are taken from H.-N. Zhang
(1985).

(83)   Tonal inventory of Zhenjiang
        a. 42   tsi   "know"
                    mu   "monster"
        b. 31   tshi   "resign"
                    mi   "rice"
        c. 35   tsi   "son"
                    mi   "riddle"
        d. 55   tsi   "self"
                    mĩ   "face"
        e. 5   tsəʔ   "duty"
                    miʔ   "destroy"

As can be seen from the data, the short tone 5 is realized on syllables ending in
glottal stop. The bisyllabic sandhi effects in Zhenjiang are summarized in the
table in (84), where phrase-initial tones are in the first column and phrase-final
tones are in the first row.

(84)   I   II   III   IV
                42   31   35   55
        42   35-42   35-31   33-35   33-55
        31   35-42   35-31   22-35   22-55
        35   35-42   35-31   35-35   22-55
        55   55-42   55-31   55-35   55-55

The short tone 5 has the same sandhi behavior as 55. We will focus on the tone
patterns of phrases ending in the high even tone 55 (Column IV in (84)). As can
be observed, the two falling tones, 42 and 31, and the rising tone 35, become
even when followed by the high even tone 55. Relevant data are given below.

(85)   a. 42-55/5 → 33-55/5
           səŋ piŋ   "fall ill"
           tshoŋ tsoʔ   "sufficient"
           çioŋ ti   "brother"
           si lu   "train of thought"
           sɛ̃n jyʔ   "March"
           foŋ jiʔ   "maple leaf"
           tshɔ tsoŋ   "operate"
           çi jaʔ   "Western medicine"

b. 31-55/5 → 22-55/5

ʐən nɛ	"endure"
tçhi si	"revelation"
lɛ̃n to	"lazy"
lən tçhi	"cold air"
tu paʔ	"gamble"
tçhiŋ khəʔ	"invite guests"
çio suoʔ	"novel"
huei miʔ	"destroy"

c. 35-55/5 → 22-55/5

çĩ huei	"virtuous"
ʐən miŋ	"human life"
jĩ li	"severe"
phũn wən	"cross-examine"
thũn tçiʔ	"unite"
huaŋ səʔ	"pornographic"
tçhỹ liʔ	"power"
tçhĩ tçiaʔ	"bind feet"

When 55 or 5 precedes 55 or 5, both tones surface, as shown below.

(86) a. 55-55/5 → 55-55/5

| tsi saʔ | "suicide" |
| tsi ɛ | "self love" |

b. 5-55/5 → 5-55/5

| tsəʔ wei | "position" |
| tsəʔ jiʔ | "occupation" |

From the above data, we observe that the non-even tones become even before the high even tone 55. This is a case of contour assimilation.

I assume that the tones in Zhenjiang have the structures shown in (87).

(87)

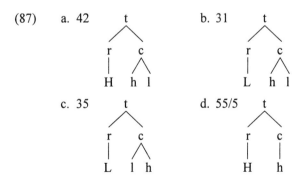

The rising tone 35 is treated as a L-registered tone because of its sandhi behavior: it surfaces as the even tone 22 when followed by the high even tone 55/5. The contour assimilation process can be captured by the spreading rule in (88).[9]

(88)   *Contour Spread*

The rule spreads a nonbranching c node, indicated by a single branch underneath the node, to the preceding tone, delinking the latter's original c node in the process. Since there is only one underlying even tone (87d), we need not mention the register or specify the contour in the rule. In (89) we see the derivations of the patterns in Column IV of (84) involving the rising and falling tones.

(89)   a.

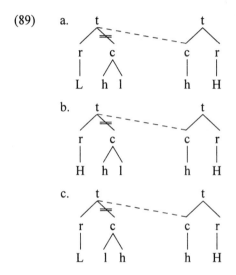

Notice that the high falling tone 42 surfaces as 33, and the low falling tone 31 surfaces as 22. This difference can be attributed to the difference in their registers: in (89a) the register of the first tone is L; in (89b) it is H. Contour spreading does not affect the registers at all.

Contour spreading creates the two structures shown in (90), (90a) from (89a,c) and (90b) from (89b):

(90)   a.   b.

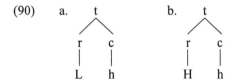

(90b) is not accounted for by (88): as an underlying tone, it surfaces as 55 in both citation and sandhi forms; as a derived tone, it surfaces as 33 (cf. (84)). Given the structures of the tones in (87), particularly the structure for the high even tone 55 in (87d), after *Contour Spread* the bisyllabic structure would be formally indistinguishable from the structure with two underlying high even tones.

(91)   a. Derived   a'. Underlying

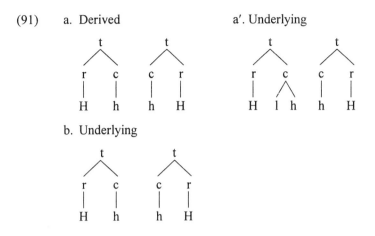

b. Underlying

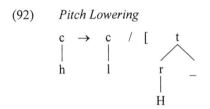

(91a) is derived from (91a'). Within the proposed model of tone, there are two ways to lower an even-contoured tone: by lowering the register from H to L, or by changing the c node specification from h to l. As noted earlier, the difference between 22 and 33 is attributable to the difference in their registers. Therefore, we need to keep the registers of the two tones in (90) distinct in their derived environment. Even if we lower the register of (90b) from H to L, we will not be able to distinguish the two structures in (90).

Alternatively, we can formulate a rule that changes the c node specification, as in (92).

(92)   *Pitch Lowering*

$$
\begin{array}{ccccc}
c & \rightarrow & c & / & [\quad t \\
| & & | & & \quad \bigwedge \\
h & & l & & r \quad \text{—} \\
& & & & | \\
& & & & H
\end{array}
$$

This rule has the effect of lowering the pitch level of an even-contoured tone in phrase-initial position. However, it will apply incorrectly to both the derived string and the underlying string, as long as they meet its structural condition. Suppose that the register of the high even tone 55 is unspecified underlyingly, as in (93a), and the H value is supplied by the default rule (93b).

(93)   a.

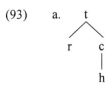

b. *Default Rule*

[ ] → [+stiff]

If so, the two structures in (91) are actually the ones given in (94), with un-specified r nodes.

(94)   a. Derived

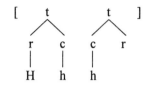

b. Underlying

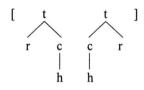

Rule (92) applies to the string in (94a), but not to (94b), since the rule requires a H register as part of its structural description. Obviously, the spreading rule applies before the default rule. The derivation of the patterns in Column IV of (84) follows.

(95)   Underlying representation

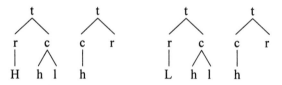

Contour Spread (88)/Conflation

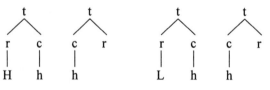

Pitch Lowering (92)

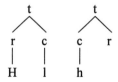

Default Rule (93b)

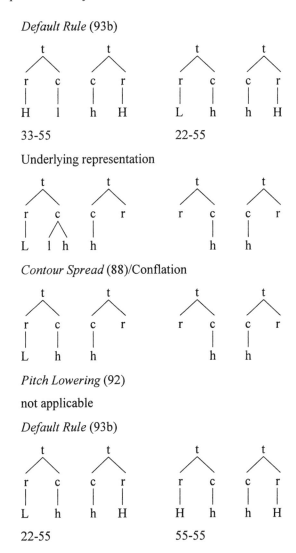

33-55   22-55

Underlying representation

Contour Spread (88)/Conflation

Pitch Lowering (92)

not applicable

Default Rule (93b)

22-55   55-55

The analysis of the Zhenjiang data thus demonstrates the existence of the c node in the geometry of tone.

3.3.3.2 Wenzhou

Wenzhou is a Wu dialect spoken in the coastal city of Wenzhou, Zhejiang Province. Like other Wu dialects, it retains voicing as a distinctive feature of its consonantal phonemes, and its tonal inventory reflects the influence of the voicing qualities of syllable-initial segments. It has eight tones in citation form, shown in (96). Unless otherwise indicated, all Wenzhou data are taken from Zhengzhang (1964b).[10]

(96)   a. 44   A. 31
        b. 45   B. 34
        c. 42   C. 22
        d. 323   D. 212

The underlined tones are the so-called "tense-throat tones," which are relatively short (Zhengzhang 1964a). 323 and 212 are derived historically from syllables ending in stop obstruents. In modern Wenzhou, such syllable types no longer exist, so the tones 323 and 212 manifest themselves as tense and relatively short. The tones in (96a-d) are used in voiceless-initial syllables, and those in (96A-D) are used in voiced-initial syllables. Note that the contours of (96b,d) and (96B,D) remain constant, giving further evidence that register and contour are separate entities.

Bisyllabic phrases surface in one of the eight phrasal tone melodies, of which we will consider patterns F and F'. These two patterns have the following tonal shapes.

(97)   Pattern   Melody   Source tones
        F.   42-21   (96b,B,C)-(96A)
                                 (96b,B,c,C)-(96c)
        F'.   21-42   (96d,D)-(96c)

The patterns are exemplified in (98) and (99), respectively.[11]

(98)   a. 45-31   kou liang   "food ration"
                          hai yuan   "seaman"
        b. 34-31   lao po   "wife"
                          dong yuan   "mobilize"
        c. 42-31   zheng ming   "prove"
                          jing tai   "mirror table"
        d. 22-31   wai po   "grandmother"
                          di qiu   "Earth"
        e. 45-42   hao huo   "good product"
                          guang po   "broadcast"
        f. 34-42   yan jing   "eye glasses"
                          niu kou   "button"
        g. 42-42   chang pian   "record"
                          fen dou   "struggle"
        h. 22-42   yun qi   "luck"
                          jiu deng   "old bench"

(99)   a. 323-42   hei bu   "black cloth"
                          zhe kou   "discount"
        b. 212-42   bai bu   "white cloth"
                          yao pian   "tablet"

One important observation we can make with respect to the tone patterns in (98–99) is that the second source tone is either 31 or 42—that is, falling in contour. The two tones that comprise patterns F and F' are both falling (we will ignore the phonetic difference between 31 and 21, which do not occur in the same environment). According to Zhengzhang, in bisyllabic phrases, the stress falls on the first syllable, except when the first source tone is either 323 or 212, in which case the stress falls on the second syllable. In pattern F, therefore, the first syllable is stressed, and in pattern F', the second syllable is stressed. Suppose that in bisyllabic phrases stress is assigned to the first syllable if the syllable carries tones other than 323 or 212 (historically such syllables end in stop obstruents); otherwise, stress is assigned to the second syllable. We can then make the observation that, in bisyllabic phrases, the stressed syllable has the high falling tone 42, and the unstressed syllable has the low falling tone 21. To derive patterns F and F', let us suppose that the two falling tones 42 and 31 (or 21) have the following structures.

(100)   a. 42

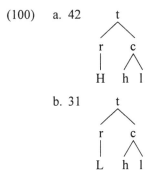

         b. 31

The two patterns can be derived in four steps:

(101)   a. Assign stress.
         b. Delete the register and contour of the source tones except the last tone.
         c. Spread the c node of the last tone
         d. Assign H to the tone in the stressed syllable and L to the tone in the unstressed syllable.

This mechanism is illustrated by the derivation in (102).

(102)   a. Assign stress (indicated by *)

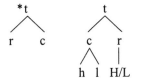

Delete register and contour

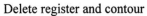

Spread contour

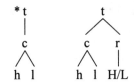

Assign register

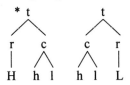

b. Assign stress (indicated by *)

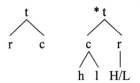

Delete register and contour

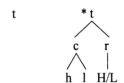

Spread contour

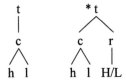

Assign register

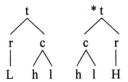

(102a) is the derivation of pattern F, and (102b) is the derivation of pattern F'. The difference between the two patterns is stress. If the first syllable carries the tone 323 or 212, stress will be assigned to the second tone; the bisyllabic phrase will then surface as 21-42, which is pattern F'. It is assumed that the rules of contour spreading and register assignment, which are not formulated, apply to the bisyllabic patterns enumerated in (97). The exceptional cases are the tonal combinations of (96c)-(96A) and (96d,D)-(96A); the former is expected to surface as pattern F, and the latter as pattern F'. This expectation, however, is not borne out; they all surface as 22-2 (pattern C).

The analysis of patterns F and F' relies crucially on contour spreading; this observation supports the postulation of the c node as an integral part of the geometry of tone. The tone pattern of trisyllabic phrases based on the bisyllabic pattern F furnishes further evidence for contour spreading. Trisyllabic phrasal tone patterns depend entirely on the last two syllables. According to Zhengzhang (1980), trisyllabic phrases of which the last two syllables would surface as pattern F have this property: if the stress is on the first syllable, the pattern is 42-21-21;[12] if it is on the second syllable, the pattern is 21-42-21. If the first syllable carries the tone 323 or 212, which are stressless, the pattern is 21-42-21. Thus, the analysis of the sandhi data in terms of contour spreading is supported by the facts of trisyllabic tone sandhi. The Wenzhou data provide empirical support for the tone model that incorporates the c node.

3.3.4   Feature Assimilation

Evidence of feature assimilation is plentiful; many tonological processes exhibit the effect of tonal feature spreading. In fact, early work in autosegmental phonology was motivated largely by evidence of this type: tone spreading can be readily analyzed as spreading of tonal features. In this section we will consider tonological evidence from one Chinese dialect, Gao'an. This dialect furnishes unequivocal data to demonstrate that the c node features (h and l) exhibit assimilatory sandhi behavior.

Gao'an has seven tones in citation form (Yan 1981).[13]

(103)   a. 55   ka   "add"
                    siu   "repair"
         A. 24   siu   "rest"
         b. 42   hou   "beg"
         c. 33   p'i   "match"
                    su   "four"
         C. 11   p'ei   "double"
                    t'i   "earth"
         d. 3   tsok   "table"
         D. 1   hok   "study"
                    çiak   "stone"

(103a,A), (103c,C) and (103d,D) are alternating pairs (pairs that are conditioned by the syllable-initial consonants) in Classical Chinese; (103a,c,d) were used with voiceless-initial syllables, and (103A,C,D) with voiced-initial syllables. Modern Gao'an, however, does not have voiced obstruents. As can be seen in the examples, *siu* 55 "repair" vs. *siu* 24 "rest" and *p'i* 33 "match" vs. *p'ei* 11 "double," the tones (103a) through (103C) are distinctive. (103d,D) are the two short tones realized on syllables ending in /p, t, k/. They are non-distinctive, derivable from (103c,C). Thus, Gao'an has an inventory of five underlying tones: three even tones (high, mid, and low), one low falling tone, and one low rising tone. The underlying tones of Gao'an may have the structures in (104).[14]

(104)

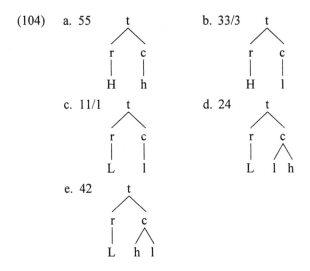

In bisyllabic phrases, the high even tone 55 becomes the high falling tone 53 when it precedes the mid and low even tones 33 and 11, as well as their short counterparts.[15] Relevant data are given in (105) (Yan 1981:105).

(105)   a. 55-33 → 53-33
           çiɛu han   "make charcoal"
           soŋ tçi   "bi-seasonal"
           siu p'i   "repair"
           sam su   "three-four"
        b. 55-11 → 53-11
           ka p'ɛi   "double"
           t'iɛn t'i   "heaven and earth"
           kuŋ çia   "commune"
           tçi han   "egg"
        c. 55-3 → 53-3
           ka k'uɛt   "broaden"
           tuŋ pɛt   "northeast"
           foŋ tsok   "square table"
           saŋ t'iɛt   "pig iron"

d. 55-1 → 53-1

tçiuŋ iok	"Chinese medicine"
k'ɛi hok	"opening of school"
tçiaŋ yot	"first month"
ts'iaŋ çiak	"stone"

No other bisyllabic phrases exhibit sandhi effects. The mid even tone 33/3 and the low even tone 11/1 form a natural class which conditions the 55→53 sandhi change, stated informally in (106).

(106)   55 → 53 / _ 33, 11, 3, 1

Formally, the two even tones 33 and 11 share the same c node, namely l, but their register specification is different: 33 is H, and 11 is L (cf. (104b, c)). The registers of the tones 33/3 and 11/1 do not figure in conditioning the 53→55 sandhi. A necessary condition is the even contour—that is, the c node of the conditioning tone must not branch. The high falling tone 53 is created by spreading the l node dominated by the c node. The rule is formulated in (107).

(107)   *Feature Spread*

Condition: the c nodes do not branch.

The derivation of the tone pattern in (105a) is as follows.

(108)   Underlying

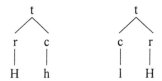

Feature Spread (107)

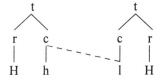

Since 55 is the only tone that has a nonbranching c node dominating h (cf. (104a)), it is not necessary to state the register of the target—the phrase-initial tone—in the structural description of the spreading rule. The register of the spreading tone cannot be mentioned, because the mid even tone and the low even tone are assumed to have different specifications for the register feature [stiff] (cf. (104b,c)). The condition in the statement of rule (107) is necessary because it prevents the l branch of the rising tone 24 from spreading to the first tone. Similarly, the c node of the first tone must be specified as nonbranching to prevent the spreading rule from applying to the rising tone 24, which would produce a convex contour. The two illicit derivations are illustrated below.

(109)   a. [...]   (*53-24)

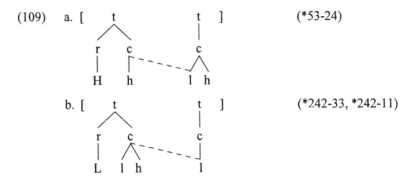

b. [...]   (*242-33, *242-11)

Note that the spreading rule (107) refers not only to the terminal feature of the c node, but also to its formal structure. This property provides further support for the existence of the c node.

The preceding analysis of the Gao'an tone sandhi depends crucially on the underlying structures we assumed for the even tones 55, 33/3, and 11/1. An alternative analysis is possible if we assume the following structures for the even tones.

(110)   a. 55   b. 33/3   c. 11/1

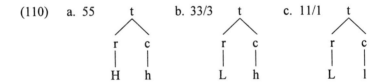

Thus, the mid and low even tones 33/3 and 11/1 belong to the same class by virtue of their register specification, which is L. The 55→53 sandhi can be seen as a process of contour dissimilation—the even contour dissimilates when followed by the two L-registered even tones. The dissimilation process can be captured by the feature-inserting rule stated in (111).

(111)   [...]

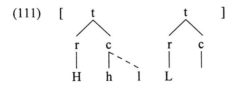

Condition: c nodes do not branch.

Rule (111) turns the even contour into the falling contour before another even-contoured tone. What is significant is that this analysis refers to the terminal feature of the c node, as well as to the formal structure of the c node that must be mentioned in the statement of the rule.

3.4   Contours and Other Matters

Having considered tonal assimilation data in the preceding section, we now turn our attention to other tonological matters that promise interesting insight into the interplay between register and contour. Specifically, I will examine the distribution of tones, the tonology of concave and convex tones, and the simplification of complex contours. I will approach these issues from the perspective of the tone model in which tone dominates register and contour.

3.4.1   Distributional Properties of Tones

Modern Chinese dialects vary tremendously in their tonal inventories, ranging in size from three tones to more than the historical eight—the *yin* and *yang* variants of the four tones, *ping*, *shang*, *qu*, and *ru* (Yuan et al. 1960). When we examine how tones distribute among tonal inventories, we need to pay attention to the tones' historical origin, and to the correlation between tonal register and obstruent voicing. In what follows, I will discuss in general terms the distribution of tones among tonal inventories of Chinese dialects.

3.4.1.1   Distribution of Even Tones

By definition, an even tone is one that maintains the same pitch height throughout the duration of the tone-bearing unit. To facilitate discussion, the structures of four even tones are given below.

(112)   Tones with even contour

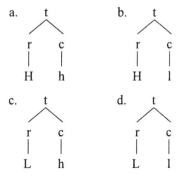

An inventory with four even tones, though rare, is nonetheless attested. Liuyang, a dialect spoken in Hunan Province, has a tonal inventory with five tones, four of which are even (Xia 1983).

(113)   Tonal inventory of Liuyang
       a. 33   pei   "cup"
                ko   "brother"
       A. 55   p'in   "poor"
       b. 24   xau   "good"
       c. 11   t'i   "big"
       d. 44   t'i   "wash"

Diachronically, (113a) and (113A) are derived from syllables with voiceless and voiced initials, respectively. Modern Liuyang, however, has lost the voiced obstruents. Hence the two tones in (113a,A) are contrastive, because both are realized on voiceless-initial syllables. Our model provides distinct formal representations for each of the four even tones in (113).

Most dialects that have been reported in the literature have in their tonal inventories no more than two even tones, at either the underlying or surface level. When we discuss the distribution of even-contoured tones, a distinction must be made between those tonal systems that exhibit register alternation conditioned by the voicing qualities of the syllable-initial consonants, and those that do not. Cross-dialectally, a tone system with register alternation involving the even contour is likely to contain the pair 44/22 (55/33) or the pair 33/11. (Henceforth I will use "alternating tones" or "alternating pairs" to refer to tones such as 44 and 22, which are in complementary distribution with respect to the voicing qualities of the syllable-initial segments.) This observation is significant because it suggests that, at least in the unmarked case, a pair of even tones alternates on the register node, leaving the c node intact. The representation of the even tones in (112) permits two ways of lowering the pitch level of a tone: by lowering the register from H to L, or by changing the nonbranching c node from h to l. Given that both tonal register and consonantal voicing are specified by the feature [stiff], the alternation between high and low even tones must involve a register-changing phonological rule. Note that alternating falling or rising tones necessarily differ in their registers—necessarily, because the proposed theory has a single representation for the falling and rising contours. Despite the fact that our theory generates four even tones, with respect to register-sensitive rules, the primary contrast among even tones is H versus L register. In this regard, the 44/22 alternation in Songjiang is typical in that the difference between the two even tones is in their register. The Songjiang tones are presented in (114a), and the structures of 44/22 are shown in (114b).

(114)   a. Alternating pairs in Songjiang (cf. (11))

ping	*shang*	*qu*	*ru*
53	44	35	5
31	22	13	3

b. Structures of 44 and 22

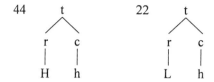

Some dialects have two alternating even tones that differ in the c node from those in (114). Shaoxin is such a dialect. It has eight surface tones, as shown in (115) (Yuan et al. 1960:80).[16]

(115) a. 51   b. 335   c. 33   d. 45
       A. 231   B. 113   C. 11   D. 12

Shaoxin still maintains voicing as a distinctive feature among its obstruents. The low tones in (115A-D) are in complementary distribution with the high tones in (115a-d). Consider now the structures of the two even tones 33 and 11 in (116).

(116) a. 33   t   b. 11   t

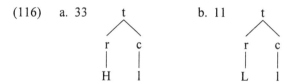

Like the 44/22 pair in Songjiang, 33 and 11 alternate only in their register. They have the same specification for the c node.

   In the two dialects Songjiang and Shaoxin, the two alternating even tones are specified either as h or as l. If the c node is h, both the high tone and the low tone are realized in the upper end of their respective registers, hence the pair 44/22 (similarly, the pair 55/33 in some dialects). If, however, the contour node is l, both the high and low tones will be realized in the lower end of their respective registers, yielding 33/11, as in Shaoxin. To my knowledge, no tone system with register alternation contains an alternating pair 55/11; such a pair, at the two extremes of the pitch scale, would require the structures shown in (117).

(117) a. 55   t   b. 11   t

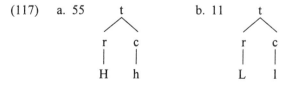

   The fact that 55 (117a) and 11 (117b) do not exist as alternating tones lends empirical support to the analysis that treats register lowering as a phonological process involving a feature-changing rule. Although it is theoretically possible to have the two tones in (117) as alternating tones, the formal relationship between these two tones involves both the register and the contour. Therefore, the formal statement that captures the relationship would be more complex—it would consist of one phonological rule to account for the register difference, and one rule to account for the contour difference. In dialects that do not exhibit register alternation, there is no restriction on the occurrence of even tones. We have seen Liuyang with four even tones (113), including 55 and 11, all of which are underlying. Other dialects that contain 55 and 11 in their tonal inventories include Taiyuan and Daning, two Mandarin dialects spoken in Shaanxi Province (Hou et al. 1986:90).

(118)   Taiyuan tonal inventory

      11   53   55   2   <u>43</u>

      Daning tonal inventory:

      35   11   55   2

Here 2 and <u>43</u> are short, i.e. *ru*, tones. In the unmarked case, the two tones 55 and 11 occur only as non-alternating tones. Like paired alternating falling or rising tones, paired alternating even tones share the same c node specification.

3.4.1.2 Distribution of Contour Tones

The proposed tonal geometry places a constraint on the number of falling or rising contours. Since the r node determines the register within which the c node specifies the tonal contour over the duration of the tone-bearing unit, we expect contours to form within a single register. Cross-dialectal evidence meets our theoretical expectation. Although it is possible for a language to have 51 and 31, or 15 and 13, as contrastive tones in its tonal inventory, it is nonetheless a statistically significant fact that the tones 51 and 31 (or 15 and 13) rarely co-occur in the same tone language. Typically, in dialects that have two contrastive falling tones, we find 53 (or 42) in opposition with 31 (or 21). The case is similar for the rising tones. Given a sufficient degree of idealization, the high variant is in the *yin* register, and the low variant is in the *yang* register. A survey of some 120 dialects of Chinese reveals the following distribution.

(119)   Tones   Number of dialects
      Fall   53 and 31   14
           51 and 31   1
           51 and 53   0
      Rise   35 and 13   5
           15 and 13   0
           15 and 35   0

In fact, the tone 15 does not occur in any of the dialects surveyed, either by itself or together with 13 or 35. The distributional pattern is statistically significant concerning tonal contours. In the great majority of cases, a tone system avoids two tones with the same start or end points but different pitch differentials. Thus, the pairs 51/53, 15/13, and 15/35 do not occur at all, and the pair 51/31 is rare. The diagrams in (120) illustrate this distribution of contour tones (adapted from Yip 1980).

(120)   a. Unmarked pairs

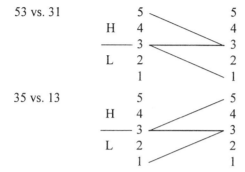

     b. Marked or non-occurring pairs

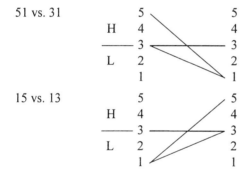

Given the proposed tone geometry, we expect an upper limit on how contours can be created—in the unmarked case, a high falling contour is not likely to fall from the highest pitch point all the way to the lowest. The distributional evidence meets the theoretical expectation.[17]

3.4.2   Convex and Concave

In section 3.1, we made the stipulation (6),

(6)   Underlyingly, the contour node may have at most two branches,

which entails the proposition (8):

(8)   Concave/convex contours are surface phenomena.

In other words, the structure of the underlying c node is either non-branching or binary-branching:

(121)   a.   c

        b.   c

We now present empirical evidence to confirm proposition (8). Formally, we represent the concave and convex contours as in (122).

(122)   a. Concave

              c

           h l h

        b. Convex

              c

           l h l

In terms of cross-dialectal distribution, complex tones exist in citation form, and to a lesser extent in sandhi form as well. There are three cases we need to consider: tone systems in which complex tones appear only in citation form; those in which they exist only in sandhi form; and those in which they exist in both citation and sandhi forms. The reduction of surface complex contours to simpler contours at the underlying level depends on two considerations: the tonal inventory of the language in question, and the sandhi behavior of the complex tones. Changzhi and Xining, both Mandarin dialects, furnish data which show that, on proper analysis of their tonal inventories and the sandhi behavior of the tones, the complex contours are derivable from simpler contours.

3.4.2.1 Changzhi

We first consider the dialect of Changzhi, which we have seen in sections 3.2.2.1 and 3.3.1.2. As shown in (56), Changzhi has a tonal inventory of five tones, plus a short tone, in citation form. For the sake of convenience I repeat the tones below, without the examples (Hou 1983).[18]

(56)   a. 213
        A. 24
        b. 535
        c. 44
        C. 53
        d. 54

Changzhi does not have voiced obstruents, and the pairs (56a,A) and (56c,C) are distinctive. Disregarding the short tone 54, we have one even tone 44, one falling tone 53, and one rising tone 24. If we treat them as underlying tones, they would have the structures in (123).

(123) a. 44

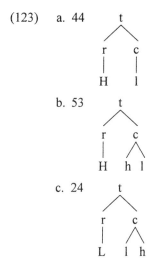

b. 53

c. 24

Given these structures, it is theoretically impossible to reduce the complex tones 213 and 535 to underlying falling or rising tones, because there would then be three underlying falling or rising tones, inexpressible within the proposed theory. The proposed structure of tone is capable of representing only two tones each for the falling and rising contours. But if we assume that the tones in (123) are all underlyingly even, we can consider the surface concave tones 213 and 535 as being derived from underlyingly falling tones. The underlying tonal inventory of Changzhi is given below.

(124) a. 44   b. 53

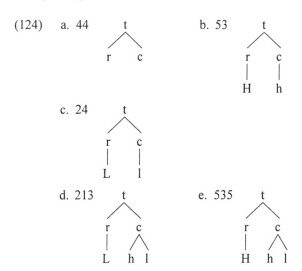

c. 24

d. 213   e. 535

In section 3.3.1.2, I argued that the tone 44 is underlyingly unspecified, as in (124a), and that two default rules supply the register and contour feature values. The default rules are repeated below as (125).

(125)   *Default Rules*
      a. [   ]   →   L
      b. [   ]   →   h

The reason to consider 44 as a L-registered tone is that in verbal reduplication, 44 surfaces as low falling 31 in phrase-initial position. To derive the citation tones from the underlying structures in (124), I propose the feature-inserting rule (126).

(126)   *Contour Formation*

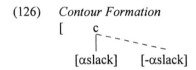

    [αslack]   [-αslack]

The rule applies to tones in citation form, and to the initial tones in reduplicated verbal phrases, as we will see shortly. Rule (126) inserts l to the right of h, and h to the right of l. It maps the underlying structures in (124) to the ones in (127).

(127)

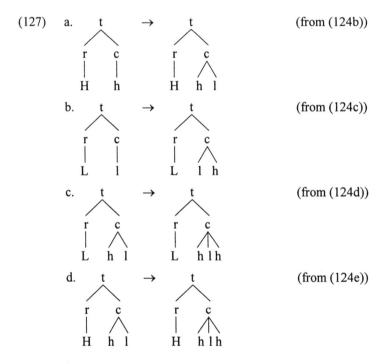

a.   (from (124b))
b.   (from (124c))
c.   (from (124d))
d.   (from (124e))

The default rules in (125) apply to the underspecified tone, deriving the following structure for the surface even tone 44.

(128)

The postulation of the underlying falling contour [hl] for the surface concave contour is justified by the sandhi behavior in verbal reduplication. The underlying falling tones exhibit different sandhi effects from the rest. With respect to the sandhi behavior of the second tone of reduplicated verbal phrases, the five tones fall into two classes based on their underlying contours. Relevant data are given below (Hou 1983:261).[19]

(129) a. 213-213 → 213-35
       saŋ saŋ   "fan"   fəŋ fəŋ   "divide"
       b. 535-535 → 535-35
       ts'ɔ ts'ɔ   "stir"   ts'əu ts'əu "look at"
       c. 24-24 → 24-53
       tɕ'iəu tɕ'iəu "seek"
       d. 44-44 → 31-53
       suaŋ suaŋ   "calculate" k'aŋ k'aŋ   "see"
       e. 53-53 → 35-53
       uŋ uŋ   "ask"   tuŋ tuŋ   "move"

In verbal reduplication, the two surface concave tones, modulo the register of the first tone, have the same tone melody—213/535-35. This is different from the reduplicated tone melodies of the other three tones. Note that 44 surfaces as 31 in verbal reduplication (129d), which is the reason we assigned L to the register of this tone by the default rule (125a).

To derive the tone patterns in (129), we first consider the behavior of tones in phrase-final position. We observe that the underlying falling tones surface as the high rising tone 35; the other tones surface as 53. The observations can be accounted for by the rule in (130a).

(130) a.

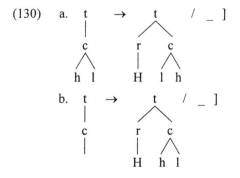

Thus, tones in Changzhi form classes according to their c nodes. Note that 44 is unspecified underlyingly, but it surfaces as 53 in phrase-final position. This indicates that the default rule applies before the rules in (130). Rule (130b) derives 53 from the underlyingly even tones 24 and 53 as well as from the underlyingly unspecified tone 44. This rule is interesting formally in that the contour is falling regardless of the internal structure of the c node undergoing the rule. It only mentions the formal property of the c node, whether it branches or not.

The tones in phrase-initial position can be derived by the feature-inserting rule (126). The derivation of the tone patterns of verbal reduplication is shown in (131); the derivation starts after reduplication.

(131)   I   II   III   IV

[L,hl]-[L,hl]   [H,hl]-[H,hl]   [L,l]-[L,l]   [H,h]-[H,h]

Default Rules (125a,b)
not applicable

Rules (130a,b)
[L,hl]-[H,lh]   [H,hl]-[H,lh]   [L,l]-[H,hl]   [H,h]-[H,hl]

Contour Formation (126)
[L,hlh]-[H,lh]   [H,hlh]-[H,lh] [L,lh]-[H,hl]   [H,hl]-[H,hl]
213-35   535-35   24-53   53-53

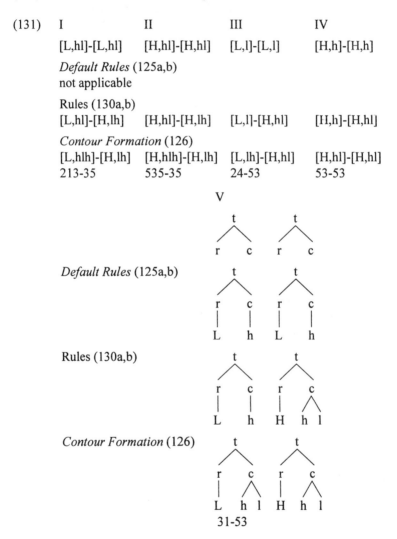

In (131IV), however, we derived the ill-formed pattern *53-53, instead of 35-53. Note that *Contour Formation* (126) creates two identical tones, and both are

high-registered falling tones. We therefore need a contour metathesis rule that changes the falling contour to rising just in case it is followed by another falling tone. This rule is given in (132).

(132)
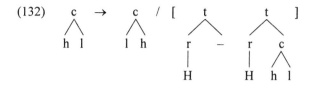

The register of the first tone must be specified so as to rule out the low falling tone 31 in (131V). The derivation of (131IV) continues as follows.

(133)
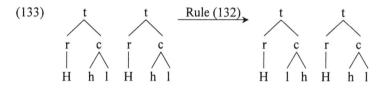

The Changzhi facts demonstrate that underlying tones may have completely different contours than the tones that surface, owing to the various rules that may apply during the derivation of surface tones. The proposition that convex and concave tones are derivative is thus confirmed by the Changzhi verbal reduplication data.

3.4.2.2 Xining

Another dialect that demonstrates the surface nature of complex contours is Xining, to which the analysis of surface complex tones in Changzhi can be extended. Xining has four tones, shown below. All Xining data are taken from C.-C. Zhang (1980:290); the apical vowel is transcribed as /i/.

(134)   Xining tonal inventory
         a. 44   ma   "ant"
                      ta   "dejected"
         A. 24   ma   "hemp"
                      t'ã   a surname
         b. 53   ma   "horse"
                      ta   "beat"
         c. 213   nu   "hungry"
                      ta   "bid"

Now consider the bisyllabic tone patterns in (135) through (138), where N is the neutral tone, and [ɣ] is syllabic.[20]

(135)   a. 44-44 → 44-N
        kɯ ta   "collusion"
        çj kua   "watermelon"
        çiõ si   "thoughts"
        tuõ çj   "thing"
     b. 44-24 → 44-N
        ia t'ɯ   "girl"
        tsa ʂi   "solid"
        tõ luõ   "lantern"
        ʂõ liõ   "consult"
     c. 44-53 → 44-N
        sõ k'ɯ   "draft animal"
        tsuõ tõ   "middle grade"
        põ ʂɯ   "aide"
        kuã k'a   "check point"
     d. 44-213 → 44-N
        kuõ tɔ   "fair"
        tçiõ ts'ɯ   "make do"
        ma j   "ant"
        yu liõ   "moon"

(136)   a. 53-44 → 53-N
        tiã çiõ   "snack"
        ta t'iõ   "find out"
        tʂ'ɛ çiõ   "care for"
        ma tʂɛ   "horse wagon"
     b. 53-24 → 53-N
        p'ɔ fa   "upset"
        tçiɯ çj   "banquet"
        tʂõ t'ɯ   "pillow"
        tʂɣ çj   "main food"
     c. 53-53 → 53-N
        ɛ tu"ear"
        lu liã   "troublesome"
        lɔ xɣ   "tiger"
        çiɔ uã   "small bowl"
     d. 53-213 → 53-N
        ta suã   "plan"
        niã luei   "tear"
        põ si   "talent"
        pã tõ   "bench"

(137)   a. 24-44 → 21-53
        miã xua   "cotton"
        ma ta   "troublesome"
        liõ kã   "decisive"
        liõ çy   "neighbor"

b. 24-24 → 21-53
   ma fã   "trouble"
   miə̃ pei   "clear"
   p'γ̣ t'ɔ   "grape"
   niɯ lə̃   "cowboy"
c. 24-53 → 21-53
   ts'ɛ xu   "match"
   tʂ'ə̃ t'γ̣   "dust"
   ɕiə̃ l̩   "luggage"
   liə̃ fə̃   a type of pastry
d. 24-213 → 21-53
   liə̃ k'uɛ   "cool"
   ʂi xua   "honest words"
   t'γ̣ tsi   "apprentice"
   niɯ ʐɯ   "beef"

(138) a. 213-44 → 21-53
          tsi fə̃   "place"
          kɔ tɕia   "self"
          tɕ'j tʂ'ɛ   "car"
          j si   "meaning"
       b. 213-24 → 21-53
          uɛ xə̃   "novice"
          ɕiɯ ts'ɛ   "intellectual"
          suã p'ã   "abacus"
          iə̃ tʂ'ɯ   "entertain (guests)"
       c. 213-53 → 21-53
          sɔ tʂγ   "bloom"
          tsɔ xu   "wood burner"
          pɔ tsi   "newspaper"
          ɕiɔ tsə̃   "principal"
       d. 213-213 → 21-53
          uei tɔ   "taste"
          ɕiɔ xua   "joke"
          kγ̣ si   "story"
          t'ɛ xɯ   "empress"

The tone patterns are summarized below (the horizontal axis is the second tone of a bisyllabic phrase; the vertical axis is the first tone).

(139)

	44	53	24	213
44	44-N	44-N	44-N	44-N
53	53-N	53-N	53-N	53-N
24	21-53	21-53	21-53	21-53
213	21-53	21-53	21-53	21-53

The Structure of Tone

The sixteen bisyllabic patterns neutralize into three phrasal tone melodies: 44-N, 53-N and 21-53. It is clear from the data that the second tone plays no role in tone sandhi; the phrase-initial tone determines the tone melody of the bisyllabic phrase. If the initial tone is 44, the bisyllabic tone melody is 44-N; if 53, it is 53-N. Interestingly, the behavior of the concave tone 213 is identical to that of the rising tone 24. Both surface in the melody 21-53. The sandhi behavior of the surface concave tone gives strong evidence that it is derived from a tone with an underlying rising contour. Assuming the structures of Xining tones to be as shown in (140),

(140)

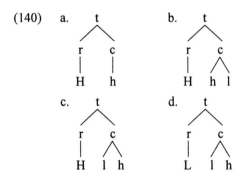

we can derive the surface bisyllabic tone patterns with the following two rules.[21]

(141)

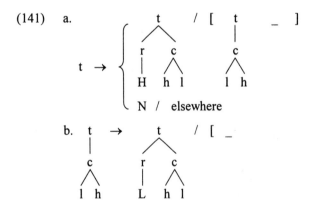

In the two rules, the rising contour [lh] is crucial. All tones become high falling 53 following the rising tones, and otherwise N (the content of rule (141a)). The rising tones become the low falling tone 21 phrase-initially; otherwise, the lexical tone remains in phrase-initial position, which is the content of (141b). The following derivation illustrates these points (T is any tone).

(142)

	[H,h]-T	[H,hl]-T	[H,lh]-T	[L,lh]-T
Rule (141a)	[H,h]-N	[H,hl]-N	[H,lh]-[H,hl]	[L,lh]-[H,hl]
Rule (141b)	–	–	[L,hl]-[H,hl]	[L,hl]-[H,hl]
	44-N	53-N	21-53	21-53

Note that if the surface concave tone is also underlyingly concave, we cannot group 24 and 213 as belonging to the same class. It would be simply accidental that the two tones exhibit the same sandhi behavior. By assuming that the surface concave tone is derived from an underlying rising tone, we provide an explanation of why the two tones 24 and 213 behave in the same way in tone sandhi. The two tones (140c,d) form a class by virtue of the fact that they have the same underlying contour. The surface concavity of (140d) in citation form can be derived by inserting [+slack] at its c node.

(143)

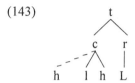

The sandhi data from Changzhi and Xining demonstrate that complex contours (concavity and convexity) can be fruitfully analyzed as derived from simpler underlying contours by means of feature-inserting rules.

3.4.3   Contour Simplification

There are three types of operation that can affect the c node: metathesis, feature insertion, and simplification. We have seen instances of the first two types. The results of metathesis and feature insertion are unique: metathesizing the falling contour gives the rising contour, and vice versa; and feature insertion often results in more complex contours, such as concavity. Contour simplification, however, is non-unique. It produces two distinct representations from a falling or rising contour:

(144)

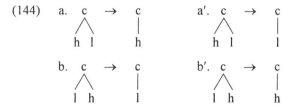

One way to constrain the dual possibilities and ensure uniqueness for contour simplification is to stipulate that for a tone language that exhibits such tone sandhi phenomena, contour simplification is either (145a) or (145b).

(145)   a. Left simplification

b. Right simplification

The process of left simplification truncates the left branch of the c node, and that of right simplification truncates the right branch of the c node. Other things being equal, if a language that contains rising and falling tones employs either of the simplification rules in (145), we expect to see two even tones with distinct c node specification as a result of simplification. The so-called "Min Circle" of the dialect of Xiamen (Amoy Hokkien) provides interesting data that indicate that contour simplification has the properties just described. In Xiamen, a tone undergoes sandhi in non-phrase-final position regardless of the following tone. This kind of tonal change is not sensitive to phonological environment; a tone in citation form corresponds one-to-one to the tone in sandhi form. The citation tones are given in (146), and the sandhi data in (147) (R. Cheng 1968:23-5).[22]

(146)   a. 55   siŋ   "rise"
         b. 35   siŋ   "succeed"
         c. 53   siŋ   "save"
         d. 31   siŋ   "holy"
         e. 33   siŋ   "prosperous"

(147)   a. 55 → 33
            sã 55   "three"
            sã 33 ki 55   "three pieces"
         b. 35 → 33
            bə 35   "no"
            bə 55 çi 35   "no money"
         c. 33 → 31
            c'ue 33   "look for"
            c'ue 31 bĩʔ 3   "look for things"
         d. 31 → 53
            si 31   "four"
            si 53 ki 55   "four pieces"
         e. 53 → 55
            kau 53   "nine"
            kau 55 ki 55   "nine pieces"

The sandhi patterns in (146) are arranged in a circular fashion in (148), hence the term "Min Circle."

(148)   55, 35 → 33 → 31 → 53 → 55

In order to derive the Min Circle, I assume that the tones in (148) have the underlying structures shown in (149).

(149)   a. 55   b. 35

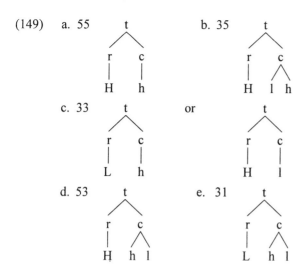

c. 33   or

d. 53   e. 31

Note that the mid even tone 33 is ambiguously specified as [L,h] or [H,l], which are neutralized phonetically.

Observe that the high rising tone 35 and the high falling tone 53 both surface in the even contour: 35 becomes the low even tone 33 (147b), and 53 becomes the high even tone 55 (147e). In other words, the rising and falling contours undergo the right simplification rule formulated below.

(150)   *Contour Simplification*

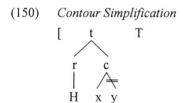

In rule (150), the H register must be specified so as not to affect the low falling tone 31—T is any tone. The rule simplifies the contour by delinking its right branch; the left branch is still dominated by the c node. The results of *Contour Simplification* (150) are given below.

(151)   a.   Rule (150)

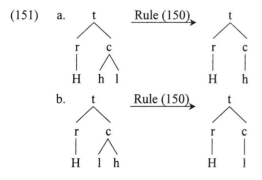

b.   Rule (150)

In addition, the high even tone 55 [H,h] lowers to 33 [H,l]. Formally the 55→33 alternation involves changing the value of [slack] from [-slack] to [+slack]. The h→l lowering could be accounted for by a rule which does just that. But in view of the fact that the high rising tone 35 undergoes *Contour Simplification* and surfaces as 33, we can derive the lowering 55→33 by first changing 55 to 35, and then simplifying the rising contour by rule (150). The rule that derives a rising tone from 55 is given in (152).

(152)

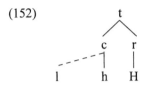

Rule (152) must be ordered before *Contour Simplification* (150), because the former feeds the latter: (152) produces the structure [H,lh] from [H,h]. We also need the two rules in (153) and (154).

(153)

(154)

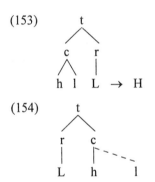

The derivation of the sandhi patterns follows. The rules must be applied in the order given.

(155)

	a.	b.	c.	d.	e.
	(149a)	(149d)	(149b)	(149c)	(149e)
	[H,h]	[H,hl]	[H,lh]	[L,h]	[L,hl]
Rule (152)	[H,lh]	–	–	–	–
Rule (150)	[H,l]	[H,h]	[H,l]	–	–
Rule (153)	–	–	–	–	[H,hl]
Rule (154)	–	–	–	[L,hl]	–
	33	55	33	31	53

The rule of interest is *Contour Simplification* (150): it generates a high even tone from a falling tone (cf. (155b)) and a mid even tone from a rising tone (cf. (155a,c)). This indicates that contours are not atomic entities, but rather are composed of the two terminal nodes of the c node.[23]

The analysis of the Xiamen data underscores a property of the mid even tone. In languages with fewer than four even tones, it is theoretically possible to represent the mid even tone 33 as either [H,l] or [L,h]. In other words, the mid even tone may be structurally ambiguous. In such languages, these two structures are not contrastive, and therefore there is no phonological reason to rule out structural ambiguity for the mid even tone. In fact, this property of the mid even tone may be empirically desirable. In the case of the Min Circle, we need not formulate rules to adjust the register and contour specifications from [H,l] to [L,h]; their contrast is neutralized phonetically. In Chapter 6 I will discuss a language (Weining Miao) which demonstrates further the advantage of dual structures for the mid even tone.

The rules involved in the derivation of the Min Circle are formally quite simple. They comprise the delinking rule (150), the lowering rule (152), the raising rule (153), and the feature-inserting rule (154). These are the elementary types of phonological rules that are widely used in segmental phonology. I will discuss rule types in tone sandhi in Chapter 5.

4

The Autosegmental Nature of Tone

In Chapter 3 I proposed the geometrical structure of tone repeated below.

(1)

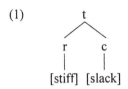

I showed how the tonal geometry accounts for various tone sandhi effects observed in tone languages. In presenting arguments, I made the assumption that tones are autosegmental. This is necessary because, as we have seen, tonal melodies undergo phonological processes independently of the segments on which they are realized. Since I claim, following many other researchers, that the geometry of tone is a substructure of the geometry of laryngeal features of the nuclear vowels, the very fact of tonal assimilation is testimony for the autosegmental treatment of tone. This can be illustrated by the register assimilation structure in (2).

(2) Syllabic

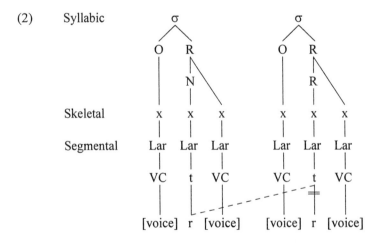

In (2), only relevant nodes are shown. Lar is the laryngeal node, and VC the vocal cord node, which specifies voicing and tone. In the theory proposed here, the VC node and the t node are formally equivalent.

116

The display in (2) is the structure of a bisyllabic phrase. We have seen sandhi processes of assimilation between the registers of two tones. If tones were segmental, as in (2), the r nodes of the two nuclei would not be adjacent. Spreading the register node of the first tone to the second crosses (as shown in (2)) the supralaryngeal nodes of the coda of the first syllable and the onset of the second syllable. The structure therefore violates a well-established condition on phonological processes: phonological rules affect elements that are adjacent at some level of representation (Goldsmith 1976, Pulleyblank 1986, McCarthy 1989, and Hewitt and Prince 1990). If tones are autosegmental, however, the two tones in (2) will be adjacent on the tonal tier, and register spreading violates no known conditions, as illustrated in (3).

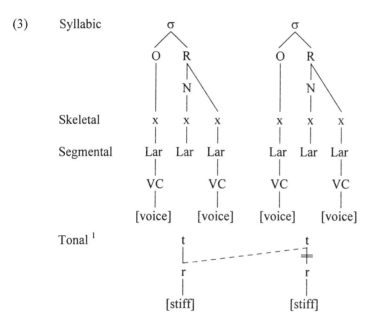

(3)   Syllabic

Skeletal

Segmental

Tonal [1]

The t node merges into the laryngeal geometry of the nuclear segment when tone is segmentalized. (See Chapter 5 for discussion of the formal properties of representation and tone sandhi rules.) The very fact of register assimilation as a type of tone sandhi supports an autosegmental representation of tone.

In this chapter I argue further that tones are autosegments. I will present three arguments: first, the lexicon may contain lexical items that are tonal, and hence lacking segmental anchors for tones (section 4.1); second, tones remain when the segmental material of the syllables in which they are realized is deleted (section 4.2); and third, tones can serve as a bridge for long-distance segmental assimilation (section 4.3). For more arguments in favor of the autosegmental representation of tone in Chinese and other Southeast Asian languages, the reader is referred to the pioneering work of Yip (1980), done within the emerging framework of autosegmental phonology, and a major contribution to our understanding of tonal phenomena.

4.1   Tonal Morphemes

In tone languages, there is a small class of morphemes that are purely tonal. Such morphemes have no fixed segmental shape. They may be lexically specified, or derived through the loss of segmental materials. The formal separation of tones from segments in autosegmental representation allows the proper treatment of such morphemes. In this section, I document a few cases of tonal morphemes in Chinese dialects.

4.1.1   Danyang Word Melodies

We have seen the Danyang data in section 3.3.1.1. There I argued that the Danyang phrasal tone patterns can best be analyzed as involving the spreading of tones as melodic units. Danyang has a tonal inventory of six tones in citation form, including two short tones realized in syllables ending in glottal stop. The tones are given in (4).

(4)			
	a. 11	lan	"rotten"
	b. 33	wang	"net"
		gao	"high"
	c. 24	fang	"house"
		dao	"arrive"
	d. 55	tu	"earth"
	e. 3	yi[ʔ]	"one"
	f. 4	fu[ʔ]	"coat"

Phrases with two, three, and four syllables exhibit the tone patterns shown in (5).

(5)		Bisyllabic	Trisyllabic	Quadrisyllabic
	a.	11-11	11-11-11	11-11-11-11
	b.	42-11	42-11-11	42-11-11-11
	c.	42-24	42-42-24	42-42-42-24
	d.	33-33	33-33-33	33-33-33-33
	e.	24-55	24-55-55	24-55-55-55
	f.	55-55	55-55-55	55-55-55-55

Phrasal tone patterns like those in (5) cannot be derived from the tones that make up the phrases. In section 3.3.1.1, I posited six base tone melodies and argued that we can derive the tone patterns in (5) by spreading, left to right, the last tones of the base tone melodies. The base tone melodies, given in (6), must be stored in the lexicon.

(6)			
	a.	[L,l]	(base melody for (5a))
	b.	[H,hl]-[L,l]	(base melody for (5b))
	c.	[H,lh]	(base melody for (5c))

d. [L,h]   (base melody for (5d))
e. [H,lh]-[H,h]   (base melody for (5e))
f. [H,h]   (base melody for (5f))

For details of the analysis, see section 3.3.1.1.

The significance of this analysis of the Danyang tone spreading facts is two-fold. On one hand, it demonstrates that tones, especially contour tones, spread as melodic units, supporting theories that treat contour tones as such. On the other hand, the postulation that the base melodies in (6) are specified in the lexicon underscores an important property of autosegments—their phonological independence from the segments in which they are ultimately realized phonetically. To the extent that such a postulation leads to a straightforward analysis of the Danyang tone spreading data, we conclude that tones are autosegmental. A segmental theory of tone does not allow tones to be postulated independently of the segments.

4.1.2 Wenzhou Definitive Morpheme

Wenzhou classifiers exhibit a peculiar tonal change. The classifiers can be pronounced with the tone 323, regardless of their lexical tones. When this happens, they acquire the additional meaning of "this." The relevant data are given below (Zhengzhang 1964b:106, [ḷ] represents voiceless [l]):

(7)   a. kai 42   "one"
           kai 323   "this one"
        b. pa 44   "group"
           pa 323   "this group"
        c. to 45   "one (flower)"
           to 323   "this (flower)"
        d. le 31   "some (people)"
           ḷe 323   "these (people)"

323 is a *yin*-registered (H-registered in our terms) tone. It is used with voiceless syllable initials, such as *ko 323* "angle." The voiced initial liquid [l] in (7d) devoices as a result of the tone sandhi. The tonal alternation exemplified in (7) is morphologically motivated. There is no discernible tonal environment that could trigger the sandhi phenomenon; and moreover, the added meaning of definitiveness cannot be explained by a purely phonological derivation. To account for these facts, I assume that the lexicon of the Wenzhou dialect contains a definitive morpheme of the following form.

(8)   Meaning   definitive
        Segmental   none
        Tonal   [H,lh],

where the high rising tone [H,lh] surfaces as concave 323. To derive the sandhi facts, we first prefix the tonal morpheme to the stem.[2] The tone then spreads to the stem, delinking its lexical tone. The derivation of *to* 323 (7c) is shown below (the tone 45 is represented as a high even tone [H,h]).

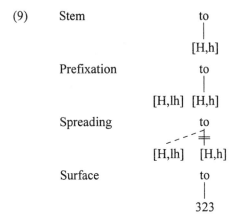

(9)   Stem   to
                                            |
                                          [H,h]

         Prefixation   to
                                            |
                                     [H,lh] [H,h]

         Spreading   to

                                     [H,lh] [H,h]

         Surface   to
                                            |
                                           323

The existence of tonal morphemes such as the definitive in (8) supports the auto-segmental representation of tone. The notion of tonal morpheme—morphemes that consist of tones but lack segmental material—is incompatible with a segmental theory of tone.

4.1.3 Cantonese Changed Tones

According to Yue-Hashimoto (1972:92), Cantonese has a total of eleven surface tones in citation form, shown in (10).

(10)   *ping*   *shang*   *qu*   *ru*
      yin   53   35   44   5, 4
                   55
      yang   21   24   33   3
                   22

The *ru* tones are short tones realized on syllables ending in /p, t, k/. We can consider the short tones as derived from "regular" tones. Yue-Hashimoto (1972:92) identifies 5 with 55, 4 with 44, and 3 with 33. The same view is expressed by Kao (1971) and Yip (1980). No argument is given to support these identifications. We will see shortly that there is evidence that 5 is derived from 35, rather than from 55.

    In addition to the tones in (10), there is the so-called "changed" tone, which surfaces phonetically as 35 and 55, depending on the phonological environment. The changed tones are derived, which we will represent with an asterisk, as *35 and *55. Words that surface in one of the changed tones acquire an added meaning; Chao (1947:35) characterizes this as "that familiar thing one often speaks of." According to Yue-Hashimoto (1972:94), the changed tone "usually carries with it some specialized meaning—familiarity seems to be the dominant note." Relevant data are given in (11). The data are cited from Yue-Hashimoto (1972:94), except (11g), which is cited from Kao (1971:99). The forms are transcribed in *pinyin* in accordance with Beijing Mandarin pronunciation, except for the endings in square brackets.

(11)   a. yu 21   →   yu *35   "fish"
         b. li 24   →   li *35   "plum"
         c. duan 33   →   duan *35   "satin"
         d. ji 44   →   ji *35   "trick"
         e. zei[k] 3   →   zei[k] *35   "thief"
         f. ta[p] 4   →   ta[p] *35   "pagoda"
         g. san 53   →   san *55   "dress"

I was not able to find data showing the alternations 5→*35 and 35→*35 in Yue-Hashimoto (1972) or Yip (1980). Kao says that "neither syllables ending in stops having the primary tone 5: nor syllables ending in other than stops having the primary tone 35: are affected by the changed tone" (1971:111). Kao uses 5: and 35: for 5 and 35 respectively; see also Chao (1947). The fact that 5 and 35 behave in the same fashion as far as the changed tone phenomenon is concerned supports the view that 5 is actually a variant of 35, rather than of 55, as assumed by Yue-Hashimoto (1972) (see section 3.2.3 for further discussion). The tonal alternations are summarized below.

(12)   a. 53/55   →   *55

         b. ⎧ 21/22 ⎫   →   *35
            ⎪ 24   ⎪
            ⎨ 44 (4)⎬
            ⎩ 33 (3)⎭

Note that tones 53 and 55 (21 and 22) are in free variation.

Yip states the changed tone phenomenon as follows: "If a tone begins at a high level (i.e., level 5), then it becomes a high level tone. If it begins at any lower level, then it becomes a rising tone ending at level 5" (1980:62-63). To account for the alternations observed in (12), Yip proposes a morpheme which consists of a floating high tone with no segmental material, something possible only if tones are viewed as autosegments.[3] I will call this morpheme "familiarity morpheme," denoted by t_f. To derive the changed tones, the familiarity morpheme is suffixed to the stem; the high tone then spreads leftward, as illustrated in (13).

(13)   a. yu   "fish"   b. li   "plum"
            ╱╲‿ ‿ ‿   ╱╲‿ ‿ ‿
            2 1   5   2 4   5

In (13), 5 is the floating tone, which spreads onto the stems *yu* "fish" (13a) and *li* "plum" (13b).

But the numbers are phonetic manifestations of underlying tones. If we consider the underlying representations of 21, 24, and the high floating tone 5, the derivation is not as straightforward as (13) indicates. In Yip's (1980) theory (see section 2.7), the three morphemes can be represented as follows.

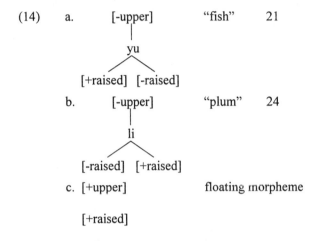

(14c) is the representation of the familiarity morpheme, which lacks segmental material. Suffixing the tonal morpheme to 21 and 24, we get the following forms.

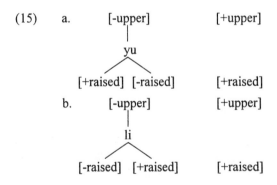

To derive the changed tone *35 from 21 and 24, [+upper] and [+raised] of the familiarity morpheme must spread simultaneously; and [+raised] of the original tones needs to be delinked, as shown in (16).

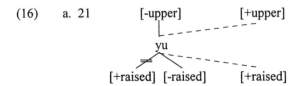

b. 24   [-upper]   [+upper]

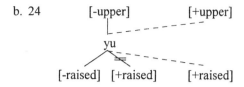

Technicalities aside,[4] Yip's analysis of the Cantonese changed tone is a convincing argument in favor of the autosegmental representation of tones. The analysis I propose below bears close resemblance to Yip's; the difference is motivated solely on the basis of theory-internal consideration.

I assume that the tones in Cantonese have the structures in (17).

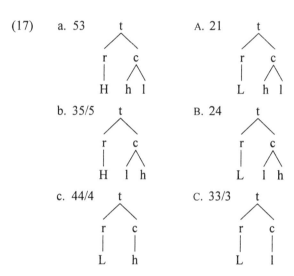

(17)   a. 53   t   A. 21   t

          r c   r c
          | /\ | /\
          H h l   L h l

        b. 35/5 t   B. 24   t

          r c   r c
          | /\ | /\
          H l h   L l h

        c. 44/4 t   C. 33/3 t

          r c   r c
          | | | |
          L h   L l

Underlyingly, 53, 35, and 5 are H-registered tones, and the rest are L-registered. Syllable-initial consonants do not affect the pitch register (Yue-Hashimoto 1972:102-109). The reason for treating the even tone 44 as the surface manifestation of the underlyingly L-registered tone (17c) stems from the fact that 44 has the same sandhi behavior as the rest of the L-registered tones: its changed tone alternant is *35 (see (11d)).[5]

There is a general sandhi process in Cantonese whereby the high falling tone 53 surfaces as the high even tone 55 when preceding 53 or 5 (Kao 1971, Yue-Hashimoto 1972). This 53→55 sandhi is exemplified below (Kao 1971:84).

(18)   a. toŋ kwa → toŋ kwa   "winter melon"
           53 53   55 53
        b. kej tok → kej tok   "Christ"
           53 5   55 5

This can be accounted for by the contour simplification rule in (19).[6]

(19)   *Contour Simplification*

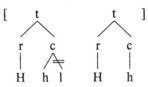

In (19) the c-node of the second tone dominates h. Only tones 53, 55, and 5 meet the condition of the simplification rule.

The treatment of 35/5 is based on two considerations. First, unlike other tones, 35 and 5 do not have a changed tone variant (Chao 1947, Kao 1971). Second, they condition the same sandhi change on the preceding tone when the segmental material of the syllable with 35 or 5 is deleted; see section 4.2.1. Note that 35 does not cause the 53→55 sandhi. This is so because the condition for the contour simplification rule (19) is not met: the rising contour begins with l under the c node. The short tone 5 is derived from 35 by the rule formulated below.

(20)

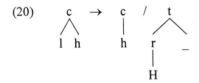

Condition: TBU ends in /p, t, k/.

This rule derives 5 from 35 just in case 35 is realized on a syllable that ends in /p, t, k/. The short tone 5, however, does condition the 53→55 sandhi (cf. (18b)). This indicates that rule (20), which derives 5 from 35, applies before the contour simplification rule (19). The derivation of the two cases in (18) is as follows.

(21)   a. Underlying

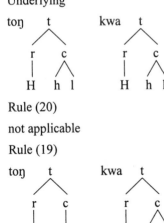

Rule (20)

not applicable

Rule (19)

b. Underlying

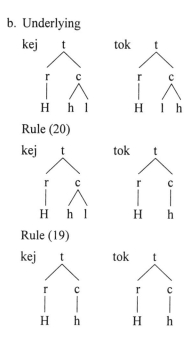

Rule (20)

kej   t   tok   t
      /⌒\   /⌒\
     r   c   r   c
     | /\ | |
     H h l   H   h

Rule (19)

kej   t   tok   t
      /⌒\   /⌒\
     r   c   r   c
     | | | |
     H   h   H   h

Following Yip (1980), I posit a morpheme of familiarity that lacks segmental material. It consists of the high even tone, as shown in (22).

(22)   Meaning   familiarity
        Segmental   none
        Tonal   [H,h]

When suffixed to a syllable with the high falling tone 53, this morpheme conditions the 53→55 change (see (11g)). The rising contour of 35 is created with the insertion of l to the c node. The insertion rule is given in (23).

(23)   *Contour Formation*

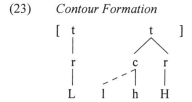

The contour formation rule inserts l to the c node of the familiarity morpheme when it follows a L-registered tone, creating a rising contour. The requirement that the register of the preceding tone be L will become apparent later; see the derivation in (25). (23) derives 35 from the underlying structure in (22), just in case the preceding tone is L-registered.

In the proposed analysis, the changed tones *55 and *35 are derived by two separate rules. The former is derived by (19), which is a general sandhi rule of

Cantonese,[7] and the latter by the rule in (23), in conjunction with the rule formulated in (24), which spreads the tonal morpheme to the stem if its lexical tone is L-registered:

(24)   *Tone Spread*

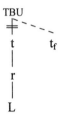

where t_f is the tonal morpheme. The derivation of *li* 24 "plum" and *san* 53 "dress" is shown below (only tones are shown; * is a tone-bearing unit):

(25)   a. Suffixation of t_f

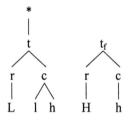

Contour Formation (23)

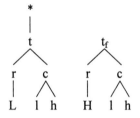

Tone Spread (24)

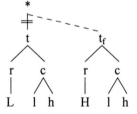

Contour Simplification (19)

not applicable

Result

*
|
*35

b. Suffixation of t_f

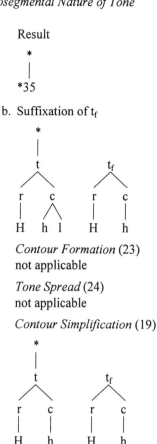

Contour Formation (23)
not applicable

Tone Spread (24)
not applicable

Contour Simplification (19)

Result

*
|
*55

The unassociated tones do not surface. Note that in (25b), the contour formation rule (23) and the spreading rule (24) are not applicable because the register of the preceding tone is H. Both rules require that the register of the preceding tone be L. Because of this, t_f is left behind, eventually to condition the simplification rule (19).

The existence of a tone-only morpheme in Cantonese supports the view that tones are autosegmental.

4.1.4 Prefixes in Jiading Miao

Jiading Miao is a Miao dialect spoken in the Jiading region of Guizhou Province in southwestern China. This dialect has a number of prefixes that perform various semantic and syntactic functions. The prefixes are grouped roughly into

two major categories in terms of the stems to which they are affixed. All data
below are cited from Yue (1979); V is any vowel.

(26)   a. Nominal markers
           qV 13   qV 31
           kV 13   kV 55
           ŋkV 13   ŋkV 55
           pV 31   lV 31
        b. Verbal markers
           tV 13   shV 13

There are some semantic restrictions on the stems to which certain nominal
markers are affixed. For instance, *kV* 55 is prefixed to stem nouns that designate
insects, and *ŋkV* 13 and *ŋkV* 55 are prefixed to stem nouns that designate birds.
When prefixed to the stem, V invariably surfaces as the vowel of the stem-initial
syllable. Relevant data are given below.

(27)   a. qV 13 (used for animate objects, their body parts, ailments)
           qi 13 pli 43   "wild cat"
           qo 13 ho 13   "head"
           qe 13 mple 55   "tongue"
           qu 13 plu 31   "rat"
           qõ 13 põ 22   "rash"
           qæ 13 plæ 13 mõ 31   "wasp sting"
        b. qV 31 (same as (a))
           qɯ 31 ʐɯ 43   "the small one"
           qɛ 31 shɛ 24   "the new one"
           qɯ 31 khɯ 55   "the skinny one (people)"
           qo 31 nzo 22   "the skinny one animal)"
        c. kV 13 (same as (a))
           ki 13 ki 43   "skin rash"
           ki 13 ki 22   "bottom"
           kɜ̃ 13 ŋkɜ̃ 13   "valley"
        d. kV 55 (used for insects)
           kɜ̃ 55 tɜ̃ 13   "ticks"
           ko 55 nsho 13   "flea"
        e. ŋkV 13; ŋkV 55 (used for birds)
           ŋki 13 si 43   "yellow-feather bird"
           ŋkə 13 sə 43   "wild chicken"
           ŋku 55 tɯ 24   a kind of bird
        f. lV 31 (used for ordinal numbers)
           li 31 i 24   "first"
           læ 31 pæ 24   "third"
           lo 31 plo 24   "fourth"
           lu 31 tɕu 55   "ninth"

g. tV 13 (used for short events)
   ti 13 si 13   "to squeeze through"
   tɛ 13 zɛ 24   "to cut vegetables"
   tə 13 sə 43   "to throw rocks"
   te 13 te 22   "to take off one's hat"
h. shV 13
   (used for continuous events)
   shu 13 lu 22 ʂu 24   "to pull"
   shə 13 tə 55   "to dance"
   shu 13 vu 22   "to ferment fertilizer"
   (used for reciprocal events)
   shu 13 tɕu 22   "to meet"
   shə 13 tə 55   "to fight (dogs)"
   shə 13 ntə 55   "to fight (people)"

Descriptively, the prefixes in Jiading Miao are all monosyllabic and take up the vowels of the stem-initial syllables. This means that these morphemes do not have a fully specified vowel in the nuclear position. Since the prefixes have their own tones, the tones therefore lack segmental anchors prior to acquiring the vowels from the stems to which they are attached. A segmental approach to tone, which requires a vowel (or sonorant) as an anchor for a tone, therefore fails to characterize the prefixes of Jiading Miao. Such prefixes pose no problems for an autosegmental approach to tone. The tones are represented on a separate plane from the segmental material. The Jiading prefixes support the view that tones are autosegmental.

To account for the facts in (27), I assume that each of the prefixes is represented in the lexicon with a syllabic template, a tone, and an onset segment, but no nuclear segment. The structure of *qV* 13 illustrates this.

(28)   Structure of *qV* 13

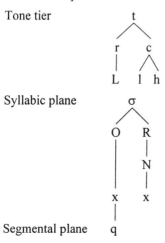

Suppose that in Jiading Miao vowels and consonants are segregated (McCarthy 1979, 1981, 1989; Prince 1987). We can then derive the patterns in (27) by spreading the stem-initial vowels on the V plane. The form *qu* 13 *plu* 31 "rat" (cf. (26a)) is derived in the following fashion (syllabic structure and tone structure are omitted).[8]

(29)   Prefixation

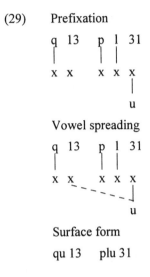

Surface form

qu 13   plu 31

A reduplication analysis of the Jiading Miao facts is also possible, but the implication remains the same: tones must be represented autosegmentally, rather than segmentally.

4.1.5 Diminutive Suffix in Shenmu and Daye

Diminutive suffixation is a common morphophonological phenomenon in Chinese, particularly among Mandarin dialects. The exact phonological property of the diminutive suffix varies from dialect to dialect. The suffix in Beijing Mandarin is a retroflex feature that is realized on the rhyme (Chao 1968, Cheng 1973a). (I use the term "rhyme" in the conventional sense of Chinese linguistics, and the term "rime" to refer to the syllabic constituent R in (28).) For this reason, this suffix is more commonly known as "retroflex suffixation," or "*er*-ification." In other dialects, owing to different historical development, this suffix may surface as an independent syllable, as an off-glide /u/ or /ɯ/ with corresponding changes in the stem vowel, or as a nasal which is resyllabified as the coda of the stem syllable (Yuan et al. 1960, Zhan 1981).

In Shenmu, a Mandarin dialect spoken in Shaanxi Province, the diminutive suffixation yields only four rhymes—/ʌɯ, iʌɯ, uʌɯ, yʌɯ/. Since it neutralizes rhyme contrasts, it is rarely used on monosyllabic words. It applies most productively to the second copy of a reduplicated word. The "suffixed" syllable carries the high fall 53, regardless of its original tone. Relevant data are shown below

all Shenmu data are cited from Xing (1996), and the tones in parentheses are
sandhi tones.

(30)   a. tɕ'iȓ 24 tɕ'iʌɯ 24 (53)   "clear"
        b. liɑ̃ 44 liʌɯ 44 (53)   "cold"
        c. tɕiȓ 213 tɕiʌɯ 213 (53)   "tight"
        d. tɕyȓ 53 tɕyʌɯ 53 (53)   "pretty"
        e. tʂəʔ 4 tʂʌɯ 4 (53)   "straight"

24, 44, 213, 53, and 4 are the five tones of Shenmu. Note that the second copy
has the rhyme /ʌɯ/, and tone 53, regardless of the base.

Although Xing (1996) considers the phenomenon exemplified in (30) to be a
case of diminutive suffixation, the data can been seen as examples of partial
reduplication. In any case, we need to postulate a morpheme that consists of the
segments /ʌɯ/ and the tone 53. Since this morpheme is never realized by itself,
and is realized productively only on reduplicated adjectives, it is in effect part of
the reduplicative morpheme. By contrast, the familiar retroflex suffixation of
Beijing Mandarin does not have such restrictions (cf. Cheng 1973a).

However we view /ʌɯ 53/, the derivation of the data requires two steps.

(31)   a. Make a copy of the original syllable
        b. Merge /ʌɯ 53/ as the rime of the second copy

These steps are illustrated in the derivation of *tʂəʔ 4 tʂʌɯ 53*:

(32)   Base   tʂəʔ 4
        Copy base   tʂəʔ 4   tʂəʔ 4
        Rhyme Merge   tʂəʔ 4   tʂʌɯ 53

Merge Rhyme is to be understood loosely; since the rhyme /ʌɯ/ could be derived
by attaching the off-glide /ɯ/ to the stem rhyme, and the phonotactics of the
dialect yield /ʌɯ/. In this case, the lexical specification of this suffix in Shenmu
would consist of the off-glide plus the tone 53. Whatever the analysis of the
processes which derive the four rhymes, /ʌɯ, iʌɯ, uʌɯ, yʌɯ/, there is little
doubt that the tone 53 is the main lexical specification of the morpheme.

While the diminutive suffix in Shenmu still contains some segmental material, either /ʌɯ/ or just the off-glide /ɯ/, the diminutive suffix in Daye, a
Mandarin dialect spoken in Hubei Province, is purely tonal. This dialect has five
tones, as follows (G.-S. Wang 1996).

(33)   a. 33
        A. 31
        b. 53
        c. 35
        d. 13

The diminutive suffix does not have any segmental material and is realized on the stem as the high falling tone, which G.-S. Wang (1996) transcribes as 553. We will deal with the proper structure of 553 in section 7.2.3, in connection with the representation of contours more complex than fall or rise. For now, we ignore the difference between 553 and 53. If the stem is bisyllabic, the diminutive suffix surfaces on the last syllable. The suffix is the typical diminutive affix, expressing the meaning of small size or endearment. Relevant facts follow (the sandhi tone 553 is in parentheses).

(34)   a. tɔ 33 (553)   "(small) knife"
           tɕ'i 35 ts'e 33 (553)   "(small) car"
        b. ɕy 53 kuẽ 35 (553)   "(small) kettle"
           tẽ 35 kua 35 (553)   "(small) jacket"
        c. tso 13 (553)   "(small) desk"
           mɑ 31 tɕ'io 13 (553)   "(small) sparrow"
        d. lɔ 53 ɕy 53 (31)   "(small) rat"
        e. t'ɔŋ 31   "pool"

The data in (34) show that the diminutive suffix surfaces as 553 if the stem tones are 33, 35, or 13, and as 31 if the stem tone is 53. According to G.-S. Wang (1996), the affix does not attach to stems with the tone 31, cf. (34e).

We will assume without argument that, underlyingly, the diminutive affix is lexically specified as 553, and that it changes to 31 just in case the stem tone has the falling contour. Given this analysis, we can argue that the suffix attaches to all stems without exception. The lack of diminutive meaning in words of the type (34e) is obviously due to the fact that the changed tone is phonetically the same as the original stem tone.

The tonal suffix may be seen as a tonal analogue of the adjective *sai* 35 "small." This word assumes the sandhi tone 553 when it precedes the head it modifies: *sai* 553 *t'ɔŋ* 31 "small pool." G.-S. Wang (1996) says that there are two ways to express the meaning "smallness" in Daye: with the adjective *sai* 35, and with the tonal suffix 553. It is not clear, however, whether the two morphemes can co-occur with a single stem.

The tones 553 and 53 present a problem for the representation of complex contours. I will take up this issue in section 7.2.3.

4.1.6 Tone as Inflectional or Derivational Affix

Chinese is not an inflectional language. There are no lexical affixes that express inflectional meanings such as number or gender. However, in a few dialects tone is used to mark number in pronouns, and distance in deictic expressions. In addition, tone is used as a category-changing derivational affix in classical Chinese, although this is no longer a productive morphological process in modern dialects. We will briefly examine the inflectional and derivational uses of tone.

In the Mandarin dialect of Shang, Shaanxi Province, the number distinction among pronouns is marked tonally (Yuan et al. 1960:50, Zhan 1981:58).

(35) a. ŋɤ 53/21   "I/we"
      b. ni 53/21   "you (sg.)/you (pl.)"
      c. t'a 53/21   "he, she, it/they"

The singular pronouns all have the high falling tone 53, and their plural counterparts have the low falling tone 21. If we assume that the pronouns are lexically specified with their segmental make-up and the falling contour, then the number distinction can be reduced to register only: H marks singular, and L plural.

This phenomenon appears to be a distinctive feature of Mandarin dialects spoken in northwestern China, which includes the provinces of Shanxi and Shaanxi. Like their counterparts in Shang, the pronouns in the dialect of Wanrong, Shanxi Province, show the same tonal inflection (Qiao 1996).

In Kejia (Hakka) dialects, deixis is expressed with the help of tone, as shown in the following data (Yuan et al. 1960:172).

(36) a. ke T2 le T1   "here"
         ke T2 p'ien T2   "this side"
         ke T2 ke T3   "this one"
         ke T2 teu T1   "these"
      b. ke T3 le T1   "there"
         ke T3 p'ien T2   "that side"
         ke T3 ke T3   "that one"
         ke T3 teu T1   "those"

See also Zhan (1981) and X.-K. Li (1994). In the data, T1, T2, and T3 stand for the traditional tonal categories: T1 for *ping*, T2 for *shang*, and T3 for *qu*. The deictic element is *ke*, which surfaces with the tone T2 for objects near the speaker, and with the tone T3 for objects farther away from the speaker.

Tone may also change the lexical category of a word. According to L. Wang (1957) and Guo (1993), many derived nouns or verbs have the *qu* tone (T3), which is realized as high fall in modern Bejing Mandarin, regardless of the lexical tone of the source. Although this process is no longer productive in modern Chinese, many such tone-derived words are fossilized and remain in the active vocabulary today. The data listed below, cited from L. Wang (1957:213-215), are transcribed in *pinyin* in accordance with the pronunciation of modern Beijing Mandarin, except for the tones.

(37) a. Noun → Verb
         yi T1/T3   "coat/to clothe"
         guan T1/T3   "hat/to put on a hat"
         zhen T2/T3   "pillow/to use as a pillow"
         want T2/T3   "king/to rule over"

b. Adjective → Verb
  hao T2/T3   "good/to enjoy"
  lao T1/T3   "tired/to comfort"
  jin T2/T3   "close/to be attached to"
  yuan T2/T3   "far away/to be distant from"
c. Verb → Noun
  guan T1/T3   "to view/viewing platform"
  fen T1/T3   "to divide/share"
  cong T1/T3   "to follow/follower"
  shi T2/T3   "to order/person who conveys orders"

As the above data show, T3, the *qu* tone, is the derivational morpheme that derives verbs from nouns or adjectives (37a,b), and nouns from verbs (37c). There is no segmental change in the process. According to L. Wang (1957), this derivational process is highly productive in classical Chinese, and, judging from the tone patterns of the so-called "regulated" poetry from that period (L. Wang 1979, Chen 1979), it has been skillfully exploited by poets since the Tang dynasty (ca. 600A.D.).

Tonal inflection and derivation provide strong evidence in support of the autosegmental view that tone is not dependent phonologically on segments, even though it is phonetically realized on them.

4.2 Tones under Segmental Deletion

Suprasegmental information often survives segmental deletion. This is one of the tonological properties that led to the development of autosegmental representation (cf. Leben 1973, William 1976, and Goldsmith 1976). Although Chinese, especially Mandarin, does not have rich segmental phonology, there are phonological processes that affect the segmental make-up of morphemes. Here, I will consider two such processes.

4.2.1 Cantonese

In the analysis proposed in section 4.1.3, we posited a floating tonal morpheme (t_f) with the meaning "familiarity." This morpheme is suffixed to the word stem. The changed tone *55 is generated by a general sandhi rule which changes the high falling tone 53 to the high even tone 55. The changed tone *35 is derived by the feature-inserting rule (23) and the spreading rule (24), which spreads t_f to a L-registered tone. This accounts for the fact that 5 and 35, which are phonetic variants of the high rising tone [H,lh] (17b), do not have a changed-tone alternant (Kao 1971:111). Another set of tone sandhi facts of Cantonese, reported in Bai (1989), corroborates the proposed analysis of the changed-tone phenomenon. The facts are also discussed in Kao (1971), Yue-Hashimoto (1972), and Yip (1980). My data come from Bai (1989).

The changed tone *35 is derived after the suffixation of the tonal morpheme t_f, which affects the meaning of the stem. *35 may also come from another source. Certain words in Cantonese with the surface tones 35 and 5 may be deleted in fast speech, but the tones remain and surface on the preceding syllable. The resultant string acquires no new meaning, since it does not involve any affixation of a new morpheme. The relevant segmental deletion data are given in (38).[9]

(38)   a. Deletion of the perfective marker *tsɔ* 35, perfective particle

mai tsɔ	→	mai	"have bought"
23 35		*35	
iau tsɔ	→	iau	"have painted"
21 35		*35	
pin tsɔ	→	pin	"have changed"
33 35		*35	
tsou tsɔ	→	tsou	"have made"
22 35		*35	
t'ɛk tsɔ	→	t'ɛk	"have kicked"
3 35		*35	
sok tsɔ	→	sok	"have been cooked"
2 35		*35	

    b. Deletion of *iat* 5 "one"

iat t'am iat t'am	→	iat t'am t'am
5 23 5 23		5 *35 23
"puddle by puddle"		
iat hɔŋ iat hɔŋ	→	iat hɔŋ hɔŋ
5 21 5 21		5 *35 21
"line by line"		
iat ts'yn iat ts'yn	→	iat ts'yn ts'yn
5 33 5 33		5 *35 33
"bunch by bunch"		
iat tam iat tam	→	iat tam tam
5 22 5 22		5 *35 22
"mouthful by mouthful"		
iat tat iat tat	→	iat tat tat
5 3 5 3		5 *35 3
"patch by patch"		
iat tip iat tip	→	iat tip tip
5 2 5 2		5 *35 2
"plate by plate"		

Other words that exhibit the same sandhi phenomenon include *tak* 5, *hai* 35, and *tou* 35. According to Bai (1989:114), two conditions must be met in order for the sandhi process exemplified in (38) to take place. First, the tones undergoing the change must be low; they are 21, 23, 33, 22, 3, and 2. The high tones 53/55, 35, and 5 are not affected. The data in (38) do not contain examples of

53, 35, or 5 undergoing the change. Second, the deleted syllable must carry the high tone 35 or 5. The facts in (38) can be readily explained, as shown in the derivation of *mai* *35 "bought" and *iat 5 tam* *35 *tam* 22 "mouthful by mouthful."

(39)   Underlying

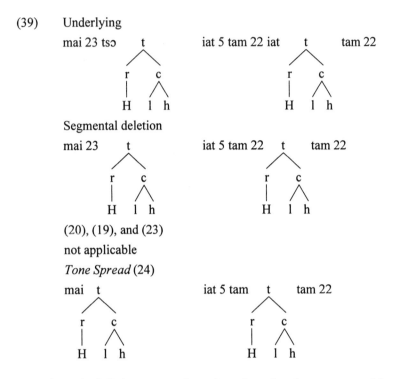

Note that rule (20) does not apply to the string after the segments of the syllable have been deleted. The rule requires that the tone-bearing unit (here, the syllabic rime) end in /p, t, k/. The deleted segments, *iat*, would have conditioned the 35→5 sandhi change.

The deletion of segments plays a crucial part in the derivation of the facts in (38). The tones survive segmental deletion. This would not be possible if tones were segmental, but the expected result if tones are autosegmental.

4.2.2 *Fanqie* Languages

Another piece of evidence in favor of autosegmental representation of tone comes from a kind of game language which Chao (1931) calls "*fanqie* languages" (Chao 1931, Yip 1982, P. J.-K. Li 1985, Lin 1988, Bao 1990a, and Duanmu 1990; see also section 5.2). *Fanqie* languages are constructed by the philological method of *fanqie*, which means literally "reverse cut." Long before the introduction of romanization schemes, Chinese philologists and classicists frequently used the *fanqie* method to specify the pronunciation of an unknown character by presenting two familiar characters. The method can best be illustrated by the following hypothetical example.

(40) ma 55 ← mo 53 pa 55

In (40), the two syllables to the right of the arrow, *mo* 53 and *pa* 55, are assumed to be familiar characters (syllables) which are used to specify the pronunciation of the previously unknown character *ma* 55. The novel character is pronounced with the initial of the first syllable and the rime of the second syllable, including its tone.

Descriptively, *fanqie* languages are created by splitting a given syllable from a source language into two parts, the initial and the final. The first segment (including the zero segment) is the initial; the rest constitutes the final. The initial is combined with a new final, and the final is combined with a new initial, generating a bisyllabic word as shown in (41):

(41) ma 55 → mo 53 pa 55

In (41) the source syllable *ma* 55 is split into the initial *m* and the final *a* 55. The initial *m* is combined with the new final *o* 53, and the final *a* 55 is combined with the new initial *p*, yielding the bisyllabic word *mo* 53 *pa* 55. *Fanqie* language formation is the reverse process of *fanqie* as a philological tool. The *fanqie* word *mo* 53 *pa* 55 could be used to specify the pronunciation of the source word *ma* 55 (cf. (40) and (41)).

Yip (1982) was the first to recognize the significance of the *fanqie* data for the autosegmental theories that were being developed at the time. Since Yip (1982), a few analyses have been proposed, among them Lin (1988), Bao (1990a), Duanmu (1990), and Chiang (1992). Because we are not concerned with the exact mechanism of *fanqie* language formation, we will not review the analyses here; interested readers can read the references cited above. Bao (1990a) argues that the derivation of *fanqie* languages involves the following two steps.

(42) a. Reduplication (cf. Steriade 1988)
      b. Substitution of onset and rime

Now consider the tone patterns of a *fanqie* language based on the dialect of Kunshan, spoken in Jiangsu Province. Following Chao (1931), I will call it Mo-pa.[10] The data are given in (43).

(43) a. pã 33 → po 33 vã 33   "country"
      b. ts'ɪ 4 → ts'o 4 zɪ 4   "seven"

Both syllables of a Mo-pa word (to the right of the arrow) have the tone of the source syllable (to the left of the arrow). Note that in the first syllable in (43a), the source segmental rime [a] is deleted and replaced with [o], but the source tone remains. Similarly, in (43b), the deletion of the source segmental rime [ɪ] does not affect the source tone. If tones are segmental, deleting the vowel will also delete the tone, and the tone pattern of Mo-pa exemplified in (43) cannot be explained. If tones are autosegmental, however, deleting a segment will not affect the tone, since segments and tones are on different planes. The derivation of *po* 33 *vã* 33 from *pã* 33 "country" is shown in (44).

(44)   Source syllable

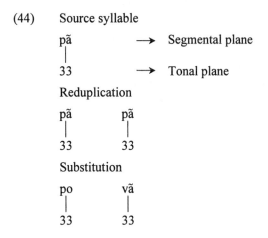

Substitution takes place on the segmental plane, hence the tones are not affected by the operation.

The *fanqie* language facts support the view that tones are autosegmental.

4.3   Bridge Effect

In nonlinear phonology, assimilation is viewed as spreading of the assimilating feature(s), which is subject to the locality condition (see, for example, Steriade 1982, Archangeli 1985, Clements 1985, Myers 1987, McCarthy 1989, and Hewitt and Prince 1990). This condition states that elements affected by phonological rules must be adjacent at some level of representation. In a multi-planar representation, it is possible for an element to assimilate into a nonadjacent element in one plane via some operation on a separate plane. I will call this phenomenon the "bridge effect." To illustrate, consider the structure in (45).

(45)

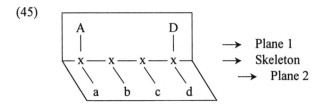

On plane 1, A and D are adjacent; on plane 2, a and d are not adjacent. The intervening b and c prevent a from spreading to d on plane 2. On plane 1, however, A and D are adjacent, and therefore A is able to spread to D. Now suppose that A spreads to D, yielding the structure in (46).

(46)

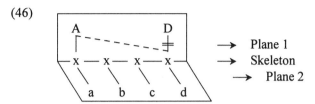

→ Plane 1
→ Skeleton
→ Plane 2

Here D is delinked. Further suppose that there is a rule that links an x-slot to a on plane 2 if it is associated with A on plane 1. Then the structure in (46) will result in the structure in (47).

(47)

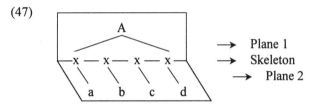

→ Plane 1
→ Skeleton
→ Plane 2

Hypothetically, the element a in effect spreads to the position formerly occupied by the element d on plane 2, via the spreading of A on plane 1. Bridge effects are possible only in a multi-planar (or multi-tiered) structure. In a linear representation, the element a cannot spread to the position marked by d without violating the locality condition.

Wuyi furnishes data that exhibit the bridge effect of tonal assimilation. Wuyi has eight surface tones in citation form, shown below. All Wuyi data are taken from Fu (1984).

(48) a. 24   sa   "raw"
      b. 55   pu   "beach"
                  p'u   "common"
      c. 53   t'ia   "supreme"
      d. 5   fo?   "duplicate"
      A. 213   za   "tailor"
      B. 13   bu   "part"
      C. 31   dia   "big"
      A. <u>212</u>   vo?   "cloth"

In our terms, the *yin* tones are H-registered; the *yang* tones are L-registered. The H-registered tones occur with voiceless obstruents in syllable-initial position, and the *yang*-registered tones occur with voiced obstruents. There is a strict correlation between consonant voicing and tonal register.[11]

We will consider the tone patterns of nominal phrases involving the tones (48a,A,c,C). Relevant data are as follows:

(49)   a. 24-24 → 24-53
             çie sa   "mister"
             kau t'oŋ   "transportation"
             ʔli ʔlu   "spider"
             t'ie koŋ   "Heavenly Lord"
         b. 213-24 → 213-53
             dʑiaŋ kaŋ   "The Yangtze River"
             ɦnie kτ   "New Year's Rice Cake"
             dzua pa   "tea mug"
             ɦaŋ tçiəu   "Hangzhou"
         c. 24-213 → 24-53
             foŋ ʔliaŋ (< ɦliaŋ)   "cool"
             hua ʔoŋ (< hoŋ)   an apple-like fruit
             çie ʔu (< ɦu)   "West Lake"
             kuaŋ ʔioŋ (< ʔioŋ)   "glorious"
         d. 213-213 → 213-31
             ɦu dʑiŋ   a Chinese musical instrument
             ɦuaŋ ɦuo   "The Yellow River"
             ɦnoŋ ɦmiŋ   "peasant"
             die dzuo   "investigate"
         e. 24-53 → 24-53
             sa ʔi   "business"
             kau tçia   "intersection"
             çiəu tçiŋ   "correct"
             fəŋ fu   "ask"
         f. 213-53 → 213-53
             ɦliŋ çia   "neighbor"
             ɦnəŋ kau   "able"
             doŋ tçiŋ   "brass mirror"
             biŋ tçiŋ   "even"
         g. 24-31 → 24-53
             sa ʔmiŋ (<ɦmiŋ)   "life"
             çy ʔnye (< ɦnye)   "school"
             sa fuo (< vuo)   "raw meal"
             hua ʔiaŋ (< ɦiaŋ)   "pattern"
         h. 213-31 → 213-31
             ɦmua da   "hemp bag"
             dʑiaŋ ʑiəu   "longevity"
             dʑiaŋ dτ   "robber"
             bi ɦmuo   "leather hat"

The tone patterns are summarized in (50); the horizontal axis is the second tone of a bisyllabic phrase and the vertical axis is the first tone.[12]

(50)   I   II   III   IV
                24   213   53   31
     24   24-53   24-53   24-53   24-53
    213   213-53   213-31   213-53   213-31

Assuming that the tones 24, 213, 53 and 31 have the structures in (51),[13]

(51)   a. 24   b. 213

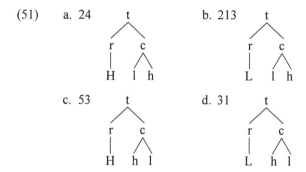

     c. 53   d. 31

we can make the following observations about the tone patterns in (50).

(52)   a. Rising tones become falling phrase-finally (Columns I and II).
       b. Given (a), the low falling tone is raised following a high tone
         (Column II and IV).

As a result of raising, the voiced syllable-initial consonants devoice (cf. (49c,g)). The sandhi facts in (50) can be accounted for in terms of the two rules in (53).

(53)   a. *Contour Metathesis*

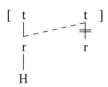

       b. *Register Spread*

          [t   t   ]
            L- - - - -≠
            r   r
            H

     As noted earlier, there is a strict correlation between tonal register and the voicing qualities of the syllable-initial segments. Because of this onset-register harmony, the registers of the tones are predictable from the syllable-initial segments. If the segment is voiceless, the register is H; if voiced, it is L. This is expressed in the following two statements.[14]

(54)   a. If the syllable-initial segment is [+stiff], the tone is [+stiff].
        b. If the syllable-initial segment is [-stiff], the tone is [-stiff].

In Chapter 5 I will argue for a set of tone adjustment rules that produces the same effect as the statements in (54). For now, I assume that in Wuyi, lexical items are associated with tones in accordance with the statements in (54). In other words, the representation to which sandhi rules apply shows the effect of onset-register harmony. A sample derivation follows.

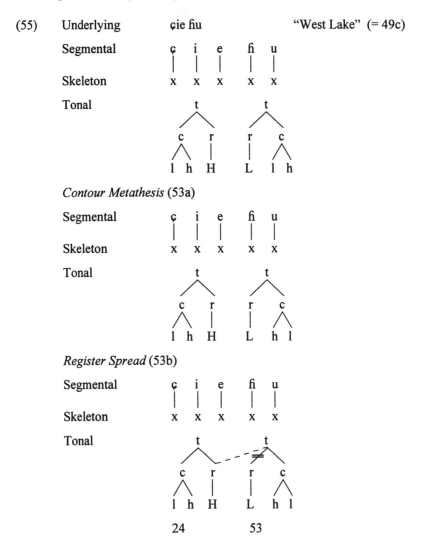

(55)   Underlying   çie ɦu   "West Lake" (= 49c)

At this stage of the derivation, after all the tone sandhi rules have applied, the tones are segmentalized—that is, they become part of the segments with which they are associated. Segmentalization merges the tone melodies with the laryngeal nodes of the nuclear segments (vowels and other syllabic segments). After segmentalization of tone, the structure in (56) is derived from the output in (55); only the laryngeal node is shown, and rt is the root node.

(56)

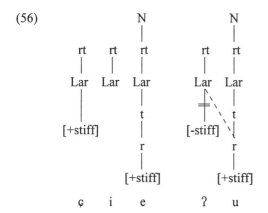

Syllable-initial devoicing results from the spreading of [+stiff] from the tone to the preceding consonant, as shown in (56). Devoicing is a late-stage assimilatory process.

This analysis of sandhi-induced devoicing in Wuyi supports the view that tones are autosegmental. As can be seen clearly from the structure in (56), onset devoicing is ultimately caused by the initial segment of the phrase-initial syllable: since it is voiceless, i.e. [+stiff], the tone is H-registered (also [+stiff]); the H register then spreads to the following L-registered tone, causing devoicing. Thus, tones serve as a bridge for voicing assimilation between the two onsets of a bisyllabic phrase.

The bridge effect is impossible to characterize if tones are considered to be segmental. A segmental analysis not only fails to account for register spreading; it also fails to account for the onset assimilation exemplified in (49c,g). In both cases lines are crossed, as shown in (57).

(57)   a. Register Assimilation

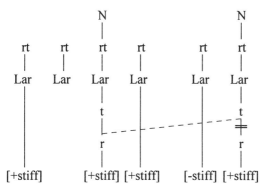

b. Onset Assimilation

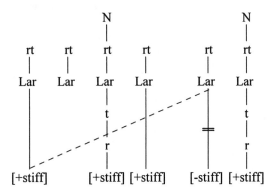

The bridge effect of register assimilation thus provides evidence in favor of an autosegmental treatment of tone.

5

Tone in Phonological Representation

5.1 Dual Nature of Tone

The relationship between tone and other elements of phonological representation was a controversial issue in early generative study of the topic. Although it has proved successful in segmental phonology, the *SPE* conception of feature bundles has its problems in dealing with familiar tonological phenomena. The controversy has centered around the representation of tone. On one hand, the segmentalists maintain that tones are a property of vowels, or other tone-bearing sonorants, while on the other, the suprasegmentalists claim that tones are a property of suprasegmental entities such as syllables. Regarding the relationship between tonal features and segmental features, W. S.-Y. Wang writes,

> In languages like Chinese the tone features are sometimes relevant for the initial consonant, sometimes for the nuclear vowel, and sometimes for the final consonant in various phonological rules. If we were to add a column of tone features to a phonological matrix of segmental features, then it becomes arbitrary where precisely to insert this column. Furthermore, segmental features are usually not relevant in the various types of tone sandhi; that is to say, the interaction of tones in a sequence is independent of the nature of the segments which occur with the tones. (1967:95)

Wang's remark underscores the relative independence of tonal features from segmental features, and that of tone sandhi processes from segmental processes. The interaction between tone and the initial and final consonants is limited to the voicing quality of the initial consonant and to the shortening effect of the final stops. Phonological independence notwithstanding, it remains true that tones are phonetically realized on nuclear segments that bear the phonological features of tone. In tone languages, tonal and segmental features together provide the articulatory instructions for the production of tone-bearing segments, particularly vowels and other syllabic sonorants. Tone is both suprasegmental and segmental.

The dual character of tone has been amply demonstrated in the discussion of tonal geometry in Chapter 3 and of the autosegmental properties of tone in Chapter 4. The geometry of tone is a substructure of the laryngeal geometry of the tone-bearing vowel, which we set forth in (1).

(1)

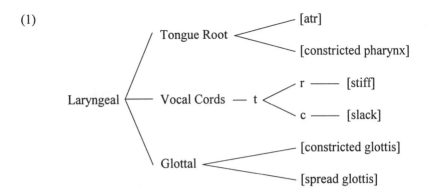

The claim is that tones are phonetically realized on the Vocal Cords node of a nuclear segment. This accounts for the segmental aspect of tone.

In autosegmental theories of phonology, the simple, linear representation of early generative phonology (Chomsky and Halle 1968) is replaced by a rich representation with three-dimensional structures consisting of levels in parallel to one another. Consider the schematic representation in (2) (P = phoneme; T = tone):

(2)   Segmental plane   P
                               |
        Tonal plane   T

The structure in (2) is abstracted from several important works in the framework of autosegmental phonology, such as Williams (1976), Leben (1973), Goldsmith (1976), Yip (1980), Halle and Vergnaud (1982), and Pulleyblank (1986). It consists of two parallel levels labeled as the segmental plane and the tonal plane.[1] Elements on each plane are linked by means of the formal device called an "association line." The phonological independence of tones from segments is captured formally in terms of plane separation. Rules that operate on one plane may leave elements on the other plane unaffected. Association lines formalize phonetic realization: tones are realized on the phonemes with which they are linked by means of the association lines. In structure (2), T is realized on P.

Plane separation, though liberating tones from vowels or other tone-bearing units, fails to capture the suprasegmental properties of tone as traditionally understood (Wang 1967, Lehiste 1970, and Hyman 1975). In a different form, the structure in (2) represents the segmentalist's view of tone, which holds that tone is a feature of vowels. Suprasegmental notions such as rime or syllable are not encoded in a way that is relevant for tone association. The early segmentalist and suprasegmentalist controversy still remains. The formal characterization of the relationship between tones and segments must be dealt with.

In autosegmental studies of tone, however, the issue has been avoided altogether. Tones are said to be associated with tone-bearing units, or TBUs The term "tone-bearing unit" is a term of convenience and has no formal status in autosegmental representation. In early work on tones within the autosegmental framework, it is assumed, either explicitly or implicitly, that TBUs are syllables or vowels, which are usually interchangeable. For example, Halle and Vergnaud (1982), in discussing Williams's (1976) *Tone Mapping Rule*, are noncommittal as to what elements can serve as tone-bearing units. This can be seen clearly in (3), their addition to Williams's formulation of the *Tone Mapping Rule*.

(3)   a. It maps from left to right a sequence of tones onto a sequence of syllables.
       b. It assigns one tone per syllable, until it runs out of tones.
       c. Then, it assigns the last tone that was specified to the remaining untoned syllables on the right, ...
       d. until it encounters the next syllable to the right belonging to a morpheme with specified tone.
       e. If the procedure above runs out of vowels (syllabic elements or syllables), more than one tone may be assigned to the last vowel only if the grammar of the language includes a stipulation to that effect.

(3e) is Halle and Vergnaud's addition. In their view, tones are assigned to vowels, syllabic elements, or syllables. Pulleyblank (1986:19) explicitly states that "there will be virtually no discussion of what constitutes a tone-bearing unit." The formal treatment of the notion of tone-bearing unit is overlooked.[2]

Given that tones are autosegments, the question arises whether it is possible to map tones onto suprasegmental entities such as rimes or syllables. If tones are conceived to form a separate plane, then the possibility of such a mapping is ruled out in current autosegmental theory, in which the x-skeleton binds the various autosegmental planes. We can state the relation between planes and x-skeleton as follows.[3]

(4)   Autosegmental planes may link to x-skeleta only.

The structure in (2) is ill-formed if the association line is interpreted as linking the tone T directly to the phoneme P. The structure in (5), however, is well-formed.

(5)   Well-formed Structure

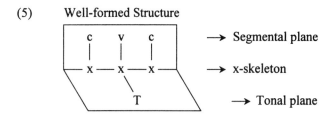

In this structure, the x-skeleton mediates the tone T and the vowel v. The condition (4) is satisfied.

With the introduction of the theory of feature geometry, the representation of phonological form was greatly enriched. In addition to the conception of tone as forming an independent autosegmental plane, as in structure (5), it is now possible to see tone as forming an autosegmental tier within the segmental plane or the syllabic plane. With respect to tone, there are three ways in which the condition (4) can be satisfied. These are shown in (6) (Rt, root node; O, onset; N, nucleus; R, rime; only relevant nodes are shown).[4]

(6) a. Tone as separate plane

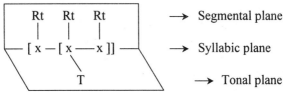

b. Tone as tier in segmental plane

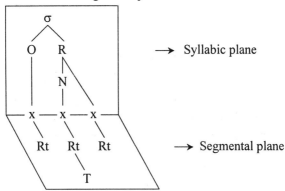

c. Tone as tier in syllabic plane

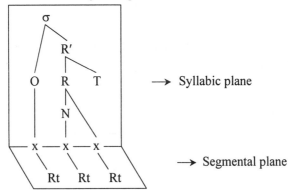

(6a) is equivalent to (5), in which the tone node T forms a separate plane and is associated with the x-slot of the syllabic nucleus. The condition in (4) is satisfied because the tonal plane, like the segmental and syllabic planes, is anchored on the x-skeleton. This is the structure assumed in various autosegmental studies on tone. In structures (6b,c), where tones do not form a separate plane, the condition (4) is satisfied vacuously. Structure (6b) is proposed by

Archangeli and Pulleyblank (1989); in it, tone is a tier of the root node on the segmental plane. Bao (1990a) proposes (6c), in which tone is represented as a tier on the syllabic plane. Note that O necessarily precedes R in time because the x-slot dominated by O precedes the x-slot(s) dominated by R. There is no temporal ordering relation between T and other syllabic constituents, since T is not associated with the x-skeleton, which comprises timing slots. However, indirectly, T is ordered before O.

The three structures in (6) make different empirical predictions concerning the behavior of tone. Note that in all three structures, tone sandhi can take place independently of the segments, because tones form an autosegmental plane in (6a), and an autosegmental tier in (6b,c). It has long been observed that phonological operations on segments do not affect tones, a phenomenon known as "tone stability." As an underlying representation, structure (6b) fails to account for tone stability; since tone is here dominated by the root node of the tone-bearing nuclear segment, phonological operations on the root node necessarily affect the tone. Tone stability is a direct consequence of both (6a) and (6c).

The structures in (6a,c) make different empirical predictions with respect to what I call "constituent operation," as opposed to "string operation." String operation is a phonological process that involves strings of segments regardless of their constituent structure. Constituent operation, by contrast, is a phonological process that involves an entire constituent—both its structural and segmental makeup. Consider two hypothetical rules of deletion, shown in (7).

(7)   a. S-deletion

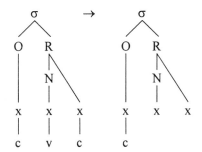

        b. C-deletion

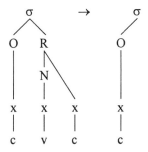

The process captured in S-deletion (7a) is a string operation, which deletes the segments on the segmental plane that are associated with the x-slots dominated by the R node; the syllabic structure is left intact. The process captured in C-deletion (7b) is a constituent operation, which deletes the entire rime constituent—its structure and segmental content. The two rules yield different sandhi effects when applied to the structures in (6), as shown in (8).

(8)   a. Tone in tonal plane

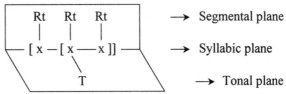

i. S-deletion (7a)   ii. C-deletion (7b)

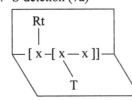   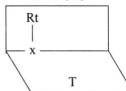

b. Tone as tier in segmental plane

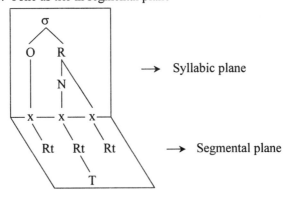

i. S-deletion (7a)   ii. C-deletion (7b)

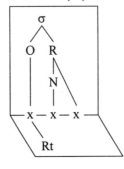   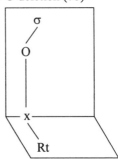

c. Tone as tier in syllabic plane

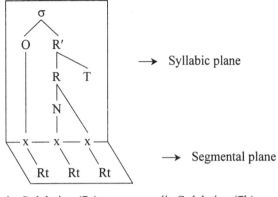

→ Syllabic plane

→ Segmental plane

i. S-deletion (7a)   ii. C-deletion (7b)

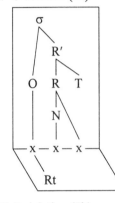   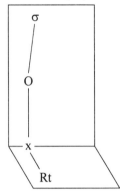

iii. C-deletion (7b)

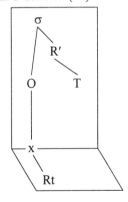

The derivations in (8a) show that if tones form an autosegmental plane separate from the segments and syllabic constituents, it is theoretically possible for tones to remain on their plane in both types of deletion processes. If tones are represented as constituent nodes of the root nodes that define tone-bearing segments, they will be deleted along with the segments in both types of operation (cf. (8b)). If, however, tones are represented as an autosegmental tier on the syllabic plane, tones will remain under S-deletion (8c-i), but they will be deleted under C-deletion (8c-ii). In (8c-ii), C-deletion is assumed to apply to the R' constituent, and T is deleted as well; in (8c-iii), it applies to the R node, and T survives deletion. Tone stability is structure-dependent. Since the structure in (6b) fails to account for tone stability, we can dismiss it as a candidate for the underlying representation of toned syllables. The structure in (6a) accounts for tone stability maximally, in the sense that tones are expected to be stable under all kinds of phonological processes (except those that expressly affect tones). The structure in (6c), however, makes an interesting prediction concerning the structure-dependency of tone stability. The prediction is stated in (9).

(9)   Given the structure

       and a structure-sensitive phonological rule P,
       T is stable if and only if P involves sub-R' elements.

This prediction is not made by the structure in (6a). This is where the empirical difference lies between the two structures (6a,c). I will show in the next section that prediction (9) is confirmed in the game languages called *fanqie* languages.

5.2   Structure-Dependency of Tone Stability

Crucial evidence in support of the structure-dependency of tone stability[5] comes from the game languages called variously "*fanqie* languages" or "secret languages" (Chao 1931, Yip 1982, P. J.-K. Li 1985, Lin 1988, Bao 1990a, Duanmu 1990, and Chiang 1992); these are described in section 4.2.2 of the present work. Consider the data from a *fanqie* language, May-ka, in (10). Unless otherwise indicated, all *fanqie* language data are cited from Chao (1931); Bao (1990a) is an analysis of Chao's data, as well as data from Li (1985) and Lin (1988).

(10)   May-ka
        a. ma   →   may-ka   "mother"
        b. pən   →   pay-kən   "book"
        c. pey   →   pay-key   "north"

An inspection of the data shows the following: (1) a *fanqie* word consists of two syllables, corresponding to a single source syllable; and (2) one of the two syllables of a *fanqie* word retains the rime of the source syllable, while the other retains the initial consonant of the source syllable. For ease of reference, I call the syllable with the original rime the "r-syllable," and the syllable with the original onset the "o-syllable." As shown in (10b), the *fanqie* equivalent of *pən* is *pay-kən*; the first syllable *pay* (the o-syllable) retains the source initial consonant, while the second syllable *kən* (the r-syllable) retains the source rime. The o-syllable obtains a new rime, and the r-syllable obtains a new onset segment. This is the general form of *fanqie* languages. The new onset segments for the r-syllable and new rimes for the o-syllable vary from one *fanqie* language to another. For example, Mey-ka differs from May-ka in that the former *fanqie* language has /ey/ as the new rime, rather than /ay/:

(11)   Mey-ka
        a. ma   →   mey-ka   "mother"
        b. pən →   pey-kən   "book"
        c. pey →   pey-key   "north"

In section 4.2.2 we saw that the derivation of *fanqie* languages involves copying and substitution. The mechanism of *fanqie* language formation is as follows (Bao 1990a).

(12)   *Fanqie* language formation (FLF):
        a. Total copying of the source syllable (Steriade 1988)
        b. Substitution operation on resultant string
        c. Substitution can operate once on a given syllable

Substitution is defined uniquely for each *fanqie* language. For example, given the syllable structure in (13), May-ka and Mey-ka can be derived by the substitution operations defined in (14) and (15) respectively.

(13)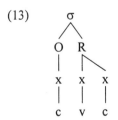

(14)   May-ka
        a. In the first syllable, replace the rime with [ay 15]$_R$.
        b. In the second syllable, replace the onset-initial with /k/.

(15)   Mey-ka
        a. In the first syllable, replace the rime with [ey 51]$_R$.
        b. In the second syllable, replace the onset initial with /k/.

Substitution preserves structure; it replaces a source constituent with a new
constituent of the same type. The following derivations involving the source
word *ma* "mother" illustrate how FLF works (a dot separates the onset from the
rime, and tones are omitted):

(16)   Copying of *ma*   m.a-m.a   m.a-m.a
        Substitution (14a, 15a)   m.ay-m.a   m.ey-m.a
        Substitution (14b, 15b)   m.ay-k.a   m.ey-k.a

Other *fanqie* languages can be derived in analogous fashion.
    We now consider the tone patterns of *fanqie* languages. The relevant data are
in (17).

(17)   a. May-ka
           ma 55   → may 15 (11)-ka 55   "mother"
           pən 15 → pay 15 (35)-kən 15   "book"
           taw 51 → tay 15 (11)-kaw 51   "path"
        b. Mey-ka
           ma 55   → mey 51-ka 55
           pən 15 → pey 51-kən 15
           taw 51 → tey 51-kaw 51
        c. Man-t'a
           ma 55   → man 55-t'a 55
           pən 15 → pən 15 (35)-t'ən 15
           taw 51 → tan 51-t'aw 51

(The tones in parentheses are derived through tone sandhi.) Of the two syllables
of a *fanqie* word, the r-syllable contains the source rime and carries the source
tone in all three *fanqie* languages. Our focus is on the o-syllable, which obtains a
new rime. The tones on the o-syllable differ from the source tones in May-ka and
Mey-ka. In Man-t'a, however, both the r-syllable and the o-syllable keep the
source tone. We now observe that in May-ka and Mey-ka the nucleus of the o-
syllable is /a/ (May-ka) or /e/ (Mey-ka), regardless of the vowel quality of the
source syllable. In these two *fanqie* languages, the o-syllable loses the source
tone. In Man-t'a, by contrast, the vowel quality of the source syllable remains the
same in both the o-syllable and the r-syllable, and the o-syllable keeps the source
tone. I express this observation in (18).

(18)   If the vowel of the source syllable remains in the o-syllable, the o-
        syllable keeps the source tone.

Now consider the tone patterns of Mo-pa, Ma-sa, and La-pi.

(19)   a. Mo-pa
           pã 33   → po 33-vã 33   "country"
           ts'ɿ 4 → ts'o 4-zɿ 4   "seven"

b. Ma-sa (Yip 1982:641)
   ma 3   → ma 5-sa 2
   ti 5   → ti 5-si 2
   kun 31 → kun 5-sun 2
c. La-pi (Li 1985, Lin 1988)
   hyaw 53 → lyaw 53 (55)-hi 53
   t'aw 13 → law 13 (33)-t'i 13
   t'at 31 → lat 31 (53)-t'it 31

In Mo-pa (19a), the source tone is retained in both the r-syllable and the o-syllable; the new rime and the new onset initial are /o/ and /p/, respectively. In Ma-sa (19b), the source tone disappears in both the r-syllable and o-syllable, and the new onset initial is /s/. In La-pi (19c), the source tone occurs on both syllables of the *fanqie* words. Furthermore, the o-syllable keeps the coda of the source syllable. The rime structure of the source syllable is preserved in the La-pi word. If the source syllable contains a coda, its La-pi equivalent contains the coda in both syllables.[6] To preserve the rime structure, the locus of substitution must be the nucleus. I define the substitution operation that derives La-pi as follows.

(20)   La-pi
   a. In the first syllable, replace the onset initial with /l/.
   b. In the second syllable, replace the nucleus with [i]$_N$.

Since the locus of the substitution operation is the nucleus, the source coda will remain in the o-syllable in La-pi. Clearly there is a correlation between the tone pattern and the presence of the source coda in the o-syllable in La-pi. I express this correlation in (21).

(21)   If the coda of the source syllable remains in the o-syllable, then the o-syllable keeps the source tone.

Recall that (18) expresses the relation between the nucleus of the source syllable and the tone pattern of the o-syllable. Generalizing, we combine (18) and (21) as in (22).

(22)   If either segmental constituent of the source rime remains in the o-syllable, then the o-syllable keeps the source tone.

To summarize, we see that the tone patterns of *fanqie* languages, as manifested on the o-syllable, fall into the five categories enumerated in (23).

(23)   a. New segmental rime; new tone (May-ka, Mey-ka)
      b. New segmental rime; source tone (Mo-pa)
      c. New coda; source tone (Man-t'a)
      d. New nucleus; source tone (La-pi)
      e. New tone on both syllables (Ma-sa)

To my knowledge, these are the only tone patterns observed in *fanqie* languages that have been reported to date.

To characterize the set of possible tone patterns, and to derive generalization (22), the structural relation of tone with respect to other aspects of the syllable—particularly the syllabic structure—is crucial. If tone is mapped onto the x-skeleton, there is no explanation of why (23) comprises the only tone patterns of *fanqie* languages, nor of why generalization (22) should govern the tone patterns of *fanqie* languages. If, on the other hand, we assume that tone is an autosegmental tier on the syllabic plane, as in (24),

(24)

then both generalization (22) and the tone patterns in (23) follow as a direct consequence of the formal mechanism of FLF. In the structure in (24), c,v are the root nodes of consonantal and vocalic segments. For ease of reference, I will call node R' the "rime," and R the "segmental rime." Note that substitution is a constituent operation defined over syllabic structure. In *fanqie* languages, the r-syllable always retains the tone of the source syllable. This is so because the locus of substitution in deriving the r-syllable is the onset initial; such an operation does not affect the tone (the T node) at all, as shown below.

(25)   New onset initial

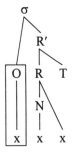

With respect to the o-syllable, there are four nodes that can serve as the locus of the substitution operation, as illustrated in (26) (the affected constituent is in the box).

(26)   a. New rime   b. New segmental rime

   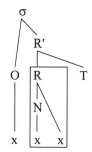

c. New coda   d. New nucleus

e. New tone

In (26a), the entire rime R' is the locus of substitution; hence the tone is also replaced. This is the tone pattern of May-ka and Mey-ka (17a,b). In (26b), substitution operates on the segmental rime R; the tone is retained because T is not dominated by R. This is the tone pattern of Mo-pa (19a). In these two cases, substitution produces the same segmental effect; the only difference is the tone.[7] In (26c), substitution affects the coda without affecting the tone. This is the tone pattern of Man-t'a, in which the o-syllable is derived by inserting a code /n/ (17c). In (26d), the nucleus serves as the locus of the substitution operation; since N does not dominate T, T is retained. This is the tone pattern of La-pi (19c). Lastly, in (26e), the substitution operation replaces the T node, in which case the *fanqie* language so derived will surface with the segmental material of the source syllable, and a new tone. This is the tone pattern of Ma-sa (19b). As for the generalization in (22), if either the source coda or the source nucleus is retained in the o-syllable, the locus of substitution must necessarily be a constituent dominated by the segmental rime node R. Tones will not be affected by such substitution operation. Thus, the tone patterns of *fanqie* languages enumerated in (23) and the generalization (22) follow from the mechanism of FLF and the structure of the syllable in (24), in which tone is represented as forming an autosegmental tier on the syllabic plane.

Suppose that tones form an autosegmental plane, as in (27).

(27)

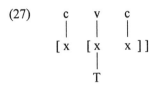

This structure satisfies condition (4), which stipulates that elements on planes must be linked to x-slots. T on the tonal plane, and c, v on the segmental plane, are all linked to the x-slots directly. Bracketing indicates the structure of the syllable. Since they form a separate plane, tones will be maximally stable and will not be affected no matter what syllabic constituent serves as the locus of the substitution operation. As an illustration, consider the derivations of May-ka and La-pi (for clarity, only abbreviated syllables and segments are shown):

(28)   a. May-ka

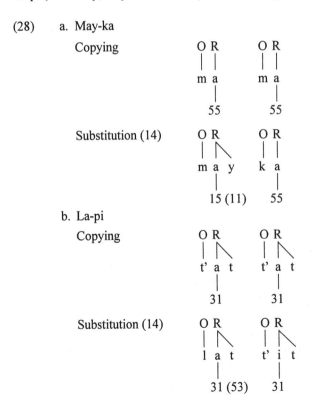

In the derivation of the La-pi example, substitution replaces the onset initial of the first syllable with /l/ and the nucleus of the second syllable with /i/. In May-ka, however, the tone is replaced along with the segmental material of the rime; tones therefore do not exhibit stability in May-ka, or other *fanqie* languages with May-ka properties. Since tones can be affected along with segments, we would expect to find a *fanqie* language that would produce the following form.

(29)   t'at 31 → lat 31-t'it 15

This hypothetical *fanqie* language is similar to La-pi with one exception: the source tone 31 is replaced by the new tone 15, along with the nucleus segment /i/. This hypothetical form is not reported in the literature on *fanqie* languages. A structure in which tones are represented on a separate plane fails to characterize adequately the tone patterns observed in *fanqie* languages. There is no principled explanation for the tone patterns in (23) and the generalization in (22).

I conclude that *fanqie* language data provide evidence for the structure proposed in (24), in which tones form an autosegmental tier on the syllabic plane. Evidence from partially reduplicated words in classical Chinese and modern dialects also supports this conclusion (Bao 1995, 1996).

5.3   Segmentalization of Tone

In this section I consider the lexical representation of tone and its segmentalization. As far as tonal phonology is concerned, the lexical representation provides the input to tone sandhi rules, after which segmentalization occurs. The phonological component of tone sandhi I assume is schematized below.

(30)   Organization of tone sandhi component

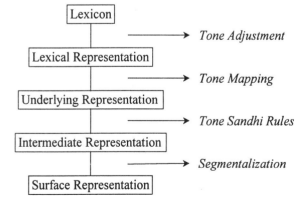

Given a monosyllabic morpheme with the segments *p, a, k*, and tone *t*, I assume that the phonological component of the morpheme has the following form in the lexicon.[8]

(31)

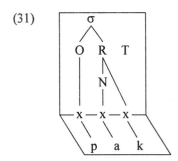

Polysyllabic strings are concatenated of repetitions of the structure in (31). Tone adjustment rules apply to strings having the syllabic structure (31); these rules, which adjust the tone in accordance with the segmental information, are of the form (32).[9]

(32)

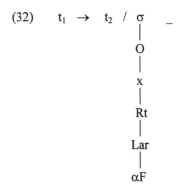

Tone adjustment rules, therefore, make reference to information on the segmental plane. Note that tone is not associated with any constituent at the time when tone adjustment rules apply. The issue of trans-planar conditioning does not arise (more on this issue later). Tone adjustment rules can be generalized to include other constituents of the syllable. For the present purpose, these rules are intended to handle co-occurrence restrictions between onset segments and tones on the following vowels within the same syllable, a phenomenon I will refer to as "onset-tone harmony." Therefore, only onset segmental information will figure in the formulation of such rules.

By "lexical representation" I mean the string that results from morpheme concatenation as modified by tone adjustment rules. *Tone Mapping* maps tones, which are unassociated in the lexical representation, to the appropriate tone-bearing units, forming an autosegmental tier of tone on which tonal computation is performed. The rules of tonal computation are referred to as *Tone Sandhi Rules*. After tone sandhi rules have applied, tones are segmentalized—that is, they are phonetically realized on the vowels (or other nuclear elements). The subcomponents in (30)—*Tone Adjustment, Tone Mapping, Tone Sandhi Rules* and *Segmentalization*—may be viewed as functions that take two representations as arguments. Thus, *Tone Mapping* relates the lexical representation of a form to the underlying representation. The schema in (30) imposes a strict ordering relation among the subcomponents. In this section, I will discuss *Tone Mapping* and *Segmentalization*. Rule types of tone sandhi will be discussed in section 5.4.

Tone mapping, however, is not as straightforward as putting tones on the syllabic plane. In many Chinese dialects, particularly of the Wu variety, a tone has two variants conditioned by the voicing qualities of syllable-initial segments. The tone/segment segregation raises questions about the trans-planar interaction between the syllable-initial segment and the tone on the following vowel. There are three cases to consider, two of which present no problem. First, in languages that do not have voiced obstruents, the laryngeal features [stiff] and [slack] are nondistinctive. There is no linguistically significant interaction between syllable-initial segments and tones in such languages, which are exemplified by most Mandarin dialects of Chinese, including Changzhi (section 3.3.1.2), Zhenjiang (section 3.3.3.1) and Pingyao (section 3.3.2). Second, there are languages that do have voiced obstruents but exhibit no interaction between the obstruents and tones. Weining Miao (section 3.2.1 and Chapter 6) is such a language. Its high tones and low tones are not in complementary distribution with respect to the voicing qualities of syllable-initial segments. These two cases present no problem because there is no interaction between segments on one plane and tones on another.

Third, there are languages that have a strict correlation between the voicing qualities of syllable-initial segments and tone registers. Songjiang is a paradigmatic example; its tone inventory is shown in (33).

(33)   Tonal Inventory of Songjiang
        Yin-register
        a. 53   ti   "low"
                    t'i   "ladder"
        b. 44   ti   "bottom"
                    t'i   "body"
        c. 35   ti   "emperor"
                    t'i   "tear"
        d. 5   paʔ   "hundred"
                    p'aʔ   "tap"
        Yang-register
        A. 31   di   "lift"
        B. 22   di   "brother"
        C. 13   di   "field"
        D. 3   baʔ   "white"

In languages that exhibit onset-tone harmony, the tone registers are predictable from the onset obstruents of the syllables on which they are realized. The bi-planar representation of tones and segments makes it difficult to characterize this onset-tone harmony. Suppose that 44 is the underlying tone from which 22 is derived. The representations of *ti* 44 "bottom" and *di* 22 "brother" (33b,B) are as follows.

(34)   a. Bi-planar structure of *ti* 44 "bottom"

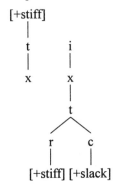

        b. Bi-planar structure of *di* 22 "brother"

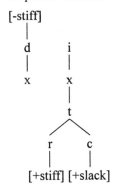

In (34) I indicate that /t/ is specified as [+stiff] and /d/ as [-stiff], without specifying the full feature trees of the two phonemes. Notice that in Songjiang, voiced obstruents always occur with [-stiff] tones, and voiceless obstruents always occur with [+stiff] tones. So the structure in (34b) must undergo some lowering process so that [L,l] will surface instead of the underlying [H,l]. It appears that the tonal register assimilates to the preceding segment, across two autosegmental planes.

The two series of tones in Songjiang's tonal inventory differ in register as conditioned by the voicing qualities of syllable-initial segments; other dialects display more complex alternations. Wenling, a case in point, has eight tones in citation form, shown in (35) (R. Li 1979).

(35)   a. 33   b. 42   c. 55   d. 5
        A. 31   B. 31   C. 13   D. 1

(35a-d) are used with voiceless initial segments, and (35A-D) are used with voiced initial segments. Note that (35A) and (35B) both surface as 31 when used with voiced-initial syllables; according to Li (1979), however, they are derived from different underlying tones because they exhibit different sandhi behavior. The tonal inventory of Wenling suggests that onset-tone harmony is not a result of register assimilation. In the case of (35c) and (35C), the alternation involves both the register (H to L) and the contour (even to rising).

To account for the phenomenon of onset-tone harmony, I assume that the lexical representation of monosyllabic morphemes in languages like Songjiang and Wenling contains a single tone regardless of the voicing qualities of the syllable-initial segments. Moreover, tones are free, unassociated with any constituent, segmental or otherwise. They are mapped to the tone-bearing units according to well-known association principles. For instance, the phonological components of the lexical entries of *ti* 44 "bottom" and *di* 22 "brother" have the structures in (36).

(36) a. Lexical entry of *ti* 44   b. Lexical entry of *di* 22

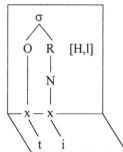 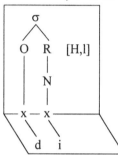

Polysyllabic morphemes are concatenated of syllables having the structure shown in (36). Tone mapping adjoins tone to the tone-bearing unit—in the case of (36), to the R node. It creates the structure in (37).[10]

(37)   R′

    R   t

In this structure, temporal precedence does not hold between R and t. The tonal tier is orthogonal to the temporal dimension. Onset-tone harmony is derived before tone mapping by means of tone adjustment rules, which must make reference to syllable-initial segments. The tone adjustment rules of Songjiang can be formulated as follows (sub-R structure is suppressed).

(38)   a. [H,l] → [L,l] / σ —

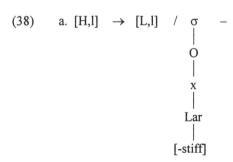

b. [H,lh] → [L,lh] / σ —
|
O
|
x
|
Lar
|
[-stiff]

c. [H,hl] → [L,hl] / σ —
|
O
|
x
|
Lar
|
[-stiff]

The rules in (38) all describe the same process, register lowering. It is possible to collapse them into a single rule, but I keep them separate for illustrative purposes. Rule (38a) derives [L,l] from [H,l] in (36b). Tone mapping adjoins tones to the R node, creating the structures below.

(39)   a.   b.

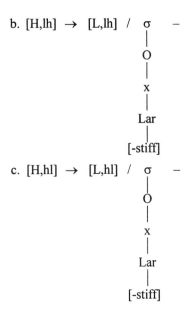

In order to see how the various rules sketched above work, let us consider the bisyllabic tone sandhi data from Wuyi. Wuyi has the following tonal inventory (Fu 1984).

(40)   a. 24   b. 55   c. 53   d. 5
        A. 213   B. 13   C. 31   D. <u>212</u>

The tones (40d,D) are short tones occurring in syllables ending in glottal stop. Historically, the pairs (40a,A), (40b,B), (40c,C), and (40d,D) are each derived from a single tone, which splits into a *yin* variant (40a), (40b), (40c), or (40d), and a *yang* variant (40A), (40B), (40C), or (40D). I will include historically related tones within braces, for example {24,213}.

In bisyllabic phrases, the first tone undergoes tone sandhi. The sandhi patterns are shown as follows; the vertical axis represents the first tone, and the horizontal axis represents the second tone.

(41)   Bisyllabic tone patterns of Wuyi

	24	213	53	31	55	13
24						
213			55-			
53						
31						
55			11-			
13						

The second tone in a bisyllabic phrase does not show sandhi effects. The tone sandhi patterns shown in (41) happen generally, with the exception of patterns {24,213}-{24,213} and {24,213}-{53,31} in phrases other than the verb-object construction. These exceptional sandhi patterns were discussed in section 4.3. Relevant data are given in (42) through (45).

(42)   a. {24,213}-24 → 55-24
         k'a tɕ'ia   "drive a car"
         ts'ɑu ɕy   "copy books"
         puɑ (< buɑ) suo   "climb mountains"
         tuo (< duo) ɕy   "take a book"
     b. {24,213}-213 → 55-213
         ka die   "plow fields"
         tsu vɑŋ   "rent a house"
         ta (< da) dɑu   "raise the head"
         tuo (< duo) dʑiŋ   "play musical instrument"
     c. {24,213}-53 → 55-53
         tsa ts'a   "plant vegetable"
         puo huo   "ship products"
         sa (< za) pu   "buy cloth"
         tsuɑ (< dzuɑ) p'ie   "check tickets"
     d. {24,213}-31 → 55-31
         tsa ʐy   "plant trees"
         ka di   "plow fields"
         tiŋ (< diŋ) die   "cut electricity"
         pia (< bia) da   "line up"
     e. {24,213}-55 → 55-55
         tɕ'iŋ ts'u   "clear"
         t'ie tɕiŋ   "courtyard"
         ʔŋuɑ (< ɦŋuɑ) ts'i   "teeth"
         toŋ (< doŋ) ʔmuo   "copper plate"

f. {24,213}-13 → 55-13

koŋ ʑia	"commune"
tsoŋ ɦɑu	"honest"
pəŋ (< bəŋ) ɦiəu	"friend"
tɕi (< dʑi) ɦimuɑ	"ride horses"

(43) a. 53-24 → 55-24

| huo tɕ'ia | "truck" |
| faŋ ɕiŋ | "at ease" |

b. 53-213 → 55-213

| t'ie dɑu | "cut hair" |
| ɕi da | "stage" |

c. 53-53 → 55-53

| ɕie tɕia | "world" |
| faŋ tɕ'i | "abandon" |

d. 53-31 → 55-31

| tɕiŋ dʑi | "politics" |
| ɕiŋ bu | "progress" |

e. 53-55 → 55-55

| pau tɕi | "newspaper" |
| kuo huo | "overdo" |

f. 53-13 → 55-13

| t'ie vu | "dance" |
| soŋ ɦilie | "give gifts" |

(44) a. 31-24 → 11-24

| duo ku | "aunt" |
| di faŋ | "place" |

b. 31-213 → 11-213

| goŋ doŋ | "common" |
| dʑi ɦiloŋ | "chopstick holder" |

c. 31-53 → 11-53

| bie ʔnaŋ | "convenient" |
| ɦinia t'ɣ | "jacket" |

d. 31-31 → 11-31

| di doŋ | "tunnel" |
| die ɦiuɑ | "telephone" |

e. 31-55 → 11-55

| di tɕy | "landlord" |
| ɦiuəi k'uo | "money order" |

f. 31-13 → 11-13

| vi dɣ | "taste" |
| duo ɦiɣ | "big rain" |

(45) a. {55,d13}-24 → 11-24

pɦu (< p'u) t'oŋ	"ordinary"
hɦuo (< huo) tɕ'a	"train"
bi k'uo	"bedding"
ɦimu tɕ'iŋ	"mother"

b. {55,13}-213 → 11-213
   bie (< pie) ɦiaŋ   "praise"
   ʐy (< ɕy) ɦu   "water kettle"
   du ʐie   "navel"
   ɦia ɦmuo   "savage"

c. {55,13}-53 → 11-53
   ga (< ka) tɕiŋ   "improve"
   kɦau (< k'au) ɕi   "examination"
   ɦŋuo tɕiŋ   "glasses"
   za kuo   "fault"

d. {55,13}-31 → 11-31
   gu (< ku) da   "antiquity"
   tsɦau (< ts'au) ɦmie   "fried noodles"
   ʐia ɦuəi   "society"
   bu da   "army"

e. {55,13}-55 → 11-55
   tɕɦii (< tɕ'i) ɕi   "begin"
   hɦuo (< huo) t'a   "ham"
   ɦna ɕy   "cold water"
   ɦy suo   "umbrella"

f. {55,13}-13 → 11-13
   gaŋ (< kaŋ) ɦnie   "make a speech"
   gua (< kua) vu   "widow"
   vu ɦmu   "parents"
   ɦau ba   "gossip"

As the data indicate, syllable-initial segments devoice if tones become H-registered as a result of tone sandhi (42); and they voice if tones surface as L-registered (45). Tone adjustment rules account for the influence of syllable-initial segments on tones. The onset-tone harmony in (42) and (45) shows that tones can also influence voicing and devoicing.

To characterize the tone patterns in (41), we focus on the first tone. Observe that {24,213} and the H variant of {53,31} surface as 55; {55,13} and 31, the L variant of {53,31}, surface as 11. Suppose that 24, 53, and 13 are the underlying tones, having the structures [H,lh], [H,hl], and [L,h] respectively. The other tones can be derived by the tone adjustment rules formulated below (only relevant structure is shown; O is the onset).[11,12]

(46)   a. [H,lh] → [L,lh] / σ _]

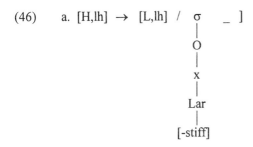

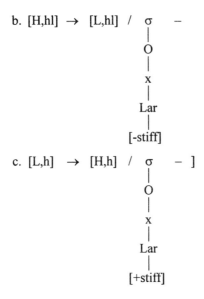

b. [H,hl] → [L,hl] / σ   –
                      |
                      O
                      |
                      x
                      |
                     Lar
                      |
                   [-stiff]

c. [L,h] → [H,h] / σ   –   ]
                    |
                    O
                    |
                    x
                    |
                   Lar
                    |
                 [+stiff]

The three tone adjustment rules in (46) do not apply in identical phonological environments. Only (46b) applies to the underlying tone [H,hl] regardless of its environment. By contrast, rules (46a) and (46c) are formulated so that they apply to tones in phrase-final position, as indicated by the right square bracket "]". They apply to tones in citation and phrase-final positions, but not in phrase-initial position. By contrast, (46b) is not restricted: it applies to tones in all positions. In citation form as well in phrase-final position, (46a) derives 213 from 24, and (46c) derives 55 from 13. (46b) derives 31 from 53 in all positions.

Given the underlying tones [H,lh], [H,hl], and [L,h], the most economical way to derive the sandhi patterns in (41) is the following rule.

(47)   c → c / [_
               |
               l

This rule applies just in case the tone is phrase-initial. The rule derives [H,l] from a H-registered tone and [L,l] from a L-registered tone. [H,l] surfaces as 55, and [L,l] as 11. Consider the derivation in (48), which involves the tone adjustment rule (46a) (full structures are suppressed).

(48)   a. Derivation of *tuo* 55 *çy* 24 "take a book"

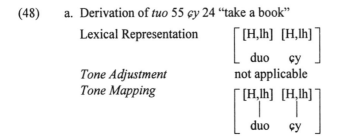

Lexical Representation   ⎡ [H,lh] [H,lh] ⎤
                             ⎣ duo   çy   ⎦
Tone Adjustment   not applicable
Tone Mapping   ⎡ [H,lh] [H,lh] ⎤
                             ⎢ | | ⎥
                             ⎣ duo   çy   ⎦

Rule (47)

Devoicing

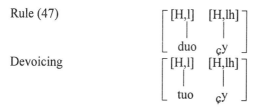

b. Derivation of *ka* 55 *die* 213 "plow fields"

Lexical Representation

Tone Adjustment (46a)

Tone Mapping

Rule (47)

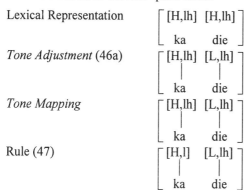

Note that tone adjustment rule (46a) does not apply to phrase-initial syllables. This accounts for the fact that the phrase-final tone [H,lh] is replaced by [L,lh], but the phrase-initial [H,lh] surfaces as [H,h], because of rule (47). The H-registered even tone eventually causes the initial consonant to devoice.

Now consider the effect of (46b) in the derivations in (49).

(49)   a. Derivation of *t'ie 55 vu 13* "dance"

Lexical Representation

Tone Adjustment

Tone Mapping

Rule (47)

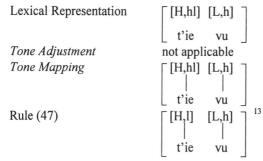

b. Derivation of *duo 11 ku 24* "aunt"

Lexical Representation

Tone Adjustment (46b)

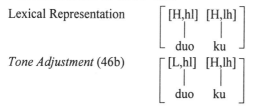

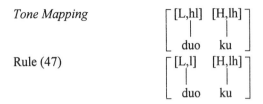

Tone Mapping

$$\begin{bmatrix} [\text{L,hl}] & [\text{H,lh}] \\ | & | \\ \text{duo} & \text{ku} \end{bmatrix}$$

Rule (47)

$$\begin{bmatrix} [\text{L,l}] & [\text{H,lh}] \\ | & | \\ \text{duo} & \text{ku} \end{bmatrix}$$

Since (46b) is not restricted to any environment, [H,hl] lowers to [L,hl] in phrase-initial position (cf. (49b)). It surfaces as the low even tone [L,l].

We now consider (46c), which is like (46a) in that it applies only to tones in phrase-initial position.

(50)   Derivation of *ʐy* 11 *ɦu* 213 "kettle"

Lexical Representation

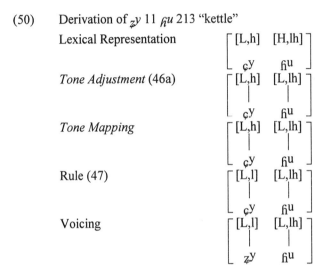

Tone Adjustment (46a)

Tone Mapping

Rule (47)

Voicing

$$\begin{bmatrix} [\text{L,h}] & [\text{H,lh}] \\ | & | \\ \text{ç}^y & \text{ɦ}^u \end{bmatrix}$$

$$\begin{bmatrix} [\text{L,h}] & [\text{L,lh}] \\ | & | \\ \text{ç}^y & \text{ɦ}^u \end{bmatrix}$$

$$\begin{bmatrix} [\text{L,h}] & [\text{L,lh}] \\ | & | \\ \text{ç}^y & \text{ɦ}^u \end{bmatrix}$$

$$\begin{bmatrix} [\text{L,l}] & [\text{L,lh}] \\ | & | \\ \text{ç}^y & \text{ɦ}^u \end{bmatrix}$$

$$\begin{bmatrix} [\text{L,l}] & [\text{L,lh}] \\ | & | \\ \text{ʐ}^y & \text{ɦ}^u \end{bmatrix}$$

In this derivation, the tone adjustment rule (46a) applies to lower the second tone, but (46c) does not apply; the underlying tone [L,h] surfaces as [L,l] after application of tone sandhi rule (47). The L-registered tone causes the initial segment to voice. In the following derivation, (46c) applies to the second tone, but not to the first tone. As a result the onset segment of the second syllable does not voice.

(51)   Derivation of *ɦy* 11 *suo* 55 "umbrella"

Lexical Representation

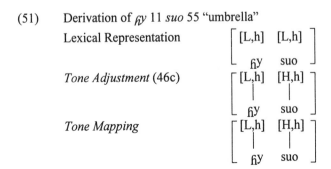

Tone Adjustment (46c)

Tone Mapping

$$\begin{bmatrix} [\text{L,h}] & [\text{L,h}] \\ | & | \\ \text{ɦ}^y & \text{suo} \end{bmatrix}$$

$$\begin{bmatrix} [\text{L,h}] & [\text{H,h}] \\ | & | \\ \text{ɦ}^y & \text{suo} \end{bmatrix}$$

$$\begin{bmatrix} [\text{L,h}] & [\text{H,h}] \\ | & | \\ \text{ɦ}^y & \text{suo} \end{bmatrix}$$

Rule (47)

The voicing and devoicing effects of tone sandhi can be seen as autosegmental spreading of the register of tone after it has been segmentalized. I state the tone segmentalization rule as follows.[14]

(52)   Segmentalization of Tone
        Link tone to the laryngeal node of the nucleus segment.

Rule (52) maps (53a) to (53b), which is equivalent to (53c).

(53)   a.

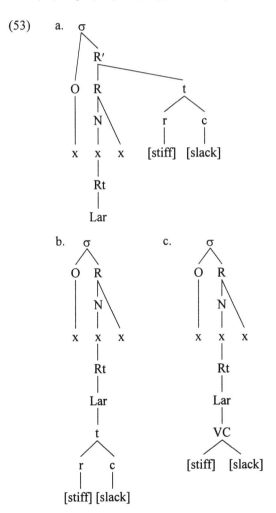

After the segmentalization of tone, voicing and devoicing can take place. These are assimilatory phenomena involving the spreading of the r node (i.e., the VC node) from the vowel to the preceding onset segment, as shown in (54). The derivation starts after the sandhi rule (47) (st = stiff; only relevant nodes are shown).

(54)   Continuation of (48a) *tuo* 55 *çy* 213

         Segmentalization

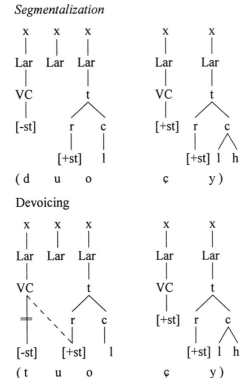

(55)   Continuation of (50) *ʐy* 11 *ɦu* 213

         Segmentalization

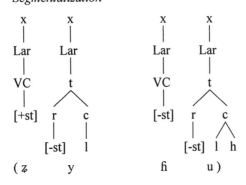

Voicing

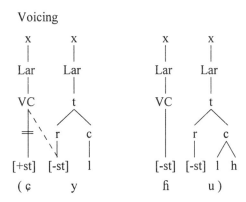

In (50) and (55), I give only the relevant details of the structure; the vowel's laryngeal node dominates t, which is intended to bring out the fact that it is the segmentalized tone. Note that in (54) the glide is not specified for the VC node. The voicing and devoicing result from the same phonological process. Tonal registers influence onset segments.

5.4   Phonological Processes of Tone Sandhi

Clements (1989) lists eight "elementary operations," which are reproduced in (56).

(56)   Elementary operations
a. Spread X
b. Delink X
c. Insert X
d. Delete X
e. Break X
f. Fuse X, Y
g. Permute X, Y
h. Map X to Y

In tonal phonology, we have seen rules involving the elementary operations of spreading and delinking (as in contour assimilation), insertion (as in contour formation), deletion (as in the deletion of lexical tones), and permutation (as in contour metathesis). Tone mapping, which involves the elementary operation of mapping, is interpreted as adjunction to a syllabic constituent. I have not been able to find unequivocal cases of tone fission (56e) or fusion (56f). In this section I will recapitulate the phonological processes that operate in tone sandhi by focusing on their formal properties. Specifically, I will discuss the formal properties of assimilation and dissimilation in contour systems. Because of the complexity of tonal geometry in a contour system, these processes often manifest themselves in different ways, and formal elucidation is called for.

5.4.1 Assimilation

We have seen four types of assimilation in tone sandhi: tone assimilation, register assimilation, contour assimilation, and feature assimilation. They are exemplified as follows.

(57)   a. Tone assimilation
               Changzhi
                   xæ təʔ   "child"
                   24 535 → 24-24
         b. Register assimilation
               Pingyao
                   xei tsuə   "river flood"
                   13 53 → 35 423
         c. Contour assimilation
               Weining Miao
                   ku nu   "ox's horn"
                   55 35 → 55 55
         d. Feature assimilation
               Gao'an
                   siu p'i   "repair"
                   55 33 → 53 33

In terms of formal operations, tone, register, and contour assimilation involve the simultaneous operation of spreading and delinking, while feature assimilation involves only the elementary operation of spreading. Consider now the spreading operation involved in the assimilation cases enumerated in (57), shown in (58).

(58)   a. Tone assimilation

$$R' \qquad R'$$

t   t

         b. Register assimilation

t   t

r   r

         c. Contour assimilation

t   t

c   c

         d. Feature assimilation

c   c

F_1 F_2

In (58a), (58b), and (58c), the target node must delink as a result of spreading. In (58d), spreading does not induce delinking of the target node. The first three instances of spreading involve non-terminal nodes, whereas the last instance involves terminal nodes. This property of assimilation can be attributed to the *Well-Formedness Condition*, which is also motivated for segmental phonology. Sagey (1986:50) stipulates that only terminal nodes may branch. The stipulation is stated as follows.

(59)   *Well-Formedness Condition*
        Contour segments may branch for terminal features only. No branching
        class nodes are allowed.

For a different approach to constraining the branching configuration of nodes, see Clements (1989). In addition to contour tones, contour segments include affricates and prenasalized stops. The tonal geometry I have introduced satisfies condition (59) because the branching nodes are the terminal feature [slack], dominated by the c node, as shown in (60).

(60)

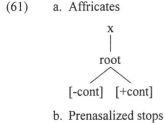

Sagey (1986) gives the structures in (61) for affricates and prenasalized stops.

(61)   a. Affricates

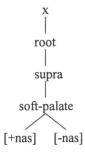

        b. Prenasalized stops

Like contour tones, the sequence of terminal features is temporally significant: in affricates, [-cont] must precede [+cont] in time; and in prenasalized stops, [+nasal] must precede [-nasal]. Another property that contour segments have in common is the fact that the contour in a contour segment can be specified only by a binary branching of the relevant features. No segment has the structure below.

(62)   a.

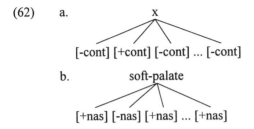

[-cont] [+cont] [-cont] ... [-cont]

        b.   soft-palate

[+nas] [-nas] [+nas] ... [+nas]

We need a supplemental constraint on the branching configuration, which I state as follows.

(63)   For any given terminal feature F, only a sequence of two F specifica-
        tions is allowed.

In section 3.1, I stipulated that c nodes are binary. This can now be seen as a special case of stipulation (63).

   There is a major difference between contour tones and affricates. Segments with the structures in (64a) do not occur in natural languages, but contour tones can have either of the two structures in (64b).

(64)   a.   root

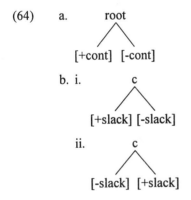

[+cont] [-cont]

        b. i.   c

[+slack] [-slack]

           ii.   c

[-slack] [+slack]

In other words, the elementary operation of permutation is possible on contour tones, but not on affricates and prenasalized stops. When contours are permuted, the falling contour becomes rising, and the rising contour becomes falling. Such an operation is behind the sandhi rule that I call *Contour Metathesis*. I will return to this process in section 5.4.2.

   Sagey's condition rules out structures in which a non-terminal node domi-nates two non-terminal nodes of the same type, but it allows two non-terminal nodes of different types to be sisters under the same node.

(65)   a. Inadmissible

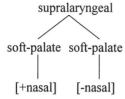

supralaryngeal

soft-palate soft-palate

[+nasal]   [-nasal]

b. Admissible

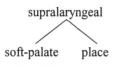

supralaryngeal

soft-palate   place

c. Admissible

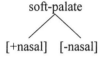

soft-palate

[+nasal] [-nasal]

A branching class node is allowed as long as its daughters are not of the same type (65b). With respect to tone, the condition makes the following restrictions.[15]

(66)   a.   t

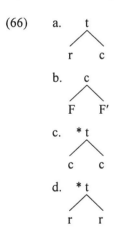

r   c

b.   c

F   F′

c.   * t

c   c

d.   * t

r   r

where F and F′ are instances of [slack]. In (66a), the structure is admissible because the non-terminal node t dominates two non-terminal nodes of different types, r and c. Structures (66c) and (66d) are not admissible because the t node dominates a sequence of two c nodes (66c) or a sequence of two r nodes (66d). The elementary operation of spreading involving the c node or r node creates precisely the ill-formed structures (66c) and (66d). The *Well-Formedness Condition* (59), however, does not include a repair strategy that will "prune" ill-formed trees to make them well-formed. A condition such as (67), proposed by Halle and Vergnaud (1982:80), is needed.

(67)   If the application of a rule results in a violation of the conditions—
        either universal or language-specific—which must be met by well-
        formed representations in the language in question, the violation is
        removed by deleting links between autosegments and core phonemes
        established by earlier rules or conventions.

Because of this condition, when spreading creates an ill-formed structure such as
(66c) or (66d), delinking is triggered automatically to remove the original autosegmental linkage. But if spreading involves features, creating the structure
(66b), delinking is not invoked.[16] This property of assimilation is observed not
only in tonal assimilation but also in segmental assimilation. Place assimilation,
for instance, necessarily induces the delinking of the target place node.[17]
    To summarize, assimilation in tonal phonology has the following formal
properties.

(68)   a. Spreading and delinking, if the assimilating node is non-terminal;
        b. Spreading, if the assimilating node is terminal.

I have shown that the properties of tonal assimilation follow from the *Well-
Formedness Condition* of Sagey (1986) in (59) and the Halle-Vergnaud
convention in (67).

5.4.2 Dissimilation

Given the tonal geometry in (69),

(69)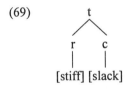

we predict three kinds of dissimilation. First, the non-branching specification of
the c node may dissimilate; second, the register may dissimilate; and third, since
the c node is possibly branching, the c node may dissimilate. These dissimilation
cases are illustrated by the structures in (70)–(71). The tones in parentheses are
sandhi tones.

(70)   Contour dissimilation
        a. Pingyao
           pu 13 (31) taŋ 35   "hatch an egg"
           13 → 31 / _ 35
           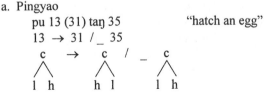

b. Tianjin[18]

    kau 21 (213) san 21   "high mountain"

    21 → 213 / _ 21

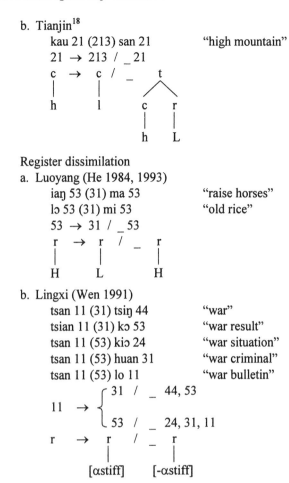

(71)   Register dissimilation

    a. Luoyang (He 1984, 1993)

        iaŋ 53 (31) ma 53   "raise horses"

        lɔ 53 (31) mi 53   "old rice"

        53 → 31 / _ 53

        r → r / _ r
        | | |
        H   L   H

    b. Lingxi (Wen 1991)

        tsan 11 (31) tsiŋ 44   "war"

        tsian 11 (31) kɔ 53   "war result"

        tsan 11 (53) kiɔ 24   "war situation"

        tsan 11 (53) huan 31   "war criminal"

        tsan 11 (53) lo 11   "war bulletin"

$$11 \rightarrow \begin{cases} 31 \ / \ \_ \ 44, 53 \\ 53 \ / \ \_ \ 24, 31, 11 \end{cases}$$

        r → r / _ r
          | |
     [αstiff]   [-αstiff]

Contour dissimilation is a simple case of the elementary operation of permutation, as (70a) shows. The data in (70b) and (71) illustrate the same process of a feature-changing operation. This operation is apparently not considered elementary by Clements (1989), since it is not in the list shown in (56). The feature-changing operation can be considered a composite of the elementary operations of deletion and insertion, as illustrated by register lowering in (72).

(72)   r r → r r → r r
        | | | | |
        H H   H   L H

In (72), the H register of the first tone is deleted first, and the L register is then inserted. This view of the feature-changing process is problematic; there is no principled way to guarantee that the feature being inserted can only be the deleted feature with a different value. I consider the feature-changing operation to be elementary.

5.4.3 Other Sandhi Effects

In addition to assimilation and dissimilation, we also find the following processes in tonal phonology.

(73)   a. Contour formation
            Pingyao
              xei 13 (35) tsuə 53 (423)   "river flood"
              53 → 423 / _]

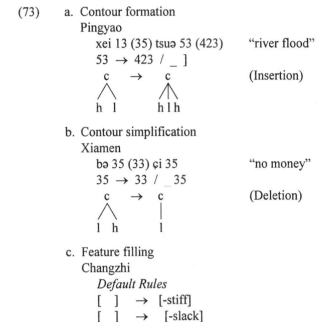

        b. Contour simplification
            Xiamen
              bə 35 (33) çi 35   "no money"
              35 → 33 / _ 35

        c. Feature filling
            Changzhi
              Default Rules
              [ ]   →   [-stiff]
              [ ]   →   [-slack]

The sandhi processes illustrated in (73) can be accounted for in terms of insertion, as in the contour formation and feature-filling processes, and in terms of delinking (or deletion), as in contour simplification.

6

The Mid Tone

6.1 Mid Tone as Default

The formal status of the mid tone has received some attention in the literature of autosegmental phonology, particularly in connection with the concerns of underspecification theories. The idea is that if tones are specified with features such as [upper] and [raised], then these features should behave like other, non-tonal features, which may be left unspecified in underlying representation. The unspecified feature values are then filled by default rules (cf. Kiparsky 1982a,b). Since tones are defined by the features, the default values define the default tone. In this chapter, I explore this empirical issue.

With respect to tone, Pulleyblank (1986) argues that the mid tone is the default tone by virtue of the universal status of the default rules shown in (1).

(1)   a. $\textcircled{V}$ →   V
                             |
                        [-upper]

         b. $\textcircled{V}$ →   V
                             |
                        [+raised]

The circled V is toneless. Translated into our terms, these two rules produce H for the r node, and l for the c node.

To support the validity of the two default rules, Pulleyblank (1986) adduces tonological evidence from two Kwa languages, Yala and Yoruba, which have a three-tone inventory. We will label the three tones as Lo, Mi, and Hi, to avoid confusing them with the register features H and L. Since the default values of the tone features need not be specified in underlying representation, the three tones are assigned lexical specification as follows.

(2)   a. Hi = [+upper]
         b. Mi = ∅
         c. Lo = [-raised]

The default rules apply, yielding the following fully specified structures for the three tones.

(3)   a. Hi = ⎡+upper ⎤
                 ⎣+raised ⎦
       b. Mi = ⎡-upper ⎤
                 ⎣+raised ⎦
       c. Lo = ⎡-upper ⎤
                 ⎣-raised ⎦

As a consequence of the default rules, Mi can only be specified as in (3b). The specification (3b′) is impossible as a default Mi tone.

(3)   b′. Mi = ⎡+upper ⎤
                  ⎣-raised ⎦

In Yala and Yoruba, the sandhi behavior of Mi can be understood if the vowel bearing it is seen as underlyingly toneless. The surface mid tone is assigned by the default rules in (1). To see the gist of Pulleyblank's argument, let us consider the data from Yoruba, shown in (4) (Pulleyblank 1986:109-111; the mid tone is not marked).

(4)   Hi-tone verb + Mi-tone-initial noun
       a. rí igbá → rígbá   "see a calabash"
       b. rí aṣọ   → ráṣọ   "see cloth"
       c. rí ọbẹ́   → róbệ   "see soup"

       Hi-tone verb + Lo-tone initial noun
       d. kọ́ èkọ́ → kẹ́kọ̌   "learn a lesson
       e. rí òbẹ   → rọ́'bẹ   "see a knife"
       f. rí àpò   → rápò   "see a bag"

In Yoruba, a vowel is deleted when it precedes another vowel. Its tone then surfaces on the following vowel, a classic example of autosegmental effect. In Pulleyblank's analysis, the Hi tone from the verb spreads to the noun-initial vowel. If the noun begins with a surface Mi tone, no further tone sandhi is observed, cf. (4a-c). (The falling tone in (4c) is due to an independent rule which turns a Lo tone into a falling tone when it follows a Hi tone.) The tone sandhi associated with V-deletion can be understood if we assume that the vowels carrying the Mi tone are underlyingly toneless. The derivation of (4a-c) involves only two rules: *V-Deletion*, which deletes the vowel of the verb, and *Hi-Spread*, which reattaches the Hi tone to the untoned vowel. This is illustrated below.

(5)   Underlying   igba   ri   igba
                            | | |
                            Hi   Hi   Hi

       V-Deletion   –   r   igba
                                                 |
                                          Hi   Hi

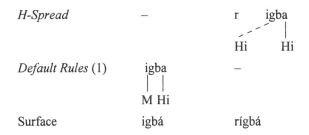

H-Spread	–	r igba
		Hi Hi
Default Rules (1)	igba	–
	M Hi	
Surface	igbá	rígbá

If the original noun-initial tone is Lo, *Hi-Spread* triggers an additional tone sandhi. The Lo tone either forms a rising tone with the following Hi (4d), downsteps the following Mi (4e), or disappears altogether when the following tone is Lo (4f). The derivation of (4d-f) is therefore more involved, and I will sketch it only briefly here After the vowel of the verb is deleted, *Hi-Spread* reattaches Hi to the following Lo-toned vowel. This creates the configuration that triggers the delinking of Lo. The sandhi behavior of the floating Lo varies. In the case of (4d), where the noun has the tone pattern LoHi, the floating Lo spreads rightward to create a falling tone, yielding the verb-noun pattern Hi-LoHi. In the case of (4e), the untoned vowel acquires Mi through the default tone rules, and is subsequently downstepped by the floating Lo. As for (4f), the floating Lo disappears because the following vowel has the Lo tone as well.

The data in (4d-f) do not bear on the status of the mid tone directly, but the data in (4a-c) are clearly relevant. Mi is indeed the default tone of Yoruba. However, we cannot conclude from the Yoruba data that the tone rules in (1) are universal. Clark (1990) argues that in Igbo, which has a two-tone inventory, the Lo tone must be lexically specified, and the Hi tone is the default, contrary to the prediction of (1).

The issue of the default tone in a language with underlying contour tones is more complicated than appears to be the case in a language without underlying contour tones. In tonological literature, a default tone is postulated to facilitate the explanation of tonological facts. However, empirical evidence from Chinese and other South Asian languages suggests that there is no bias in favor of any particular tone as the default tone, analogous to schwa /ə/ being the "universal" default vowel. For example, in Changzhi, the default tone is 44, which we have argued to be [L,h] (cf. section 3.3.1.2). This is compatible with the default rules in (1). But in Zhenjiang, our analysis makes it necessary to treat 55, or [H,h], as the default tone (cf. section 3.3.1.2). This will make [+upper] the default value for the register feature—exactly like the situation in Igbo. Furthermore, as we will see shortly, the mid tone may be the phonetic realization of two distinct structures. It appears that there cannot be a single set of default tone rules, universal or otherwise, that are responsible for default tones. The default tone varies from language to language and can be postulated only on language-specific sandhi facts.

I now proceed to examine the behavior of the mid tone in languages with underlying contour tones.

6.2 Dual Structure of the Mid Tone

The tone model introduced in Chapter 3 makes available four even-contoured tones. They have the structures shown in (6).

(6)

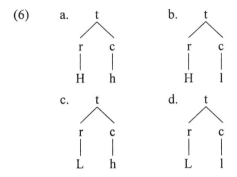

The two structures (6b) and (6c) formally encode tones which phonetically occupy the mid-range of the pitch scale—the former being higher in pitch than the latter. In languages that make use of four even tones, all the structures in (6) surface as distinctive tones. However, in cases where there are fewer than four even tones, there is a degree of indeterminacy concerning the structure of the mid tone. This state of affairs arises when we consider a tonal inventory such as (7).

(7)   55   33   11

We can assign structure (6a) to 55, and (6d) to 11. But we have two structures available for the mid tone 33: it can be either [L,h] (6c) or [H,l] (6b). This indeterminacy can be resolved by examining the sandhi behavior of the mid tone. Suppose that R is a register-sensitive rule. If 55 and 33 undergo or trigger R but 11 does not, then 33 must be a H-registered tone; on the other hand, if 33 and 11 undergo or trigger R but 55 does not, we conclude that 33 is a L-registered tone.

The matter, however, is not so simple. For any given register, there are two possible c node specifications. Thus, if 33 is a H-registered tone, it necessarily differs in its c node specification from the other H-registered tone, 55. The c node of 33 is l, and that of 55 is h. 33 as [H,l] would fall in the same class as 11, which is [L,l], by virtue of the c node specification. 55 and 33 belong to the same class by virtue of their registers. The structural indeterminacy of the mid tone 33 often leads to different analyses of the same sandhi phenomenon. In section 3.3.4 we saw the sandhi phenomenon of Gao'an, whose tonal inventory contains the three even tones in (7). Recall that in this dialect of Chinese, 55 becomes 53 when it precedes either 33 or 11. There are two equally plausible analyses available, depending on our formulation of the sandhi rule and our assumption about the structure of the mid tone 33. Suppose that 33 has the structure (6c), namely [L,h]. 3 and 11 are L-registered tones. The 55→53 sandhi can be viewed as a case of contour dissimilation: the even contour becomes the falling contour before another even-contoured tone. Formally, this can be accounted for by the rule in (8).

(8)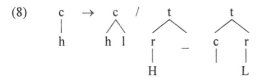

Note that the second c node is nonbranching (i.e., even contour). The formal significance of this rule is that it refers to the structural property of a non-branching c node. The terminal nodes it dominates do not figure in the sandhi process.

Alternatively, we can assume that 33 has the structure in (6b)—[H,l]. Under this assumption, 33 and 11 are both l-contoured tones. The 55→53 sandhi can be viewed as an assimilatory spread of l.

(9)   [c_ _ _ _ _ _ c]
         ⌐   ⌐
         h   l

The contour of the first tone becomes falling as a result of l-spreading. These two analyses of the Gao'an sandhi facts are equally plausible; both are allowed by the theory developed in this study.

The Gao'an data show the theoretical possibility of analyzing the same sandhi phenomenon differently depending on the structure assumed for the mid even tone 33. Furthermore, each analysis has a unique structure for the mid tone. In section 3.4.3, we saw that the optimal analysis of the Min Circle in Xiamen requires that the two structures [H,l] and [L,h] be realized as 33. Recall that Xiamen has two even tones 55 and 33. As part of the Min Circle, the high even tone 55 lowers to 33. There is a contour simplification process in the derivation of the Min Circle. The rising tone 35 simplifies to 33, and the falling tone 53 simplifies to 55. The 35→33 sandhi suggests a derivation of the 55→33 lowering in which l is first inserted to the c node of 55, yielding the rising tone 35; the rising contour is then simplified, yielding the mid even tone 33. In other words, the derivation process is 55→35→33. The derivations of the three sandhi effects are shown in (10).

(10)   a.   (55→35→33)

       b.   (35→33)

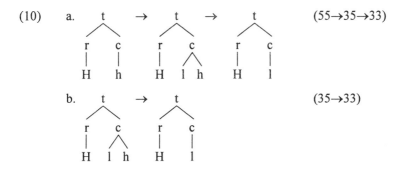

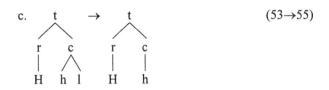

The output in (10) indicates that the mid even tone 33 has the structure [H,l] (cf. (10a,b)), which contrasts with [H,h] (cf. (10c)), the structure for the high even tone 55.

In addition to the sandhi effects shown in (10), we see in the Min Circle that the even tone 33 becomes the low falling tone 31. This can be accounted for by a single feature-inserting rule if we assume that 33 has the structure [L,h]. The derivation is shown below.

(11)   (33→31)

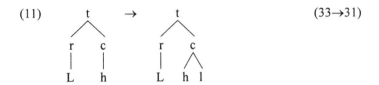

In other words, 33 has the underlying structure [L,h]; and l-insertion results in [L,hl], which is the structure for the low falling tone 31. The analysis of the Min Circle in Xiamen leads to the conclusion that 33 is the phonetic manifestation of the two structures [H,l] and [L,h].

The Gao'an and Xiamen data demonstrate the dual status of the mid tone. In the case of Gao'an, the analysis of the sandhi facts depends on the structure assumed for the mid tone 33; in the Min Circle of Xiamen, the two contrastive structures [L,h] and [H,l], one underlying and the other derived, are neutralized phonetically. Such dual status is a consequence of the theory, which provides two distinct representations for the phonetically mid tone. This property of the theory is desirable. If the theory does not allow dual characterization of the mid tone, we would need more rules to derive the sandhi facts of the Min Circle. By shifting the burden from rule to representation, we are able to account for the facts with less use of phonological rules.

This theoretical possibility is further supported by empirical facts concerning the mid tone from Weining Miao, which we first saw in section 3.2.1. Weining Miao has seven tones in citation form, shown in (12) (F.-S. Wang 1957).

(12)   a. 55   ku   "I"
        b. 33   ko   "root"
        c. 11   ku   "be"
        d. 53   ly   "willow"
        e. 31   la   "friend"
        f. 35   v'ae   "that"
        g. 13   v'ae   "grab"

The tones in Weining Miao do not show the effect of syllable-initial consonants. This can be seen in the pairs (12a,c) and (12f,g). The voiceless velar stop
/k/ is used with the high even tone 55, the mid even tone 33, and the low even
tone 11. Similarly, the voiced aspirated fricative /v'/ is used with both the high
and low rising tones. We cannot reduce the number of underlying tones on
account of the voicing qualities of syllable-initial segments. The tones have the
structures in (13).

(13)

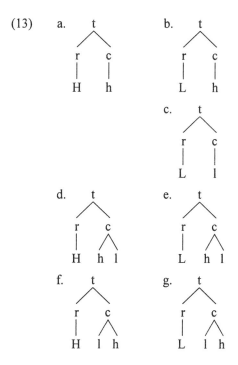

The mid even tone 33 is represented in (13) as [L,h]. Weining Miao has all the
theoretically possible tones except the missing structure in (14).

(14)

I will argue that the optimal analysis of the sandhi behavior observed in numerals
and classifiers in the language leads us to conclude that (14) is the derived
structure that surfaces as the mid tone 33. The mid tone is therefore the surface
manifestation of two structures, (13b) and (14). Weining Miao's tonal inventory
thus contains all the theoretically possible tonal contrasts.

The sandhi process that affects the numerals and classifiers in the language
has the following general properties.

(15)   In numerals,
        a. the mid even tone 33 lowers to the low even tone 11 when the
           preceding tone is H-registered;
        b. the low falling tone 31 becomes the low rising tone 13 when the pre-
           ceding tone is H-registered.
        In numeral-classifier phrases,
        c. the high even tone 55 and the mid even tone lower to 33 and 11
           respectively, when the preceding tone is H-registered;
        d. the mid even tone 33 does not trigger the sandhi phenomena observed
           in (a,b,c).

(The classifiers that exhibit the sandhi behavior (15c) belong to the categories II
and IV; see section 6.4 for details.) The mid even tone 33 and the high even tone
55 exhibit the same sandhi behavior as an undergoer of the lowering process
(15a,c); but 33 differs from 55 and other H-registered tones in that it does not
trigger the lowering process. In this regard, 33 behaves like a L-registered tone.
Details and analysis follow for the sandhi data in Weining Miao's numeral and
classifier system. All Weining Miao data are taken from F.-S. Wang (1957).

6.3   Numerals

The number system in Weining Miao is strictly decimal. The numbers one
through ten are given in (16).

(16)   i 55   "one"
        a 55; ni 31   "two"
        tsi 33   "three"
        tlau 55   "four"
        puɯ 55   "five"
        tlau 33   "six"
        çau 33   "seven"
        ẓ'i 31   "eight"
        dẓ'a 35   "nine"
        g'au 31   "ten"

        The tone of *g'au* 31 "ten" changes to 13 when it is preceded by a H-registered
tone, as the data below show.

(17)   a. ni ng'au   "twenty"
           21 31 → 21 31
        b. tsɾ dẓ'au   "thirty"
           55 31 → 55 13
        c. pu dẓ'au   "fifty"
           55 31 → 55 13

d. dʑ'a dʑ'au   "ninety"
   35 31 → 35 13
e. ʑ'i dʑ'au   "eighty"
   31 31 → 31 31

One segmental change can be observed from the data. The voiced, aspirated velar obstruent /g'/ in *g'au* 31 changes to the pre-nasalized, aspirated velar stop /ng/ when preceded by *ni* (17a), and to /dz'/ otherwise. The 31→13 sandhi can be captured by the contour metathesis rule formulated in (18):

(18)   *Contour Metathesis*

The rule is triggered by the preceding H register. The mid even tone 33 does not trigger *Contour Metathesis*, as (19) shows.

(19)   a. tlau dʑ'au   "sixty"
           33 31 → 33 31
        b. çauɯ dʑ'au   "seventy"
           33 31 → 33 31

Thus, 33 behaves as if it is a L-registered tone, having the structure in (13b).
    The unit number *ts'ie* 55 "thousand" does not exhibit any sandhi effects: *i* 55 *ts'ie* 55 "one thousand." The unit number *vau* 53 "ten thousand" has similar sandhi behavior as *g'au* 31 "ten." The data are shown below.

(20)   a. i vau (-v'au)   "ten thousand"
           55 53 → 55 13
        b. dʑ'a vau (-v'au)   "ninety thousand"
           35 53 → 35 13
        c. pi dʑau vau (-v'au)   "tens of thousands"
           55 53 53 → 55 53 13
        d. tlau vau (-v'au)   "sixty thousand"
           33 53 → 33 31
        e. tsɾ dʑ'au vau   "three hundred thousand"
           33 31 53 → 33 13 31
        f. i pa vau (-v'au)   "one million"
           55 33 53 → 55 11 31

As we can see, the tone for the word *vau* is 31 if the preceding tone is L-registered (20d,e,f), but 13 if the preceding tone is H-registered (20a,b,c). As a result of tone sandhi, the initial obstruent of *vau* becomes aspirated. This suggests that the high falling tone 53 in citation form is not the underlying tone—rather, the low falling tone 31 is. The citation tone 53 can be derived by a L→H raising rule which applies to numerals in citation form. *Contour Metathesis* derives the tone patterns observed in (20).[1] Note again that 33 does not trigger *Contour Metathesis* (20d).

The word *van* 53 "ten thousand" has some idiosyncratic sandhi patterns. If it is preceded by a single lexical tone 31, *Contour Metathesis* applies as well (21a); but if it is preceded by the sequence 33 31, *Contour Metathesis* is blocked (21b) (I give 31 as the tone of *vau*, instead of 53).

(21)   a. ʐ'i vau (-v'au)   "eighty thousand"
           31 31 → 31 13
       b. tlau dʐ'au vau (-v'au)   "six hundred thousand"
           33 31 31 → 33 31 31 [2]

(21b) is the expected result; (21a) is not. I take this to be a lexical idiosyncrasy of the word *vau* 53 "ten thousand."

In (20f), the unit *pa* 33 "hundred" lowers to *pa* 11 when it follows a 55 tone. More data concerning this word follow.

(22)   a. a pa   "two hundred"
           55 33 → 55 11
       b. dʐ'a pa   "nine hundred"
           35 33 → 35 11
       c. pi dʐau pa   "several hundred"
           55 53 33 → 55 53 11
       d. ʐ'i pa   "eight hundred"
           31 33 → 31 33
       e. tlau pa   "six hundred"
           33 33 → 33 33
       f. çaɯ pa   "seven hundred"
           33 33 → 33 33

Descriptively, the mid even tone 33 lowers to the low even tone 11. Like *Contour Metathesis*, the 33→11 lowering is triggered by the preceding H-registered tone (22a,b,c), but not by L-registered tones (22d). Again, 33 does not trigger the lowering (22e,f). With respect to contour metathesis and lowering, 33 behaves like a L-registered tone. Given the structure [L,h] (cf. (6b)), the lowering process can be captured formally by the rule in (23).

(23)   *C-Lowering*

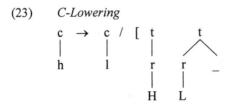

The rule derives [L,l] (i.e. 11) from [L,h] (i.e. 33). In the number system of Weining Miao, H-registered tones trigger sandhi processes that involve the c node, namely, *Contour Metathesis* and *C-Lowering*.

Alternatively, we can view the 33→11 sandhi as a case of register dissimilation. Given the structure in (24a), we can formulate the rule in (24b), which lowers the register from H to L.

(24)   a.

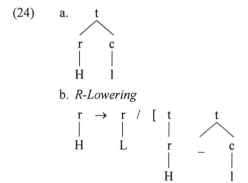

    b. *R-Lowering*

The two lowering rules, *C-Lowering* in (23) and *R-Lowering* in (24b), are comparable in terms of formal complexity; both are rules which change feature values. Despite that fact that they are able to derive the 33→11 sandhi, the two rules have different empirical consequences. Since the c-lowering analysis assigns [L,h] as the structure of 33,[3] it provides a ready explanation for the fact that the mid even tone 33 does not trigger *Contour Metathesis* or *C-Lowering*. The r-lowering analysis fails to capture this fact. Since 33 has the structure [H,l], the r-lowering analysis predicts that 33 would trigger *Contour Metathesis* or *R-Lowering*, just like as other H-registered tones. This prediction is not correct, however. The sandhi facts of the numerals appear to support the c-lowering analysis.

We now turn to the sandhi phenomenon found with the classifiers.

6.4   Classifiers

F.-S. Wang (1957:78) groups the classifiers into seven categories, depending on their initial consonants and tones. The seven categories are as follows.

(25)   Categories   Attributes

	Categories	Attributes
	I	voiceless initials; high even tone
	II	voiced initials; high rising tone
	III	voiceless initials; high even tone
	IV	voiceless initials; mid even tone
	V	voiced initials; mid even tone
	VI	voiced initials; high falling tone
	VII	voiced initials; high even tone

Note that classifiers with voiceless initials and high even tones fall into two categories, (25I) and (25III). The difference between these is their sandhi behavior: the high even tone exhibits a tone sandhi effect in Category (25I), but not in Category (25III). In fact, this is the only criterion used by F.-S. Wang for determining the category of a classifier with a voiceless initial and high even tone. Some classifiers are shown in (26) (F.-S. Wang 1957:113-118):

(26)   a. 55   faɯ   for plants
                  so   for bee hives, etc.
                  ʈə   for flowers, leaves
                  ntsɾ   "slice"
       b. 35   dz'o   for ropes, etc.
                  nd'aɯ   "section (as of rope)"
       c. 33   lo   for sentences
                  ti   "layer"
                  baɯ   for rivers
                  mɯ   "litter (of pigs)"
                  di   "handful"
       d. 53   zae   "pair"
                  ʑi   "family (of people)"
                  dla   for books, letters

No classifier has the tone 11, 31, or 13. If the mid even tone 33 is H-registered, the distribution of tones among the classifiers can be stated as follows.

(27)   Tones of classifiers are H-registered.

However, we see in section 6.3 that the rule of *C-Lowering* in numerals is triggered by H-registered tones, and 33 does not trigger the lowering process. This means that 33 is L-registered. Therefore, the proposition in (27) is not compatible with the conclusion we were led to make with respect to the sandhi behavior of the mid even tone in numerals.

The sandhi behavior of the mid even tone is also observed in the classifiers. The phrases under consideration have the form Numeral-Classifier-Noun. The tone sandhi patterns of classifiers of the categories (25III) and (25IV) are given in (28) (the horizontal axis represents tones of the numerals, and the vertical axis, tones of the classifiers).[4]

(28)   a   b   c   d   e   f   g   h   i
              55   33   31   35   13   11   53   33-31 x-55
   III 55   33   55   55   33   55   55   33   55   33
   IV   33   11   33   33   11   33   33   11   33   11

We observe that when the preceding numeral has a H-registered tone, 55 lowers to 33 and 33 lowers to 11 (columns a,d,g,i). No lowering takes place when the preceding tone is L-registered (columns c,e,f,h). The mid even tone 33 does not trigger lowering either (column b), indicating that 33 is a L-registered tone. Relevant data are given in (29).

(29)   a. a   tşau   "two kinds"
           two CL
           55 55 → 55 33

        b. tsſ ʈə   "three (flowers)"
           three CL
           55 55 → 55 33

        c. tsſ   tso so   "three threads"
           three CL thread
           55 33 55 → 55 11 55

        d. çaɯ tso   "seven pieces"
           seven CL
           33 33 → 33 33

        e. i   ts'ae nɢ'ae   "one piece of meat"
           one CL   meat
           55 33 35 → 55 11 35

I found no further examples in F.-S. Wang's corpus of data. The tone sandhi effects in (28), as exemplified in (29), take place only in numeral-classifier phrases. In other types of phrases, 55 and 33 are not lowered, as the following examples show.

(30)   a. n'au ts'ae nɢ'ae   "eat the piece of meat"
           eat CL   meat
           35 33 35 → 35 33 35

        b. ti   lɯ ni   "these (people)"
           few CL this
           55 55 55 → 55 55 55

In (30a), 33 does not lower to 11 even though it follows a H-registered tone 35; and in (30b), the high even tone 55 does not lower to 33 following another 55. Both the high rising tone 35 and the high even tone 55 trigger lowering on the following even tones in numeral-classifier phrases.

In section 6.3, we saw that the mid tone 33 of the numeral *pa* 33 "hundred" lowers to 11 when it follows a H-registered tone (22). We note that the 33→11 sandhi can be accounted for with the rule *C-Lowering* (cf. (23)) if we assign the structure [L,h] to the mid even tone, or with *R-Lowering* (cf. (24b)) if we assign the structure [H,l]. Both rules derive [L,l] (i.e., 11) from their respective input structures. In the numeral-classifier construction, the mid even tone 33 lowers in the same tonal environment. Thus, the lowering process observed in numeral-classifier phrases is the same process that can be observed in the numerals. Again, we have two possible analyses—the c-lowering analysis and the r-lowering analysis. Both rules need to be modified as in (31) to accommodate the lowering of 55.

(31)   a. *C-Lowering*

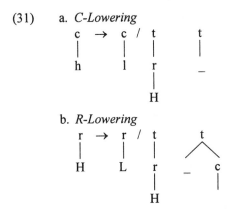

        b. *R-Lowering*

Here the c node of the second tone (that of the classifiers) in the formulation of *R-Lowering* (31b) is nonbranching. Formally, *C-Lowering* is not as complex as *R-Lowering*, since the latter rule must refer to the c node as well. In the formulation of *C-Lowering*, the r node is superfluous. Because of its formal simplicity, the c-lowering analysis is to be preferred.

To be sure, both analyses derive the sandhi effects correctly from the underlying structures assumed for the tones in question. The derivation is shown in (32) and (33).

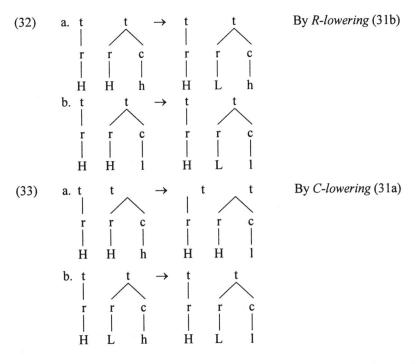

(The first tone is specified only for the H register.) In the r-lowering analysis (32), 33 is the phonetic realization of [H,l] and [L,h]—[H,l] being the underlying structure (32b), and [L,h] the derived structure (32a). In the c-lowering analysis (33), [H,l] and [L,h] are also neutralized phonetically to 33; in this case, however, [L,h] is the underlying structure (33b), and [H,l] the derived (33a). As a result of the structures they postulate for the mid even tone, the two analyses make different empirical predictions. In the r-lowering analysis, the mid even tone 33 is H-registered; it therefore predicts that when a numeral with the tone 33 precedes a Category III or Category IV classifier, it will trigger lowering. But we have seen that 33 does not trigger lowering. Thus, *çaɯ* 33 *tso* 33 "seven pieces (thread)" (29d) does not surface as *çaɯ 33 *tso* 11. But the r-lowering analysis predicts otherwise.

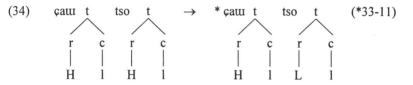

(34)   çaɯ t   tso t   →   * çaɯ t   tso t   (*33-11)

The c-lowering analysis makes the right prediction. The underlying structure for the mid even tone is [L,h], and therefore it does not trigger lowering. However, the proposition stated in (27) cannot be maintained. It is seen as an accidental fact about Weining Miao that no classifier has the tone 13, 31, or 11.

6.5 R-Lowering Reconsidered

The tone sandhi facts that need to be captured are summarized below.

(35)   In numerals,
        a. 31 metathesizes to 13 when it follows 55, 35, 53;
        b. 33 lowers to 11 when it follows 55, 35, 53.
    In numeral-classifier phrases,
        c. 55 lowers to 33 when it follows 55, 35, 53;
        d. 33 lowers to 11 when it follows 55, 35, 53;
        e. Classifiers have only 53, 35, 53, 33.

The trigger of contour metathesis (35a) and lowering (35b,c,d) is a preceding H-registered tone. Our focus will be on lowering—the sandhi behavior of 55 and 33, particularly the latter. The peculiar behavior of the mid even tone 33 is that it does not serve as a trigger, suggesting that it is a L-registered tone; yet it undergoes lowering in the same environment as the H-registered even tone 55, suggesting that it is a H-registered tone. This apparently contradictory behavior can be attributed to the possibility of characterizing the mid even tone as underlyingly either [H,l] or [L,h].

Intuitively, the lowering involving 55 and 33 is a case of register dissimilation, since lowering occurs only when they are preceded by a H-registered tone. The r-lowering analysis is more intuitively appealing than the c-lowering analysis. In numeral-classifier phrases, the r-lowering analysis is preferred because, if we assume that the mid even tone we see in classifiers has the structure [H,l], we are able to account not only for the lowering by *R-Lowering* (24b), repeated below, but also for the generalization (27) (cf. (35e)).

(24)   b.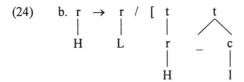

The assumption that the mid even tone in classifiers is H-registered cannot be tested, since a classifier does not precede another classifier, which would enable us to see whether the first 33 triggers lowering of the second 33. A sequence of two 33s cannot come from a sequence of two classifiers—the language does not allow classifier-classifier combination. In numeral-classifier phrases, if both the numeral and the classifier have the tone 33, the second 33 does not undergo *R-Lowering*. This will then force us to assume that the mid even tone in the numerals is L-registered; that is, it has the structure [L,h]. If so, we have to use *C-Lowering* to derive the 33→11 tone sandhi in numerals. This is the consequence that threatens the plausibility of the r-lowering analysis, as I pointed out in section 6.4. The 33→11 tone sandhi is exactly the same phenomenon in numerals as in numeral-classifier phrases. It would thus be natural to assume that the same phonological process is responsible for it.

    To provide a unified account of the tone lowering phenomenon in numerals as well as in numeral-classifier phrases, let us suppose that classifiers that surface with the mid even tone 33 have the underlying tone [H,l]; and the numerals that surface with the mid even tone 33 are underlyingly unspecified for tone. The following rule assigns either [H,l] or [L,h] prior to *R-Lowering*, depending on the environment (Num = numeral).

(36)   *Tone Assignment*

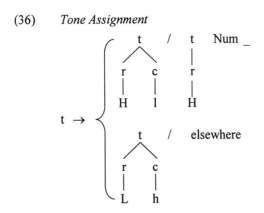

This rule assigns [H,l] to a toneless numeral just in case it follows a H-registered tone. *R-Lowering* then applies. Sample derivations of numerals follow.

(37)   a.

"two hundred" (22a)

b.

"nine hundred" (22b)

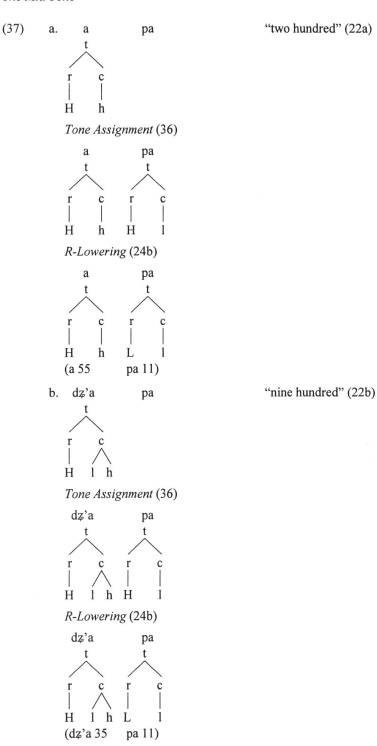

c. tlau   pa   "six hundred" (22e)

Tone Assignment (36)

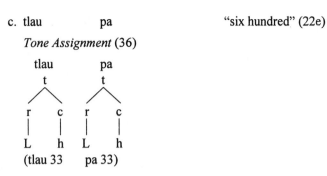

(tlau 33   pa 33)

In (38) are the derivations of some of the tone patterns of numeral-classifier phrases.

(38)   a.   tsi   țə   "three (flowers)" (29b)

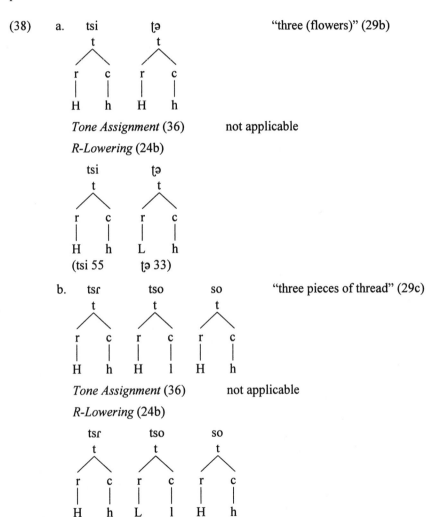

Tone Assignment (36)   not applicable

R-Lowering (24b)

(tsi 55   țə 33)

b.   tsɾ   tso   so   "three pieces of thread" (29c)

Tone Assignment (36)   not applicable

R-Lowering (24b)

(tsɾ 55   tso 33   so 55)

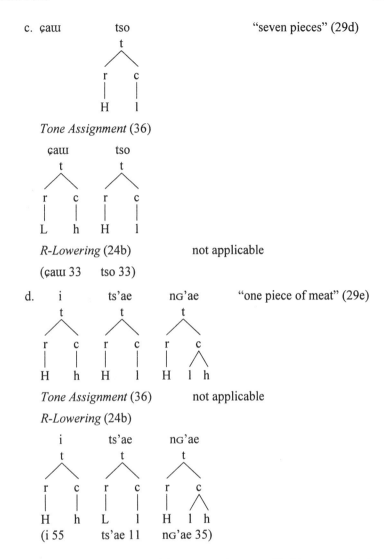

c. çaɯ   tso   "seven pieces" (29d)

Tone Assignment (36)

çaɯ   tso

R-Lowering (24b)   not applicable

(çaɯ 33   tso 33)

d.   i   ts'ae   nɢ'ae   "one piece of meat" (29e)

Tone Assignment (36)   not applicable

R-Lowering (24b)

i   ts'ae   nɢ'ae

(i 55   ts'ae 11   nɢ'ae 35)

Given the assumption that the mid even tone is unspecified in numerals, the r-lowering analysis is able to capture all the facts enumerated in (35) in an intuitively appealing way. The lowering process involving the two even tones 55 and 33 is now seen as a simple case of register dissimilation.

7

Epilogue

7.1 Contour System versus Level System: A Parametric View

It has been observed that tone languages fall into two general types, the contour system and the level system, or using Pike's (1948) term, the register system. The theory of tone proposed in this study vindicates the typological divide between the level systems characteristic of African languages, and the contour systems characteristic of Asian languages.[1] In this section, I will explore the typological differences in light of the theory of tone proposed in this study.

On the difference between the two systems, Pike writes:

> Contour systems differ from register systems in a number of points: (1) The basic tonemic unit is gliding instead of level. (2) The unitary contour glides cannot be interrupted by morpheme boundaries as can the nonphonemic compounded types of a register system. (3) The beginning and ending points of the glides of a contour system cannot be equated with level tonemes in the system, whereas all glides of a register system are to be interpreted phonemically in terms of their end points. (4) In the printed material examined contour systems had only one toneme per syllable, whereas some of the register tone languages, like the Mazateco, may have two or more tonemes per syllable. (1948:8)

Canonical register systems are found in African-type tone languages, in which contour tones are arguably concatenations of level tones; canonical contour systems are found in Asian languages, mainly in the Sino-Tibetan family. Since the term "register" has technical meanings in this book, we will use the term "level system" instead. Our investigation into the range of tone sandhi facts found in contour systems in Chinese and other Asian tone languages vindicates Pike's original insight. Contour systems are typologically different from level systems, and the former cannot be reduced to the latter.

In the theory being developed here, a contour system can be characterized formally in terms of a branching c node. This contrasts with a level system, which does not allow the c node to branch. To capture Pike's insight, I propose the *Contour Parameter*, as follows.

200

(1)   *Contour Parameter*
Given the structure   t

                 /\

              r   c

a tone system is a contour system if and only if the c node of at least one tone has a branching structure; a tone system is a level system if it is not a contour system.

The typological difference between the two tone systems that Pike recognizes is parameterized in terms of the structural configurations of the c node. With the possibility of a branching c node, a contour system is more complex structurally than is a level system. Any tone language contains a setting of the *Contour Parameter* and is expected to exhibit tonal properties in accordance with its parametric setting. The properties of the two systems need not be entirely different. In fact, we would expect a contour system to exhibit properties that are also found in a level system, but not vice versa, since a contour system can have level (even-contoured) tones in its tonal inventory, while a level system cannot have contour tones in its tonal inventory. A level system, however, may lack tonal properties that are found in a contour system—particularly properties related to the c node. Given the formal apparatus, the properties noted by Pike in the cited passage can be interpreted as follows:

(2)   a. In a contour system, contours are basic; in a level system, they are derivative; cf. Pike's (1).

        b. In a contour system, contour remains intact under morpheme concatenation; in a level system, it dissolves; cf. Pike's (2).

        c. In a contour system, the end points of a contour tone result from the interaction between the branching c node and the r node, and hence contour is relativized to register; in a level system, the end points are independent; cf. Pike's (3).

        d. In a contour system, the relation between tone-bearing units and tones is one to one; in a level system, it is one to many; cf. Pike's (4).

In addition, the distribution of contour tones in a contour system differs from that in a level system. This is stated below.

(2)   e. In terms of distribution, contour tones are free in a contour system, but restricted to peripheral positions in a level system (Yip 1989).

Unlike (2a,b,c), (2d) is not a direct consequence of the formal apparatus spelled out so far. Rather, it is in part a consequence of the association conventions (Goldsmith 1976, Pulleyblank 1986), which stipulate a one-to-one relation between tone-bearing units and tones. In a level system, contour tones, which are represented as a one-to-many association between tone-bearing units and level tones, are a consequence of rule application (Pulleyblank 1986). Contour tones cannot be created in this manner in a contour system, however.

With respect to (2e), we have seen that in a contour system such as Danyang (section 3.3.1.1), contour tones are not restricted to the edges of a domain (a phrase, in Danyang): they occur freely. Yip (1989:153) gives examples of Beijing Mandarin borrowings which show the contour tone 35 to occur phrase-initially (3a,e), phrase-medially (3c,d), and phrase-finally (3a).

(3) a. He 35 lan 35   "Holland"
     b. Ma 315 ke 51 si 55   "Marx"
     c. Qiu 55 ji 35 er 315   "Churchill"
     d. qiao 315 ge 35 li 51   "chocolate"
     e. mo 35 tuo 55   "motor"

In a level system, however, the distribution of contour tones is restricted. This is best illustrated by Tiv. According to Pulleyblank (1986), contour tones in Tiv occur only in word-final position. This can be seen from the data below (Pulleyblank 1986:216).

(4) a. ùnyìnyà mbâ   "there are horses"
     b. íwá ngî   "there are dogs"
     c. ngòhôr   "accepted (recently)"
     d. swâm   "wild boar"

Pulleyblank shows that contour tones are created by a rule of tone attachment, which links "a final floating tone to the last vowel of a word in pre-pausal position."

Given the formal difference in tonal geometry that the parametric settings entail, we expect to find certain tone sandhi processes in one system but not in the other. We will address this issue from the perspective of the synchronic "universal tone rules" proposed in Hyman and Schuh (1974) and enumerated below.

(5) a. *Tone Shifting*
        A tone shifts from one syllable to another.
     b. *Dissimilation*
        An underlying tone changes to the opposite of the tone of an adjacent syllable.
     c. *Replacement*
        An underlying tone is replaced by another.
     d. *Displacement*
        A tone is realized on syllables away from its original syllable.
     e. *Downstep/Downdrift*
        Tones are realized with lower pitch than that of preceding tones within the same tone group.
     f. *Copying*
        A toneless syllable receives a copy of the tone of an adjacent syllable.

g. *Polarization*
A toneless syllable receives the opposite of the tone of an adjacent syllable.

See also Hyman (1975) and Maddieson (1978). These rule types all exist in level systems.
With regard to contour systems, we have seen the following types of tone sandhi processes.

(6) a. *Assimilation*
    i. Register assimilation, i.e. register spread
    ii. Contour assimilation, i.e. contour spread
    iii. Tone assimilation, i.e. tone spread
    b. *Dissimilation*
    i. Register dissimilation
    ii. Contour dissimilation

In a contour system, assimilation involves register, contour, and tone as a melodic unit, while dissimilation affects register and contour. Tone dissimilation can be thought of as a composite process involving both register and contour at the same time. Only tone assimilation and dissimilation have their analogues in level systems, as *Tone Shifting* (5a) and *Dissimilation* (5b). Because of the complex geometry of tone in a contour system, its phonological processes are correspondingly more complex than those found in level systems.

Replacement (5c) is also attested in contour systems, and it may involve the register, the contour, or the entire tone. Replacement is not easily distinguishable from instances of assimilation (tone shifting) or dissimilation. Context provides a clue: replacement is not context-sensitive, whereas assimilation and dissimilation, by definition, are sensitive to neighboring tones. Given this characterization, we have seen examples of tone replacement in the Min Circle (section 3.4.3), the deictic expressions in Kejia, and the tone-derived verbs or nouns in classical Chinese (section 4.1.6). Register replacement is found in the pronouns of Shang, Shaanxi Province, where the high falling tone 53 marks the singular, and the low falling tone 21 marks the plural (section 4.1.6). So far, I have been unable to find examples of contour replacement.

Displacement (5d) is attested in a contour system when a morpheme loses its segmental materials but its tone shows up somewhere else. This is the classic autosegmental effect of tone. In Cantonese, for example, the perfective aspect can be marked tonally (Yuan et al. 1960:218), as shown in (7).

(7) a. ŋɔ 13 sik 2 (35) la 33
    I   eat   Particle
    "I have eaten"
    b. k'œy 13 lɐi 21 (35) la 33
    he   come   Particle
    "He has come"

c. ŋɔ 13 k'am 31-mat 2 hœy 33 (35) kwɔŋ 35-tsau 55
   I   yesterday   go   Guangzhou
   "I went to Guangzhou yesterday"

In Cantonese, the perfective aspect is marked by /tsɔ 35/, which occurs after the verb. So the tone change observed in the above data can be accounted for if we assume that the segmental materials of the perfective marker are lost, and the tone 35 is "displaced" onto the verb. The sentences in (7) are then derived from those in (8); the perfective marker is underlined for clarity.

(8)   a. ŋɔ 13 sik 2 <u>tsɔ 35</u> la 33
       b. k'œy 13 lɐi 21 <u>tsɔ 35</u> la 33
       c. ŋɔ 13 k'am 31-mat 2 hœy 33 <u>tsɔ 35</u> kwɔŋ 35-tsau 55

See similar tone sandhi facts of Cantonese discussed in section 4.1.3.
    Another dialect that provides an example of displacement is Daye, which we have seen in section 4.1.5. Daye has an interesting tonal morpheme which marks diminutive affixation. This morpheme is suffixed to the last syllable of the stem and surfaces as 31 if the stem tone is falling, or as 553 otherwise (G.-S. Wang 1996).

(9)   a. kɔŋ 553 (< 33)   "small jar"
          mɑ 31 tɕ'io 553 (< 13)   "small sparrow"
          tɔŋ 553 (< 35)   "small pit"
       b. lɔ 53 ɕy 31 (< 53)   "small rat"

Stems with the lexical tone 31 do not undergo this diminutive tone sandhi. They can be modified by *sai* 35, which literally means "small." Interestingly, its tone changes to 553.

(9)   c. sai 553 (< 35) t'ɔŋ 31   "small pool"
          sai 553 (< 35) ny 31   "small fish"

The 35→553 sandhi happens only to *sai* 35. *Sai* 35 can also modify the words in (9a,b), with the same tone sandhi. It appears that the surface realization of the diminutive suffix, 553, may not be coincidental. The phenomenon exhibited in (9a,b) may be related to the tone sandhi on the word *sai* 35. In other words, it could be analyzed as a case of displacement: the segments of the morpheme are deleted, and the tone 553 is displaced onto the stem-final syllable. We illustrate this analysis with the derivation of *ma* 31 *tɕ'io* 553 *(< 13)* "small sparrow" below.

(10)   sai 35 mɑ 31 tɕ'io 13
       Tone sandhi   sai 553 mɑ 31 tɕ'io 13
       Segment loss   _ 553 mɑ 31 tɕ'io 13
       Displacement   mɑ 31 tɕ'io 553

Note that the target of the displaced tone is the stem-final syllable, which may not be adjacent to the source syllable *sai* 35. Examples of displacement, though attested, are nevertheless not as common as assimilation or dissimilation in contour systems.

The other tone rules in Hyman and Schuh's (1974) list are not attested in any contour system. We might argue that the reason for the lack of *Copying* and *Polarization* (5e,f) is that in contour systems, especially in Chinese, the vast majority of the morphemes, monosyllabic or otherwise, have lexically specified tones. The question of a toneless syllable just does not arise. As for the absence of downstep (or downdrift), we can argue that floating tones, especially floating low tones, are exceedingly rare in contour systems. The "floating" tones we have seen in Chinese and other tone languages are morphemes in their own right, either lexically specified, or set "afloat" when the segmental content of the morpheme is deleted. Since downstep is typically caused by a floating low tone, the absence of downstep in contour systems is expected.

Based on the tone model of Yip (1989), M. Chen (1992) proposes a formal account of the reason why downstep does not occur in contour systems. There are two interrelated aspects to Chen's account. One has to do with the formal relationship between tonal features; the other concerns the planar structure of tonal representation. In the autosegmental literature, downstep is often analyzed as the rightward spread of the L register.[2] In Yip's model, register features dominate contour features; register spread is therefore formally indistinguishable from whole-tone spread. In other words, downstep is formally equivalent to whole-tone spread (tone copying or shifting) in a contour system. This aspect of Chen's formal explication works for Yip's model, but not for the model of tone proposed in this study, where register and contour are formally separate, and register spread does not affect contour at all. In addition, it is not at all clear that Yip's notion of register is applicable to the L register involved in downstep, or to the H register involved in upstep.

The other aspect of Chen's account may shed some light on the absence of downstep. In contour systems, tone has co-planar structure: one plane for register (or the feature [upper]), and the other for contour (or the feature [raised]); but in level systems, tone has multi-planar structure, which is capable of encoding more formal contrasts. This is essentially the proposal made in Hyman (1993) (see section 2.12). Note that the notion "register" in the analysis of downstep is not the same as the notion in Yip's tone model, nor in the tone model developed in this book. For convenience we will call it "super-register." Super-register is encoded on a separate plane. The downstepped H can have the structures below, depending on the specific model of tone being used:

(11)   a.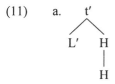

b.

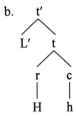

L' is the super-register that downsteps the H tone, and t' represents tone that contains the super-register. This structure allows long-distance spread of the super-register. Typically, downstep affects all tones subsequent to the location of the L super-register. The typological difference between level and contour systems is reduced to the super-register plane: in the former it is part of the tonal representation, and in the latter it is not.

We summarize the way Hyman and Schuh's (1974) universal tone rules are manifested in contour systems as follows.

(12)   a. *Tone Shifting*   Shifting of register, contour and tone
        b. *Dissimilation*   Dissimilation of register and contour
        c. *Replacement*   Tone, possibly register, replaced
        d. *Displacement*   Tone displaced due to segmental loss
        e. *Downstep*   Not attested
        f. *Copying*   Not attested
        g. *Polarization*   Not attested

7.2   Some Problematic Cases for the Theory

The proposed theory of tone is capable of accounting for a wide range of tone sandhi facts found in contour tone languages. However, it has consequences that may turn out to be problematic. There are three areas where the theory could be falsified. First, the theory has no mechanism for handling the tonal effects of syllabic obstruents (if such things should exist). Since vowels are unspecified for the laryngeal features, the use of the vocal cord features [stiff] and [slack] for tones is not problematic. But laryngeal features must be specified for obstruents, particularly where they are distinctive. Potential problems arise when obstruents are interpreted as occupying the syllabic nucleus. Second, the theory is capable of accounting for four level (even-contoured) tones, two rising tones, and two falling tones. A tonal inventory with five contrastive level tones, or more than two contrastive falling or rising tones, is a real problem for the theory. Third, there are tone systems that have, at the level of underlying representation, complex tones in violation of the *Obligatory Contour Principle*. I now proceed to address these three issues.

7.2.1 Syllabic Nasals and Obstruents

Syllabic nasals are quite common in Chinese dialects, particularly the southern dialects, and in non-Chinese languages spoken in China and Southeast Asia. These syllabic segments do not pose a problem for our theory; on the contrary, the tonal distribution in syllabic nasals in at least one Chinese dialect provides evidence for the interaction of voicing and tonal register. This dialect is Wenzhou, a Wu dialect spoken in Zhejiang Province. Wenzhou has eight surface tones in citation form (all Wenzhou data are taken from Zhengzhang 1964a).

(13)	a. 44	pa	"father"
		p'a	"climb"
	b. 45	pa	"board"
		p'a	cracking sound
	c. 42	pa	"act"
		p'a	"petal"
	d. 323	pa	"hundred"
		p'a	"pat"
	A. 31	ba	"firewood"
	B. 34	ba	a kind of fish
	C. 22	ba	"perform"
	D. 212	ba	"white"

The underlined tones are the so-called "tense" tones, as opposed to the "lax" tones, which are not underlined. The tones fall into two series: (13a–d) are the *yin* (H-registered) tones, and (13A–D) are the *yang* (L-registered) tones. The paired tones (13a,A), (13b,B), etc., are in complementary distribution with respect to the voicing qualities of the syllable-initial segments. In addition to voiced and voiceless obstruents, Wenzhou also has voiced and voiceless nasals. The nasals, especially the velar nasal, can be syllabic, as exemplified in (14).

(14)	a. ŋ 31	"Wu (name of a region)"
	b. ŋ 34	"I"
	c. ŋ 22	"two"
	d. ŋ 212	"fish"

No other syllabic nasals occur as lexical items. The syllabic velar nasal in (14) is voiced and does not occur with *yin* tones. The voiceless syllabic velar nasal in (14e,f), denoted by /ŋ̊/, is often used onomatopoetically.

(14)	a. ŋ̊ 44	sound of moaning
	c. ŋ̊ 42	sound of answering

It is important to note that the voiced velar nasal is used with *yang* (L-registered) tones, whereas its voiceless counterpart is used with *yin* (H-registered) tones. Moreover, Zhengzhang observes that the voiceless nasals are pronounced with "somewhat tight vocal cords" (1964a:31). This is precisely the predicted result of the proposed theory: voicing and tone are specified by the Vocal Cord features [stiff] and [slack].

A potentially damaging case comes from syllabic obstruents. To my knowledge, only a few tone languages have been reported as having the syllabic [ɣ]. Xining has lexical items with the syllabic [ɣ] (Zhang 1980).

(15)   a. fɣ̩ 44   "bran"
           ts'ɣ̩ 44   "out"
           ɣ̩ 44   "room"
        b. xɣ̩ 53   "tiger"
           ɣ̩ 53   "five"
           ts'ɣ̩ 53   "elbow"
           fɣ̩ 53   "rat"
        c. ɣ̩ 213   "teacher"
           kɣ̩ 213   "past"
        d. p'ɣ̩ 24   "grape"

As we have seen in section 3.4.2.2, Xining has four tones: 44, 53, 213, and 24. So the syllabic [ɣ] occurs with all tones, and with a wide range of obstruents in the onset. Interestingly, there are no voiced obstruents in Xining except [ɣ], which, judging from the data given in Zhang (1980), does not appear to occur in the onset. But this peculiar property of the sole voiced obstruent [v] does not make the problem disappear. The theory developed here predicts that the syllabic [ɣ] will occur only with L-registered tones, but in fact it occurs with all the tones of the dialect. We cannot say that the four tones in Xining are all L-registered tones, since, as we have demonstrated in section 3.4.2.2, the contrast between the two tones 213 and 24 lies in their registers: the former is L-registered, and the latter H-registered. So the syllabic [ɣ], if it is indeed an obstruent, poses a problem for the theory.

Another language that has the syllabic [ɣ] is Bai, a language spoken in the southwestern part of China. This language has three tones realized on syllables with tense vowels, three tones realized on syllables with lax vowels, and one tone realized on syllables with either tense or lax vowels. The tones are exemplified as follows (Xu and Zhao 1964:323).[3]

(16)   Lax Vowel
        a. 33   to   "top"
        b. 31   to   "fight"
        c. 55   to   "meet"
        d. 35   to   "do"
        Tense Vowel
        e. 42   to   "big"
        f. 44   to   "drop"
        g. 21   to   "do"
        h. 55   to   "fight"

The even tone 55 occurs with both tense and lax vowels (cf. (16c,h)). For ease of exposition, I will call the tones in (16a-d) "lax tones," and those in (16e-h) "tense tones." There does not appear to be any correlation between pitch height and vowel tenseness. Syllabic [ɤ̍] and its nasalized counterpart [ɤ̃] occur with both lax and tense tones.

(17) Lax
  a. 33   tsɤ̃̍   "wine"
           ŋɤ̍   "five"
  b. 31   fɤ̃̍   "powder"
           sɤ̃̍   "sick"
  c. 55   kɤ̍   "call"
           tɤ̍   "escape"
           fɤ̍ (-tɕa 42)   "old friend"
  d. 35   (khɯ 35-) fɤ̍   "overcome"

  Tense
  e. 42   fɤ̩   "tie"
           ŋɤ̩   "ten thousand"
  f. 44   tsɤ̩   "candle"
           tɤ̩   "dig"
           thɤ̩   "stop"
           tɤ̩̃   "frozen"
  g. 21   kɤ̩   "group"

I have not been able to find an example of tense syllabic [ɤ̩] occurring with the tense high even tone 55 (note that 55 occurs with both tense and lax vowels). As in Xining, Bai has no voiced obstruents other than [ɤ̍] and its nasalized equivalent. As is evident from the data in (17), the syllabic obstruent [ɤ̍] (and [ɤ̃]) in Bai occurs with all tones, and there is no apparent phonotactic constraint on the onset.[4]

Again, the tonal effects of the syllabic obstruent [ɤ̍] contradict the theory. I leave this issue open.

7.2.2 Unusual Tonal Inventories

The tone model being proposed here is capable of generating four even tones, two rising tones, and two falling tones, for a total of eight contrastive tones. The eight theoretically possible tonal contrasts are sufficient to account for the tonal inventories of the vast majority of tone languages. Languages with more than four level tones, or more than two tones of each contour are problematic for the theory. They are, however, rare—a fact pointed out by W. S.-Y. Wang (1967) and Yip (1980). Even in the rare cases with five even tones, such as the Miao dialect reported by W. S.-Y. Wang (1967), we do not have tone sandhi facts that indicate whether the five phonetically even tones are phonologically even. The existence of five even tones (or three contour tones, for that matter) in citation forms is not in itself sufficient evidence of five underlying even tones. Often citation tones are not reliable indicators of their underlying structure. In the case of Changzhi, as we have demonstrated in section 3.4.2.1, the citation contour (falling and rising) tones are derived from underlying even tones. One can readily imagine that among the five surface even tones, some are underlying contour tones. If so, we would expect that those even tones that are derived from underlying contour tones might have sandhi behavior different from that of those that are even on the surface as well as underlyingly. Unfortunately, no firm conclusion can be drawn, because we lack sandhi data from languages with five surface even tones.

We are faced with the same paucity of data when we consider languages with more than two falling or rising tones. Such languages are not common. Yip (1980:206) reports a language with five falling tones. This language, a Min dialect of Kienyang, has the following tonal inventory.

(18)   Level   33
        Rising   35
        Falling   53, 31
                     43, 32, 21

There are no sandhi data to help us decide whether the five falling tones are indeed falling underlyingly. In all likelihood, the three falling tones 43, 32, and 21 are underlyingly even. If so, Kienyang makes nearly full use of the theoretically possible tonal contrasts: four even tones, two falling tones, and one rising tone, as Yip (1980) points out. Kienyang can be explained away as a counterexample to the two-feature system that is at the core of the proposed theory.

Another dialect of Chinese, Xinzhou, has three falling tones—53, 42, and 31. 42, however, does not occur in citation form and is derived from 313. Xinzhou has the following tonal inventory (Wen 1985).[5]

(19)   53   313   2
        31

313 becomes 31 in phrase-final position, and 42 in phrase-initial position, so that Xinzhou has three surface falling tones: 53, 42, and 31. Assuming that 53 and 31 are underlyingly even, and 313 underlyingly falling, the phonetic realization of the underlying falling tone is contextually conditioned, surfacing as 42 phrase-initially and as 31 phrase-finally. The difference between 42 and 31 is thus simply a surface phenomenon.

Yip (1980) proposes the addition of Woo's feature [modify] to handle languages that genuinely possess more than four even tones or two falling or rising tones. Exactly how this feature figures in the geometry of tone cannot be decided without adequate tone sandhi data. We can speculate that [modify] is a register feature which "modifies" the [-stiff], i.e. L, register. The two features [stiff] and [modify] then define three registers, as shown in (20).

(20)   H   M   L
    stiff   +   -   -
    modify   -   +

The structure of tone would then look like (21).

(21)

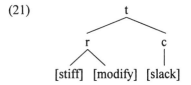

[stiff] [modify] [slack]

Alternatively, we can assume that [modify] interacts with the contour feature [slack], with the slightly modified structure shown in (22).

(22)

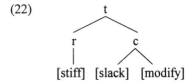

[stiff] [slack] [modify]

However, we do not have adequate data to decide where the feature [modify] fits into the overall geometry of tone.

An alternative proposal is suggested by Duanmu (1990); see section 2.14. In Duanmu's work, the features [stiff] and [slack] both specify the register, and the features [above] and [below] further refine the pitch differences. Instead of the two features [above] and [below], we can use one feature, say [above]. Interpreted within the present theory, the three features will have the geometry shown below.

(23)

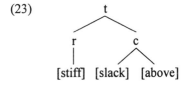

[stiff] [slack] [above]

The c node feature [above] defines h and l, and it is allowed to branch. Interpreted in accordance with Halle and Stevens (1971), [stiff] and [slack] yield three registers. This model will specify three falling tones, three rising tones, and six even tones, which is sufficient for the unusual inventories we have noted.

7.2.3 Convex and Concave

In our analysis of tonal contour, we stipulate that underlyingly, only [hl] or [lh] are allowed. Convex and concave contours, which are quite common in Chinese, are derived. This constraint may be problematic. There are tonal systems with convex or concave tones that cannot be reduced to underlying tones with simpler contours. Moreover, we have to admit the possibility of [hhl] or [llh], in violation of the *Obligatory Contour Principle*. We will consider two such systems, one from Daye, a Mandarin dialect spoken in Hubei Province, and the other from Bunu, a language of the Miao-Yao branch of the Sino-Tibetan language family.

Daye has five citation tones, as follows (G.-S. Wang 1996):

(24)   a. 33   A. 31
         b. 53
         c. 35
         d. 13

In addition to these citation tones, there are two sandhi tones, which G.-S. Wang transcribes as high even-fall 553 and low even-fall 331. These two tones occur in diminutive affixation (cf. section 4.1.5), in reduplication, and in certain other constructions. The reduplication data are shown below (G.-S. Wang 1996).

(25)   a. ts'o 33 ts'o 33 (331)
         b. tse 53 tse53 (331)
         c. k'u 13 k'u 13 (331)
         d. tsau 35 tsau 35 (553)

Together with the tonal change there is also segmental change, which is not reflected in the transcription. Stems carrying 31 are reduplicated without tone sandhi.

The citation tones 553 and 331 present a problem. Given the constraint against underlying complex contours—contours with more than two terminal feature specifications—there is no mechanism formally to distinguish 53 from 553, or 331 from 31. If we relax the constraint on complex contours, we can represent the tones as follows.

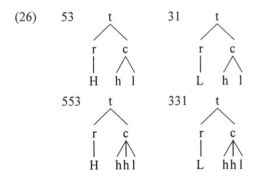

But the contour [hhl] violates the OCP.

Bunu presents a problem as well. This language has eight basic tones, enumerated below (Meng 1985).

(27)   a. 33   tɔ   "deep"
        b. 13   tɔ   "to come"
        c. 43   tɔ   "to knock"
        d. 232   tɔ   "to read"
        e. 41   tɔ   "to kill"
        f. 221   tɔ   "to die"
        g. 32   tɔ   "to stamp"
        h. 21   tɔ   "to bite"

On the surface, Bunu has one even tone 33, one rising tone 13, four falling tones 43, 41, 32, 21, one convex tone 232, and one even-falling tone 221. Such a tonal inventory cannot be formally specified within a two-feature theory. One might argue that the eight tones in (27) are surface tones derived from an underlying, well-behaved tonal inventory. We might, for example, consider 232 as rising, and 43, 32, and 221 as even-contoured. Although such a move is theoretically possible, as we have shown with respect to complex tones in Changzhi and Xining (section 3.4.2), it will not work for Bunu. The reason is that the first four tones, (27a-d), undergo tone sandhi in a stressed syllable. Relevant data are presented in (28) (Meng 1985), with sandhi tones parenthesized.

(28)   a. 33 → 55
          tɬa 33 ka 33 (55)   "chicken feather"
          pen 13 tɬo 33 (55)   "white flower"
    b. 13 → 35
          lo 33 ŋka 13 (35)   "to cook meat"
          ŋka 13 ʐoŋ 13 (35)   "mutton"
    c. 43 → 54
          luŋ 33 nɔŋ 43 (54)   "this one"
          nɔŋ 13 tɕI 43 (54)   "eat for free"
    d. 232 → 454
          tɬa 33 tuŋ 232 (454)   "four pieces"
          no 13 lo 232 (454)   "old people"

According to Meng (1985), bisyllabic phrases have the iambic rhythm, so that the second syllable is longer and more prominent than the first syllable. The interaction between stress and tone is straightforward if we assume that the citation tones are L-registered, and the sandhi tones are H-registered. Under this assumption, stress induces register raising. Note that the contour of the tones remains intact. We formulate the rule as follows.

(29)   r   →   r   when in stressed syllable
        | |
        L   H

This rule accounts for the data in (28). Thanks to the register raising rule, we now have a total of twelve tones in Bunu.

(30)   a. Even   33 55
        b. Rising   13, 35
        c. Falling   43, 54, 41, 32, 21
        d. Convex   232, 454
        f. Even-Falling   221

Even if we treat 221 as even to avoid the OCP-violating contour of [hhl], we are still left with two concave tones and five falling tones in the inventory. The theory of tone proposed in this study simply cannot accommodate such an unusual tonal inventory.

7.3   Concluding Remarks

The study of tone has a tenuous history in generative phonology. *The Sound Pattern of English* (Chomsky and Halle 1968), which is the foundation of generative phonology, skips the issue of tone entirely. In the general spirit of the time, early work on tonal phenomena within generative phonology tended to treat tone as defined by features which are part of the feature bundles of tone-bearing segments. This is characteristic of works such as W. S.-Y. Wang (1967) and Woo (1969). The segmentalist approach was a major departure from the more conventional, pre-*SPE*, suprasegmental approach, which viewed tone not as a property of segments but as a property of syllables, or rimes. This view was prevalent not only in traditional Chinese philology (cf. L. Wang 1956), but also in works of the Prague School and of the London School of prosodic analysis (cf. Anderson 1985). The suprasegmental properties of tone proved intractable for segmental analysis, which led to the abandonment of simple linear represent-ation consisting of feature bundles, in favor of complex, multi-dimensional representation. Phonological theory must provide for segmental as well as suprasegmental entities. Autosegmental phonology fills this need.

Although the structure of phonological representation is the central concern of autosegmental phonology, the internal structure of tone is nevertheless an important issue for an adequate theory of suprasegmental phonology. Most early work on tone in the history of autosegmental phonology drew data from African tone languages, where level systems predominate. Indeed, the languages—such as Tiv and Margi—that provide most of the data for such pioneering works as Williams (1976) and Leben (1973), have relatively small inventories of level tones; contour tones, if any, behave as if they were concatenations of the more basic level tones. The question arises whether contour tones in all tone languages can be analyzed as concatenations of level tones. The success of concatenation analysis of contour tones in level systems encourages a positive answer to the question, reinforced by the philosophical considerations of ontological parsimony in theory-building.

When we turn to Asian tone languages, where contour systems predominate, the tonological phenomena are much more complicated, and contour tones cannot be analyzed in the same way they are analyzed in level systems. Yip

(1980) is exceptional among early works of autosegmental phonology in drawing most of its data from Chinese dialects. Two properties of Yip's theory of tone are worth noting. First, tone is a complex phonological entity composed of two autosegmental features; second, tonal contour is concatenated of the sub-register feature [raised], not of tone per se. In other words, tone, whether level or contour, has internal structure. Further developments in generative phonology, particularly the development of feature geometry theories, have directed attention to the geometry of tonal features, by which the internal structure of tone is articulated.

It is within this intellectual milieu that this study has been conducted. The central themes are the internal structure of tone, and how tone fits in the overall structure of phonological representation.

On the first theme, we argued in Chapter 3 that tone must contain register and contour, which are represented as sister nodes under the tonal root node t, as shown below.

(31)

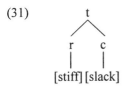

[stiff] [slack]

The c node can optionally branch. To establish the structure, we use the familiar array of diagnostic tools in phonological argumentation. One such diagnostic tool is the OCP. In tone languages, a tone may change its contour in the environment of another tone with the same contour; this is the OCP-effect in tonal phonology. Contour must be available in the representation of tone to allow the OCP to determine the identity of tones. In the model of (31), the OCP operates on the c node.

In addition to OCP-related contour metathesis, we also considered natural classes as evidence for the postulation of underlying tonal contour. In some languages, tones with the same contour exhibit the same sandhi behavior. An adequate theory of tone, therefore, must be able to define natural classes on the basis of tonal contour. This is not possible if tonal contour is treated as a surface phenomenon arising from a many-to-one association of tone and tone-bearing unit. The tone model in (31) makes it possible to define natural classes in terms of tonal contour.

By far the most extensive sandhi processes we have examined are those of tonal assimilation. We find that assimilatory processes can involve all components of tone. An issue of methodological concern should be noted here. In the literature on feature geometry, assimilation is analyzed as spreading, and features that spread together are interpreted as sharing a common mother node. In feature-geometric terms, these features are dominated by the same mother node, and it is the mother node, not the individual features, that spreads. If, on the other hand, a node spreads without affecting other nodes, then there is no domination relationship between them. Given this methodological consideration, the fact that register and contour assimilate independently of each other is sufficient evidence in favor of the formal separation of register and contour. In Chapter 3 we discussed ample evidence for register assimilation that does not affect the contour, and, to a lesser extent, contour assimilation that does not affect the register. Since contour tones also spread as melodic units in contour-tone languages, we conclude that register and contour must be sisters under the t node. Evidence from assimilatory tone sandhi supports the tone model in (31).

A note on contour assimilation is in order. The attested contour assimilation typically involves the even contour, as in the case of Zhenjiang (section 3.3.3.1). Tones rarely assimilate to the falling or rising contour of neighboring tones. This is quite peculiar, given the fact that the c node is available in the tone model of (31). This phenomenon has been interpreted to mean that contour does not exist in the formal representation at all (cf. Duanmu 1994); or if it does exist, it is not an independent node (cf. Chen 1992, Yip 1992). I would like to offer two reasons to explain why the falling or rising contour does not spread. First, affricates, pre-nasalized segments and post-nasalized segments, which have been analyzed as contour segments (cf. Sagey 1986), do not spread their contour properties. The behavior of contour tones falls into this general pattern. A theory that admits contour segments must also admit contour tones. If spreading is taken as suf-ficient evidence for the postulation of a node in feature geometry, the lack of spreading does not imply the lack of a common node. Even if we do not have convincing cases of spreading of the falling or rising contour, other tonological considerations support the postulation of the c node. Second, there is a tendency in Chinese dialects for tones within a given domain to have different contours—the classic OCP-effect. Spreading of a falling or rising contour creates just the opposite pattern. It is therefore not at all surprising that tones do not assimilate to the falling or rising contour.

Chapter 4 detailed some of the autosegmental properties of tonal phenomena in Chinese dialects. These properties are familiar ones that appear to transcend the typological divide between contour and level systems. Of special interest, perhaps, is the role of tonal contour: in the pronouns of some northwestern Mandarin dialects, number is marked by the register, and the contour—in this case falling—remains intact. This is possible if contour is formally represented.

It has long been recognized that tone is not a segmental property, at least phonologically. This recognition predates generative phonology. In traditional Chinese philology, tone is considered a property of the rhyme (rime), or final. In autosegmental phonology, however, the term "tone-bearing unit" conveniently circumvents the issue. Tone as an autosegment is maximally free from its tone-bearing unit. One of the main arguments in favor of autosegmental representation is tonal stability: when a vowel is deleted, or otherwise rendered incapable of bearing tone, its original tone does not disappear with the vowel. Instead, it shows up in the neighboring tone-bearing unit. Tonal stability is a pervasive phenomenon in tone languages. But when we examined phonological processes that affect tone, such as partial reduplication and game languages in Chinese dialects, we found that tonal stability is sensitive to the structure of the tone-bearing unit. In Chapter 5 I argued that tone is adjoined to the rime, creating the structure in (32).

(32)   R'

R   t

This structure reflects the general view that tone is a suprasegmental property. It allows us to account for the tone patterns of partial reduplication and game languages encountered in Chinese dialects.

The behavior of the mid tone was treated in Chapter 6. Theoretical interest in the mid tone has been linked to theories of underspecification. Pulleyblank (1986) argues that the mid tone is the default tone by virtue of the universal default rules shown in (33).

(33)   a. [ ] → [-upper]
         b. [ ] → [+raised]

In other words, L is the default r node specification, and h is the default c node specification. We argued in Chapter 6 that there is no empirical basis for the postulation of a universal default tone; default tones, and consequently default tone rules, must be motivated by the empirical facts of particular languages. The mid tone has two possible structures—[L,h] in some tone systems and [H,l] in others; in some systems, moreover, the mid tone may be the phonetic realization of both these structures. Positing this ambiguous structure for the mid tone has analytical advantages.

The theory of tone proposed in this study has its empirical problems, some of which are addressed in section 7.2. Despite its limitations, I hope that this study has shown with a good degree of certainty and clarity the general properties of tone and tone sandhi in contour systems. Those properties cannot be fully accommodated in reductionist theories. A parametric approach is required to study tone and tonal phenomena across the world's tone languages.

Notes

Chapter One

1. It is possible to invoke the *Obligatory Contour Principle* (OCP) to rule out the structures in (3). For discussions on the theoretical status of the OCP, see McCarthy (1986), Odden (1986, 1988), and Yip (1988), and the references cited therein. The OCP effect in tonal phonology is discussed in section 3.2.3.
2. Pulleyblank (1986) makes the following stipulation: "Autosegmental tiers can only link to slots in the skeletal tier." According to Pulleyblank's terminology, tiers are equivalent to planes. See discussions in chapter 5.

Chapter Two

1. Unless otherwise stated, tones are listed in accordance with their historical origin, as follows:

    (i) (a,A) represent the *ping* ("even") tones.
         (b,B) represent the *shang* ("rising") tones.
         (c,C) represent the *qu* ("departing") tones.
         (d,D) represent the *ru* ("entering") tones.
    (ii) (a, b, c, d) represent the *yin* tones.
         (A, B, C, D) represent the *yang* tones.

2. Chao (1930) stipulates that points 2 and 4 cannot be used in combination with 1, 3, or 5. This reduces the number of tones considerably. But this stipulation is often ignored in later work on tones.
3. It is possible to view the short tones 5/3 as derived from 44/22. In the absence of positive phonological data, the decision to treat 5/3 as derived from 53/31 is admittedly arbitrary, but nothing hinges on the issue.
4. Yip (1980) uses the feature [high]; the Tone feature [raised] was due to Pulleyblank (1986). Yip adopts [raised] in her subsequent work on tone. Following Yip, we will use [raised].

    Gruber, as reported in Fromkin (1972) and Snider (1988), has a two-feature system that can specify up to four distinct level tones. Gruber calls the features [high] and [high 2], and the four level tones are specified as follows:

high	+	+	-	-
high 2	+	-	+	-

    According to Fromkin, implicit in Gruber's proposal is "the claim that the basic distinction in any tone language is between high tones and non-high tones, with all other tonal contrasts being made within these two disjunctive sets" (1972:47). Gruber's system anticipated Yip's.

5. The phonetic difference between 53 and 42 is phonologically irrelevant. Often, it is a perceptual or notational idiosyncrasy of the field linguist. W. S-Y. Wang (1967:98) lists two reports of the Suzhou dialect (spoken in Suzhou, Jiangsu Province) prepared at roughly the same time, as follows:

44	13	52	412	31	5	2
44	24	41	513	331	4	23

Wang writes that the difference between the two reports in regard to the phonetic pitch of the tones is "probably more spurious than real." Under a certain degree of idealization, the difference between 53 and 42 is no more real than that between 52 and 41. What needs to be stressed is that 51/31 remains observationally rare.

Chapter Three

1. Lin and Repp (1989) report that in Taiwanese, F_0 height and movement are the most important factors in tonal perception. Among tones with the same or similar contour, the F_0 height (i.e., the register) is the most prominent; among tones with the same or similar register, the F_0 movement (i.e., contour) is the most prominent factor. The report strongly supports the psychological reality of tonal contour.
2. In sonorant-initial syllables, (11a,A,b,B) and (11C,D) are attested. See the Appendix for the sound system of Songjiang.
3. The values given in (15) must be understood in a relative sense. F.-S. Wang (1957:121) notes that when pronounced, 35 is 24, 13 is 12, 33 is 44, 11 is 22, and 31 is 21. But Y.-S. Li et al. (1959) give the same tonal values as shown in (15).
4. The short tone 54 exhibits two patterns. If the syllable had a voiced initial consonant in classical Chinese, the tone pattern is the same as 53; if the syllable had a voiceless initial consonant, the tone pattern is 44-44. I will ignore the complication of the short tone.
5. The two rules in (60) are essentially the default rules Pulleyblank (1986:126) proposes for the features [upper] and [raised], as follows.

(i) V → V
            |
         [-upper]

(ii) V → V
            |
         [+raised]

Pulleyblank takes the default rules to be universal. Note that [-upper] corresponds to [-stiff], and [+raised] to [-slack]. See section 6.1 for further discussion of the default rules.

   The reason to treat 44 as a L-registered tone is that in verbal reduplication the tone 44 surfaces as the low falling tone 31 in initial position, see section 3.4.2.1.
6. For further evidence of register spreading, see section 4.3.
7. The tones in (65) can be represented without underlying contour, as in (i).

(i) a. 13   [L, l]
     b. 35   [H, l]   c. 53   [H, h]

(ii)   c
      _ _ _ _ _ _ ⌐
  [αslack]   [-αslack]

The feature-inserting rule (ii) applies to the forms in (i), yielding the tones in (65). However, this move is of peripheral interest for our purpose. Since underlying contour is permissible, I will use the structures in (65) as the underlying representation of Pingyao tones.

8. All Pingyao data are taken from Hou (1980), with slight modification in transcription. I use /i/ to transcribe the apical vowels that appear after alveolar and retroflexed fricatives and affricates, and /n/ for both the alveolar and palatal nasals. The palatal nasal occurs before the high front vowel /i/. I will follow this practice where appropriate throughout this book.

9. Zhang (1985:195-6) proposes three rules to derive the bisyllabic sandhi patterns in (84). The rules, formulated in terms of the contour notions falling, rising, and even, are as follows.

    (i)   Falling → Rising / _ Falling
    (ii) Falling → Even / elsewhere
    (iii) Rising   → Even / _ Even

    The spreading rule in (88) does not cover the same range of facts as any of the rules individually. For instance, the spreading rule does not account for the fact that the two falling tones surface as even before the rising tone as well. This fact is accomplished by Zhang's rule (ii).

10. The same sandhi phenomenon, slightly revised, can be found in Zhengzhang (1980). In both articles Zhengzhang discusses two varieties of the Wenzhou dialect, those of the city proper and of a suburban area called Yongzhong. I discuss the variety spoken in the city proper.

11. A note on transcription is in order. Zhengzhang uses Chinese characters as examples, so the transcription of data, except tones, is in *pinyin*, based on Mandarin pronunciation.

12. In Zhengzhang (1980), Pattern F is given as 42-1, where 1 is a low neutral tone. He explains that in slow speech, Pattern 42-1 surfaces as 42-21. I stay with the slow-speech version.

13. In addition to the seven tones in (103), there is also the so-called neutral tone, which is omitted here.

14. The reason to treat 42 as an underlying low register tone has to do with the existence of 53, which is derived from the underlying high even tone 55. 53 does not exist underlyingly or in citation form. This move underscores the relative nature of tonal pitch. For some systems, 42 would be considered as high falling. But in the presence of a 53 and the absence of a 31, I think it is justified to consider 42 as low falling underlyingly, although on the surface it is fairly high in pitch.

15. 55 becomes 53 before the neutral tone as well.

16. Shaoxin has one of the rare tonal inventories with the surface falling tone 51 in citation form. This tone, however, does not alternate with 31. See section 3.4.1.2 for discussion of the distributional properties of contour (falling or rising) tones. Underlyingly, 51 may be represented in the same way 53 is represented. There is no formalism within the proposed theory to distinguish between 53 and 51. I take it as a phonetic detail that has little phonological relevance.

17. The distributional properties of the contour tones also follow from Yip's (1980) theory, since our tone features are functionally equivalent to Yip's [upper] and [raised].

18. We see Changzhi in section 3.3.1.2, where I analyze the tone spreading phenomenon induced by the nominal and adjectival suffixes.

19. The short tone 54 shows diachronic influence on the verbal reduplication tone melodies. If the syllable has a voiced onset historically, then the tone melody is that of the surface tone 53, in (129e); otherwise, it has the same pattern as the even tone 44, in (129d).

20. In Xining, tone sandhi does not take place in all bisyllabic phrases. Consider the two phrases in (i).

(i)   a. tuə̃ piã   "east side"
          44-44 → 44-N
      b. iə̃ t'iã   "cloudy day"
          44-44 → 44-44

The two phrases have the same Adjective-Noun structure, but (ia) undergoes tone sandhi, whereas (ib) does not. The reason for this difference is obscure, and I assume that it is lexical. In (135) I give only the tone patterns of the phrases that do show sandhi effects.

Some phrases with the pattern 44-24 surface as 44-44, rather than 44-N. (ii) is an example.

(ii) tɕiə̃ niã "this year"
      44-24 → 44-44

Again, this appears to be lexically conditioned.

21. If we treat the neutral tone as lack of tone, then the mechanism of deriving the tone patterns will involve the deletion of the phrase-final lexical tones. The *elsewhere* clause of rule (141a) will not be necessary.

22. In our discussion of Xiamen tone sandhi, the short tones 31 (*sik* 31 "clever") and 55 (*sik* 55 "cooked") are omitted. The Xiamen data have been studied extensively; among the studies are R. Cheng (1968), Yip (1980), Wright (1983), and Shih (1986), and, from a different perspective, M. Chen (1987b), J.-W. Lin (1994), and Bao (1997).

23. Wang (1967:103), using the primitive contour features [falling] and [rising], defines the Xiamen tones as follows.

	55	35	53	31	33
High	+	+	+	-	-
Falling	-	-	+	+	-
Rising	-	+	-	-	-

He captures the Min Circle in a single rule schema,

(i) $\begin{bmatrix} \alpha\text{high} \\ \beta\text{falling} \end{bmatrix} \rightarrow \begin{bmatrix} \beta\text{high} \\ -\alpha\text{falling} \end{bmatrix}$

from which the following rules can be extracted:

(ii) $\alpha = +; \beta = +$

$$\left[\begin{array}{c} \text{+high} \\ \text{+falling} \end{array}\right] \rightarrow \left[\begin{array}{c} \text{+high} \\ \text{-falling} \end{array}\right]$$

(iii) $\alpha = +; \beta = -$

$$\left[\begin{array}{c} \text{+high} \\ \text{-falling} \end{array}\right] \rightarrow \left[\begin{array}{c} \text{-high} \\ \text{-falling} \end{array}\right]$$

(iv) $\alpha = -; \beta = +$

$$\left[\begin{array}{c} \text{-high} \\ \text{+falling} \end{array}\right] \rightarrow \left[\begin{array}{c} \text{+high} \\ \text{+falling} \end{array}\right]$$

(v) $\alpha = -; \beta = -$

$$\left[\begin{array}{c} \text{-high} \\ \text{-falling} \end{array}\right] \rightarrow \left[\begin{array}{c} \text{-high} \\ \text{+falling} \end{array}\right]$$

See also Wright (1983) on the Min Circle.

Chapter Four

1. In Chapter Five I argue that tones form an autosegmental tier on the syllabic plane. They do not form a separate, autosegmental plane. In the discussion to follow, I will represent tones as if they are an autosegmental plane. This is solely for convenience in exposition.
2. It does not matter whether the tonal morpheme is a suffix or prefix. Either assumption will serve to illustrate the existence of tonal morphemes.
3. Chao (1956:1) describes the changed tone as a "non-syllabic and non-segmental suffix." Yip's analysis takes advantage of the theoretical devices available in the emerging framework of autosegmental phonology.
4. Note that 21 and 22 are in free variation. Yip (1980:357) assumes 22 to be the underlying tone, and 21 derived. This avoids the technical difficulty facing her analysis.
5. The tones that Yue-Hashimoto represents as 44 and 33 are given the values of 33 and 22 respectively by Kao (1971) and Yuan et al. (1960). Kao (1971:93) posits six "tonal phonemes," as in (i).

(i) a. 53 (55,5)   A. 21
    b. 35   B. 23
    c. 33 (3)   C. 22 (2)

Yuan et al. (1960:208) give the following tone inventory.

(ii) a. 55 or 53   A. 21 or 11
     b. 35   B. 13
     c. 33   C. 22
     d. 5,33   D. 2

It must be emphasized that these numbers are relative values of auditory impression. It is hardly surprising that different authors give different values to the same tones.

6. Zong (1964) raises serious doubt that 55 is derived from 53. He argues that 55 and 53 are contrastive tones in Cantonese.

7. Chao (1947:26) says that the changed tone *55 is not the same as 55 derived from the underlying tone 53, because the former "is associated with a special kind of function and meaning, irrespective of tonal environment." Chao's observation is correct in that words with the changed tone *55, as in *san* *55 "dress" (< *san* 53) (cf. (11g)), have the meaning of "familiarity." By contrast, 55 in *kej* 55 *tok* 5 (> *kej* 53 *tok* 5) (cf. (18)), which is derived from 53 by the sandhi rule *Contour Simplification* (19), does not have the added meaning "familiarity." But the meaning "familiarity" comes from the morphemic tonal suffix, which is present in *san* *55, but not in *kej* 55. The phonological condition for contour simplification is met in both cases. Given the analysis being proposed here, the changed tone *55 is derived by rule (19), since t$_f$, being H-registered, conditions the 53→55 sandhi change just like any other H-registered tone. There is no need to view the changed tone *55 in *san* *55 (< *san* 53) any differently from 55 in *kej* 55 (< *kej* 53). Both are derived by rule (19). The difference is the trigger: the presence versus the absence of the familiarity morpheme.

8. In Marantz's (1982) theory, a reduplication analysis starts out with a CV prefix with C and tone prespecified. The derivation of *qu* 13 *plu* 31 is as follows.

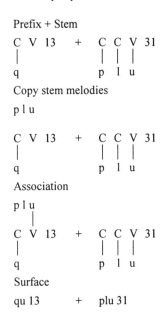

Prefix + Stem

C V 13   +   C C V 31
| | | |
q   p l u

Copy stem melodies

p l u

C V 13   +   C C V 31
| | | |
q   p l u

Association

p l u
|
C V 13   +   C C V 31
| | | |
q   p l u

Surface

qu 13   +   plu 31

See Marantz (1982) for details of the theoretical apparatus behind this derivation.

9. Bai (1989) postulates the following tone inventory of Cantonese.

High tones   55, 53, 35, 5
Low tones   21, 23, 33, 22, 3, 2

10. Chao (1931) names a *fanqie* language after its word for *ma* "mother." The name "Mo-pa" is derived from *ma*, hence the name for this *fanqie* language based on the dialect of Kunshan.

11. Wuyi has two series of sonorants, as shown below.

(i)   ?m   ?n   ?l   ?ɲ   ?ŋ
(ii)   ɦm   ɦn   ɦl   ɦɲ   ɦŋ

The sonorants in (i) are glottalized, and those in (ii) are voiced. The *yin* tones occur with the sonorants in (i); the *yang* tones occur with the sonorants in (ii).

12. Other tones undergo tone sandhi in bisyllabic phrases as well. They are as follows.

Citation tone	Sandhi	Environment
24, 213	55	before 55,13,5,212
53	55	before all tones
5, 212	5	before all tones
55, 13, 31	11	before all tones

Except for (50), none of the tones undergoes sandhi in phrase-final position. For an analysis of the above sandhi data, see section 5.3.

13. The concave tone 213 is underlyingly low rising, since it has basically the same tone sandhi behavior as the high rising tone 24. We need the contour formation rule below to derive the contour.

Since this rule is not crucial for the purpose of our discussion, I will simply use the numerical representation, 213.

14. Apparently we cannot express the onset-tone harmony as a result of assimilatory spreading, because tones and syllable-initial segments are on different planes.

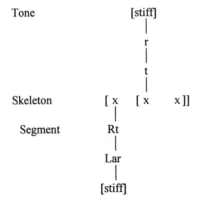

Autosegmental spreading involves tiers on the same plane. The current conception of planar representation precludes the possibility of trans-planar spreading such as that shown above.

Chapter Five

1. Archangeli defines the terms *plane* and *tier* as follows: "*Tier* refers to plane-internal sequences of matrices parallel to the core skeleton. *Plane* refers to the entire melody (or structure) anchored in the core skeleton" (1985:336). My use of the terms essentially follows Archangeli's.
2. The theoretical indifference for the segmentalist versus suprasegmentalist controversy can be traced much earlier. Hyman writes: "It appears that the syllable approach and the segment approach are readily translatable into each other. ... We can assume that this is due to the fact that syllables are defined in terms of segments and, as a result, it is always possible to avoid talking about syllables and talk instead of the segments which define them" (1975:215).
3. The condition in (4) is essentially a paraphrase of Pulleyblank's (1986) stipulation: "Autosegmental tiers can only link to slots in the skeletal tier."
4. The segments are assumed to be on a single plane. The discussion of tone is independent of the issues of v/c-segregation. For discussion, see Prince (1987), and references cited therein.
5. This section is a modified version of the analysis presented in Bao (1990a); for details of argumentation and other theoretical assumptions, see that work.
6. In La-pi, the coda consonant of the o-syllable defaults to the alveolar stop /t/:

tsap	→ lap-tsit (*-tsip)	"ten"
t'at	→ lat-t'it	"kick"
pak	→ lak-pit (*-pik)	"peel"

    [p] and [k] in the second syllables surface as *tsat* and *pat* respectively.
7. This is the reason we cannot strengthen the generalization (22) into a bi-conditional:

    Either segmental constituent of the source rime remains in the o-syllable if and only if the o-syllable keeps the source tone.

    That is, it is possible that no segmental material of the source syllable is retained in the o-syllable even if the o-syllable keeps the source tone, as in Mo-pa.
8. Strictly speaking, the segments *p,a,k* should be the root node of the feature geometry that defines the segments. Since the discussion does not hinge on the geometrical structure of the segmental feature trees, I use the segments as shorthand symbols.
9. Tone adjustment rules look like readjustment rules in the sense of Chomsky and Halle (1968) and Halle (1990), but there is a crucial difference. Readjustment rules are "feature-filling" redundancy rules, while tone adjustment rules can be viewed as feature-changing. Take (38a), for example. In this tone adjustment rule, the feature [stiff] changes from [+stiff] to [-stiff]. Other tone adjustment rules have more complex feature-changing operations (cf. rules in (45)), but readjustment rules and tone adjustment rules are similar in that both "prepare" the input structure for the phonological component. In Chinese, the need for tone adjustment rules results from historical tonal split: one tone splits into two variants after voicing has become nondistinctive. Tonal variants often reveal their common historical origin in tone sandhi. In Wuyi, 24 and 213 on the one hand, and 55 and 13 on the other, have exactly the same sandhi behavior. For this reason {24,213} and {55,13} are referred to as "tone categories" in Chinese linguistics. Historically, {24,213} is derived from the *ping* (even) tone in classical Chinese, and {55,13} from the *shang* (rising) tone.

10. Instead of considering tone mapping as an adjunction rule, we can assume that the structure in (37) is part of the syllable structure pre-specified in the lexicon. The syllable structure for Mandarin Chinese may thus look like the following.

Tone is pre-specified as a node dominated by R'.

11. The reason to represent 13 as [L,h] has to do with the fact that 13 surfaces as 11 in sandhi environment. The surface rising contour is derived by the feature-inserting rule, given below.

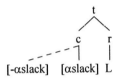

The rule inserts l to the c node of 13, giving rise to [L,lh]. The same rule also derives 213: [L,lh]→[L,hlh].

12. The rules in (46) all involve the register; it appears to be possible to formulate a single rule that produces the same effect. This approach is not desirable, however, since the three tone adjustment rules in (46) apply in different environments.

13. The tone [L,h] surfaces as 13. See footnote 11.

14. It is possible to formulate the segmentalization rule as involving the *head* of the syllabic constituent that serves as the tone-bearing unit. If we view syllabic structure as the projection of vowels (sonorants), then vowels are heads in the same way that a verb is the (lexical) head of VP.

15. A branching r node would be well-formed because it dominates two terminal nodes:

The two structures are ruled out conceptually: the tonal geometry expressly states that only the c node branches; cf. section 3.1.

16. The Halle-Vergnaud convention is rewritten as the *Branch Pruning Convention* by Clements (1989):

> *Branch Pruning Convention*
> Given a branching configuration (5), remove the older of the two branches.

The configuration (5) is the *No Branching Condition*, as follows.

No Branching Condition

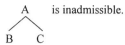

A   is inadmissible.

A is a non-terminal node, B and C are either terminal or non-terminal. I adopt the Halle-Vergnaud condition because the c node is ruled out as inadmissible by the *No Branching Condition*. This condition works only when B and C are non-terminals of the same type.

17. In fact, to satisfy Sagey's condition, either deletion or delinking will do. Both operations result in a singly linked non-terminal node.

(i) Result of delinking

t   t

r   r

(ii) Result of deletion

t   t

r

Delinking creates a floating tone, but deletion does not. A floating tone is not equivalent to a deleted tone, and some phonological phenomena, notably downdrift, are triggered by the presence of a floating tone (cf. Pulleyblank 1986, Clark 1990). In this study, however, nothing hinges on whether illegal nodes are deleted or merely delinked.

18. I assume that underlyingly Tianjin has only even tones, so the surface contours in the examples result from a feature-inserting rule which creates the contour of rising. For Tianjin data, see Li and Liu (1985), Chen (1986a), Hung (1987), Tan (1987), Zhang (1987), and Milliken et al. (1997).

Chapter Six

1. If 31 is the underlying tone for *vau*, underlyingly the initial obstruent [v] must also be aspirated. The derivation of the citation form *vau* 53 involves raising the register and de-aspirating the initial obstruent.

2. F.-S. Wang (1957:77) gives 11-31-31 as the tone pattern for "six hundred thousand." The pattern shows the lowering of the phrase-initial tone 33 to 11. I do not use this form for two reasons: first, 33 does not lower to 11 in this position elsewhere, cf. (19); and second, it is not crucial for the purpose at hand.

3. I will call the analysis that postulates *C-Lowering* the "c-lowering analysis," and the one that postulates *R-Lowering*, the "r-lowering analysis."

4. Other tonal combinations also show sandhi effects; the complete table of tone sandhi in the numeral-classifier system in Weining Miao is reproduced in the Appendix. Note that in columns (28h,i), two tones of the numerals are listed as the trigger of *C-Lowering*. The effect of this is not obvious in the sandhi patterns of Category III and IV classifiers, since 33-31 does not trigger lowering, and x-55 does, as expected. In Category V classifiers, the mid even tone 33 becomes 13, and the initial obstruent of the classifier is aspirated, when the preceding numeral has the tone 31; it becomes 31

when the preceding numerals have the tone sequence 33-31. Therefore, it not sufficient to refer to the immediately preceding tone to handle the sandhi behavior of Category V classifiers.

Chapter Seven

1. The areal characterization of tonal systems is descriptively convenient; it does not preclude the possibility of African languages with contour systems, nor of Asian languages with level systems. In the tonological literature, it has been argued that contour tones such as falling or rising are different from the high-low or low-high sequences in the African Grebo and Hausa languages (Newman 1986, 1995). Conversely, tone sandhi in the Wu dialects of Tangsic and Shanghai has properties often associated with African languages (Kennedy 1953, Zee and Maddieson 1979, Cao and Maddieson 1989, Selkirk and Shen 1990, Chen 1992, and Bao 1997).
2. Hyman's (1985) analysis of Dschang tonology is representative of the autosegmental treatment of downstep. In the associative construction, N_1 *of* N_2, the associative marker for class 7 nouns is *á*, which carries underlying H tone. This tone spreads rightward, dislodging the original tone of the target. If the dislodged tone is L, it downsteps the following H, but not the following L (Hyman 1985:51).

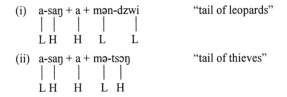

(i) a-saŋ + a + mən-dzwi   "tail of leopards"
     L H   H   L   L

(ii) a-saŋ + a + mə-tsɔŋ   "tail of thieves"
     L H   H   L H

The form in (i) surfaces as [à-sáŋ+á+mə́n-dzwì], and the form in (ii) as [à-sáŋ+á+mə́n-tsˈɔ́ŋ]. The formal analysis of downstep depends on the model of tone; see, among others, Clements (1979, 1983, 1989), Hyman (1986, 1993), Inkelas (1987), Snider (1988, 1990), and Laniran and Clements (1996). The tone models proposed in these works are discussed in Chapter Two. Despite their formal differences, these works all treat downstep as a phonological phenomenon that should be analyzed in the same way as other phonological processes, such as assimilation. Clark (1990) proposes an alternative account of downstep. She treats downstep as a result of phonetic interpretation: T is interpreted lower in pitch if it follows H; and the presence of a floating L is not necessary.
3. The authors of the field report do not provide detailed phonetic descriptions of tense or lax vowels, which are marked with tones. There is a strict correlation between tone and vowel tenseness.
4. The fricative [v] can be used as an onset as well, but the pronunciation differs. Xu and Zhao describe the phonetic characteristic of the syllabic [ʋ] thus: the upper teeth lightly touch the lower lip, and the tongue position is toward the front. François Dell (personal communication), who has field experience with the language, informs me that the syllabic [v] is definitely a fricative.
5. The tone 313 is derived from two historical sources in classical Chinese, *yin ping* and *shang*. The sandhi behavior of 313 is in part determined by its historical source. Since it is not crucial for our purpose, I cite only the sandhi behavior of 313 derived from the ancient *shang* tones.

Appendix

This appendix contains the sound systems of Chinese dialects and other languages whose tone sandhi phenomena have been analyzed to some extent in this book. For the Chinese dialects, the tones are presented in a format that conforms to the practice of the Chinese linguistics circle. The phonetic symbols follow as closely as possible the conventions of the sources, except where noted. The retroflexed and non-retroflexed apical vowels are not contrastive; they are therefore denoted by /ɿ/, and the zero-initial is not given, since it occurs in vowel-initial syllables across the dialects. The palatalized nasal is written /ny/.

The appendix contains the sound systems of the following dialects and languages: (1) Bai (Tibeto-Burman); (2) Danyang (Wu); (3) Changzhi (Mandarin); (4) Gao'an (Mandarin); (5) Pingyao (Mandarin); (6) Songjiang (Wu); (7) Weining Miao (Tibeto-Burman); (8) Wenzhou (Wu); (9) Wuyi (Wu); (10) Xiamen (Southern Min); and (11) Zhenjiang (Wu).

1. Bai (Xu and Zhao 1964)

Initials

P	ph	m	f	v
t	th	n		l
ts	tsh		s	
tɕ	tɕh		ɕ	j
k	kh	ŋ	x	ɣ

Finals

i	ĩ	ao		ui	uĩ
e	ẽ				
ɛ	ɛ̃	iɛ	iɛ̃	uɛ	uɛ̃
a	ã	ia	iã	ua	uã
o	õ	io	iõ		
u					
ɯ	ɯ̃	iɯ	iɯ̃		
v	ṽ				

Note: Nasality is marked on the main vowels of nasalized rhymes.

Tones Lax   33 31 55 35
       Tense 42 44 21 55

2. Danyang (Lü 1993)

Initials

p	p'	m	f	v
t	t'	n		l
ts	ts'		s	z
tɕ	tɕ'	ny	ɕ	
k	k'	ŋ	x	ɣ

Finals

ɨ	i	u	y	ɑŋ	iɑŋ	uɑŋ	yɑŋ
	ɪ		Y	eŋ	ieŋ	ueŋ	yeŋ
ɑ	iɑ	uɑ	yɑ	ɔŋ	iɔŋ		
æ		uæ	yæ	oŋ			
e	ie	ue	ye		iʔ		yʔ
ə				ɑʔ	iaʔ	uɑʔ	yɑʔ
ɔ	iɔ			æʔ	iæʔ	uæʔ	yæʔ
o				ɔʔ	iɔʔ		
ŋ	iŋ		yŋ				

Note: /ŋ/ may be syllabic.

Tones

	ping		*shang*		*qu*		*ru*	
	yin	*yang*	*yin*	*yang*	*yin*	*yang*	*yin*	*yang*
Literary	33		55		24		4	
Colloquial	33	24	55	24	24	11	3	4

Note: Many characters have two readings, the literary reading and the colloquial reading. The tones are realized differently. The *yin* and *yang*
distinction is lost in the literary reading, but in the colloquial reading,
yang ping, yang shang, and *yin qu* all merge into a single tone.

3. Changzhi (Hou 1983)

Initials

p	p'	m	f
t	t'	n	l
ts	ts'		s
tɕ	tɕ'		ɕ
k	k'		x

Finals

ɑ	iɑ	uɑ	
ə	iE	uə	yE
ɨ	i	u	y
æ		uæ	
ɔ	iɔ		
ei		uei	
əu	iəu		
ɑŋ	iɑŋ	uɑŋ	yɑŋ
əŋ	iŋ	uŋ	yŋ
ɑʔ	iɑʔ	uɑʔ	yɑʔ
əʔ	iəʔ	uəʔ	yəʔ

Tones

ping		shang		qu		ru	
yin	yang	yin	yang	yin	yang	yin	yang
21	24	535		44	53	4	<u>54</u>

4. Gao'an (Yan 1981)

Initials

p	p'	m	f
t	t'	n	l
ts	ts'		s
tɕ	tɕ'		ɕ
k	k'	ŋ	h

Finals

am				ap			
om				op			
ɛm		iɛm		ɛp		iɛp	
		im				ip	
an	uan	ian		at	uat	iat	
on			yon	ot			yot
ɛn	uɛn	iɛn		ɛt	uɛt	iɛt	
ɵn	un	in	yn	ɵt	ut	it	yt
aŋ	uaŋ	iaŋ		ak	uak	iak	
oŋ	uoŋ	ioŋ		ok	uok	iok	
	uŋ	iuŋ			uk	iuk	

Note: Gao'an has three syllabic nasals as well.

Tones

ping		Shang		qu		ru	
Yin	yang	yin	Yang	yin	yang	yin	yang
55	24	42		33	11	3	1

234   *Appendix*

5. Pingyao (Hou 1980)

Initials

p	p'	m		
t	t'	n		l
ts	ts'	nz	s	z
tʂ	tʂ'	ɳ	ʂ	ʐ
tɕ	tɕ'	ny	ɕ	
k	k'	ŋ	x	

Finals

ɑ	iɑ	uɑ	yɑ
ɨE	iE		yE
		uə	yə
æ		uæ	
ɔ	iɔ		
ɨ	i	u	y
ɿ		ɥ	
ər			
ei		uei	
əu	iəu		
ɑŋ	iɑŋ	uɑŋ	
əŋ	iŋ	uŋ	yŋ
ʌʔ	iʌʔ	uʌʔ	yʌʔ

Tones

ping		shang		qu		ru	
yin	yang	yin	yang	yin	yang	yin	yang
13	13	53		35		23	54

Note: The *ping* tones are merged in citation form, but exhibit different sandhi behavior.

6. Songjiang (Jiangsu 1960)

Initials

p	t	ts	tɕ	k
p'	t'	ts'	tɕ'	k'
b	d		dʑ	g
m	n		ny	ŋ
f		s	ɕ	h
v		z		ɦ

Finals

ɿ	i	u	y
e		ue	
ɛ	iɛ	uɛ	
ɑ	iɑ	uɑ	
ø			yø
ɤ	iɤ		
o			
ɔ	iɔ		
	iu		
ər			
Ã̃	iã		
ã		uã	
ən	in	uən	yn
oŋ	ioŋ		
	iɿʔ		yɿʔ
ɛʔ	iɛʔ	uɛʔ	
ɑʔ	iɑʔ		
əʔ	iəʔ	uəʔ	
ɔʔ		uɔʔ	
oʔ	ioʔ		

Tones

ping		shang		qu		ru	
Yin	yang	yin	yang	yin	yang	yin	yang
53	31	44	22	35	13	5	3

Tones and Initials

	53	31	44	22	35	13	5	3
Vl obstruents	+	-	+	-	+	-	+	-
Vd Obstruents	-	+	-	+	-	+	-	+
Nasals, Lateral	+	+	+	+	-	+	-	+

Note: + indicates co-occurrence; - otherwise.

7.   Weining Miao (F.-S. Wang 1957)

Consonants

p	p'	b	b'	mp	mp'	mb	mb'
t	t'	d	d'	nt	nt'	nd	nd'
ʈ	ʈ'	ɖ	ɖ'	nʈ	nʈ'	nɖ	nɖ'
k	k'	g	g'	nk	nk'	ng	ng'
q	q'	ɢ	ɢ'	nq	nq'	nɢ	nɢ'
ts	ts'	dz	dz'	nts	nts'	ndz	ndz'
tʂ	tʂ'	dʐ	dʐ'	ntʂ	ntʂ'	ndʐ	ndʐ'
tɕ	tɕ'	dʑ	dʑ'	ntɕ	ntɕ'	ndʑ	ndʑ'
tl	tl'	dl	dl'	ntl	ntl'	ndl	ndl'
f		v	v'	m̥		m	m'
s		z	z'	n̥		n	n'
ʂ		ʐ	ʐ'			ɳ	ɳ'
ɕ		ʑ	ʑ'	ny̥		ny	ny'
x		ɣ	ɣ'	ŋ̊		ŋ	ŋ'
χ							
h		ɦ					
l̥		l	l'				
		w					

Vowels

Monophthongs   i   a   o   u   y   ɯ   ə   ɨ   ɥ
                      Note: /ɨ, ɥ/ are retroflexed after retroflexed
                            obstruents.

Diphthongs   ie   ae   au   aɯ   œy

Glides   i   (u   y)

Tones   55   33   11
                      53   31
                      35   13

Tone Sandhi in Numeral-Classifier Phrases

	55	33	31	35	13	11	53	33-13	x-55
I 55	55	55	55	55	55	55	55	55	55
III 55	33	55	55	33	55	55	33	55	33
IV 33	11	33	33	11	33	33	11	33	11
II 35	55	35	35	55	35	35	55	35	55
V 33	31	33	13'	13'	31	31	31	31	13'
VI 53	13'	31'	13'	13'	31'	31'	13'	31'	13'
VII 55	55	35	35	55	35	35	55	35	55

Note: Classifiers in Classes I, III, and IV have voiceless onset initials; those
      in Classes II, V, VI, and VII have voiced onset initials. The row is the
      tone of numerals; the column is the tone of classifiers. The "'" sign
      after a tone indicates aspiration, which the syllable-initial consonant
      acquires as a result of tone sandhi. The two tones in the last two col-
      umns together trigger the sandhi process; x is any tone.

8. Wenzhou (Zhengzhang 1964b)

Initials

ө	p'		m̄		b	m	
		f		v̄			v
t	t'		n̄	l̄	d	n	l
ts	ts'	s			dz		z
tɕ	tɕ'	ɕ	nȳ	j̄	dʑ	ny	j
k	k'		ŋ̄		g	ŋ	
		h					ɦ

Finals

a	ɛ	e	ø	ə	o
ʋ	y	i	ɨ		
iɛ	yɔ	uɔ	ai	aʋ	eʋ
ei	øy	ɤʋ	aŋ	eŋ	oŋ

Note: There are three nasal finals in Wenzhou.

Tones

Ping		shang		qu		ru	
Yin	*Yang*	*yin*	*yang*	*yin*	*yang*	*yin*	*yang*
a	A	b	B	c	C	d	D
44	31	45	34	42	22	323	212

Bisyllabic Tone Patterns

Tone Melodies		Source Tones
A.	22-33	a,A - a
B.	42-33	b,B,c,C - a
C.	22-2	a,A,c,d,D - A
D.	43-34	a,A,b,B,c,C - b,B
E.	213-43	a,A - c,C
F.	42-21	b,B,c,C - c
G.	42-22	b,B,c,C - C
H.	43-12	a,A,b,B,c,C - d,D

Note: 213 is a variant of 22.

9. Wuyi (Fu 1984)

Initials

I	II	I	II
p	b	p'	pɦ
t	d	t'	tɦ
ts	dz	ts'	tsɦ
tɕ	tɕ	tɕ'	tɕɦ
k	g	k'	kɦ
ʔ	ɦ	h	hɦ
f	v	ʔm	ɦm
		ʔn	ɦn
s	z	ʔl	ɦl
ɕ	ʑ	ʔɲ	ɦɲ
		ʔŋ	ɦŋ

Finals

	i	u	y
ɤ, ɯ	ie		ye
a	ia	ua	ɥa
		ua, ɯɔ	
		iəu	uəi
au	iau		
əŋ	iŋ	uəŋ	yəŋ
aŋ	iaŋ	uaŋ	yaŋ
oŋ	ioŋ		
æʔ	iæʔ	uæʔ	yæʔ
ɤʔ	ieʔ		yeʔ
aʔ	iaʔ	uaʔ	
		uɑʔ	yɑʔ
oʔ	ioʔ	uoʔ	
ɑuʔ	iɑuʔ		

Note: /m n l/ can be syllabic.

Tones

ping		shang		qu		ru	
Yin	yang	yin	yang	yin	yang	yin	yang
24	213	55	13	53	31	5	212

Note: *yin* tones co-occur with Class I initials; *yang* tones co-occur with Class II initials.

10. Xiamen (Cheng 1968)

Consonants

	Obstruents	Affricates	Spirants
vl. unasp.	p t k	c	s
vl. asp.	ph th kh ʔ	ch	h
voiced	b l g	j	

Note: /b,l,g/ surface as [b,l,g] before oral vowels, [n,m,ŋ] elsewhere.

Vowels   i   e   a   o   u   ə

Tones   55   35   53   31   33

11. Zhenjiang (Zhang 1985)

Initials

p	t	ts	tɕ	k
ph	th	tsh	tɕh	kh
m	n			
	l			
f		s	ɕ	h
w		ʐ	j	

Finals

	i, ɨ	u	y, ỹ
ɑ	iɑ	uɑ	
ɛ	iɛ	uɛ	
ər, o, ɔ	iɔ		
ei		uei	
əu	iəu		
ɛ̃n	iɛ̃n	uɛ̃n	
ən		uən	
ũn			
ɑŋ	iɑŋ	uɑŋ	
iŋ			yŋ
oŋ	ioŋ		
ɑʔ	iɑʔ	uɑʔ	
əʔ	iʔ	uəʔ	yʔ
oʔ	ioʔ	uoʔ	

Tones:

ping		*shang*		*qu*		*ru*	
Yin	*yang*	*yin*	*yang*	*yin*	*yang*	*yin*	*yang*
42	35	31		55		5	

References

Glossary of Chinese language journals

Fangyan	Dialects
Minzhu Yuwen	Minority Languages
Yuyan Yanjiu	Language Research
Yuyanxue Luncong	Linguistics Forum
Zhongguo Yuwen	Chinese Language
Zhonguo Yuyanxue Bao	Bulletin of Chinese Linguistics

Anderson, Stephen R. (1978). Tone Features. In *Tone: A Linguistic Survey*, edited by Victoria A. Fromkin. New York: Academic Press.

Anderson, Stephen R. (1985). *Phonology in the Twentieth Century*. Chicago: University of Chicago Press.

Archangeli, Diana (1985). Yokuts Harmony: Evidence for Coplanar Representation in Nonlinear Phonology. *Linguistic Inquiry* 16, 335–373.

Archangeli, Diana, and Douglas Pulleyblank (1989). Yoruba Vowel Harmony. *Linguistic Inquiry* 20, 173–218.

Bai, Wanru (1989). Guangzhou hua zhong de shenglue xing bianyin (The Changed Tone under Deletion in Guangzhou). *Fangyan* 1989, 114–120.

Bao, Zhiming (1989). On the Nature of Contour Tones. Paper presented at the Annual Conference of the Linguistic Society of America, Washington, D.C.

Bao, Zhiming (1990a). *Fanqie* Languages and Reduplication. *Linguistic Inquiry* 21, 317–350.

Bao, Zhiming (1990b). *On the Nature of Tone*. Ph.D. dissertation, MIT.

Bao, Zhiming (1995). Syllable Structure and Partial Reduplication in Classical Chinese. *Journal of East Asian Linguistics* 4, 175–196.

Bao, Zhiming (1996). The Syllable in Chinese. *Journal of Chinese Linguistics* 24, 312–354.

Bao, Zhiming (1997). Local Tree Geometry and the Syntax-Phonology Interface. In *Interfaces in Phonology*, edited by Ursula Kleinhenz. Berlin: Akademie Verlag.

Cai, Junming (1991). *Chaozhou fangyan cihui* (*A Dictionary of Chaozhou Dialect*). Hong Kong: Institute of Chinese Culture, Chinese University of Hong Kong.

Cao, Jianfen, and Ian Maddieson (1989). An Exploration of Phonation Types in Wu Dialects of Chinese. *UCLA Working Papers in Phonetics* 72, 139–60.

Chan, Marjorie K.-M. (1989). Contour-Tone Spreading and Tone Sandhi in Danyang Chinese. Ms., Ohio State University, Columbus.

Chang, Kun (1953). On the Tone System of the Miao-Yao Languages. *Language* 29, 374–378.

Chang, Kun (1975). Tonal Developments among Chinese Dialects. *Bulletin of the Institute of History and Philology, Academia Sinica* 46, 636–709.

Chang, M.-C. Laura (1992). *A Prosodic Account of Tone, Stress, and Tone Sandhi in Chinese Languages.* Ph.D. dissertation, University of Hawaii.

Chao, Yuen Ren (1930/1980). A System of Tone-Letters. *La Maitre Phonetique* 45, 24–47. Reprinted in *Fangyan* 1980, 2, 81–82.

Chao, Yuen Ren (1931). Fanqie yu ba zhong (Eight Varieties of Languages Based on the Principle of *Fanqie*). *Bulletin of the Institute of History and Philology, Academica Sinica* 2, 320–354.

Chao, Yuen Ren (1947). *Cantonese Primer.* Cambridge, Mass.: Harvard-Yenching Institute.

Chao, Yuen Ren (1956). Formal and Semantic Discrepancies between Different Levels of Chinese Structure. *Bulletin of the Institute of History and Philology, Academia Sinica* 28, 1–16.

Chao, Yuen Ren (1968). *A Grammar of Spoken Chinese.* Berkeley: University of California Press.

Chen, Matthew (1979). Metrical Structure: Evidence from Chinese Poetry. *Linguistic Inquiry* 10, 371–420.

Chen, Matthew (1986a). The Paradox of Tianjin Tone Sandhi. *Chicago Linguistic Society* 22, 98–154.

Chen, Matthew (1986b). An Overview of Tone Sandhi Phenomena across Chinese Dialects. Ms., University of California, San Diego.

Chen, Matthew (1987a). Introductory Remarks. *Journal of Chinese Linguistics* 15, 203–227.

Chen, Matthew (1987b). The Syntax of Xiamen Tone Sandhi. *Phonology Yearbook* 4, 109–149.

Chen, Matthew (1992). Tone Rule Typology. In *Proceedings of the Special Session on the Typology of Tone Languages, Eighteenth Annual Meeting of the Berkeley Linguistic Society.* 54–66.

Chen, Zangtai, and Li Rulong (1991). *Min yu yanjia* (*A Study of Min*). Beijing: Language Press.

Cheng, Chin-chuan (1973a). *A Synchronic Phonology of Mandarin Chinese.* The Hague: Mouton.

Cheng, Chin-chuan (1973b). A Quantitative Study of Chinese Tones. *Journal of Chinese Linguistics* 1, 93–110.

Cheng, Robert (1968). Tone Sandhi in Taiwanese. *Linguistics* 41, 19–42.

Chiang, Wen-yu (1992). *The Prosodic Morphology and Phonology of Affixation in Taiwanese and Other Chinese Languages.* Ph.D. dissertation, University of Delaware.

Chomsky, Noam, and Morris Halle (1968). *The Sound Pattern of English.* New York: Harper and Row.

Clark, Mary M. (1990). *The Tonal System of Igbo.* Dordrecht: Foris.

Clements, George N. (1979). The Description of Terraced-Level Tone Languages. *Language* 55, 536–558.

Clements, George N. (1983). The Hierarchical Representation of Tone Features. In *Current Approaches to African Linguistics*, vol. 1, edited by Ivan R. Dihoff. Dordrecht: Foris.

Clements, George N. (1985). The Geometry of Phonological Features. *Phonology Yearbook* 2, 225–252.

Clements, George N. (1989). On the Representation of Vowel Height. Ms., Cornell University.

DeFrancis, John (1984). *The Chinese Language: Facts and Fantasy.* Honolulu: University of Hawaii Press.

Duanmu, San (1990). *A Formal Study of Syllable, Tone, Stress and Domain in Chinese Languages.* Ph.D. dissertation, MIT.

Duanmu, San (1994). Against Contour Tone. *Linguistic Inquiry* 25, 555–608.

Fromkin, Victoria A. (1972). Tone Features and Tone Rules. *Studies in African Linguistics* 3, 47–76.

Fromkin, Victoria A. (1974). The Phonological Representation of Tone. In *UCLA Working Papers in Phonetics* 26, 1-17.

Fu, Guotong (1984). Wuyi fangyan de lianxü biandiao (Tone Sandhi in the Wuyi Dialect). *Fangyan* 1984, 109–127.

Fujimura, Osamu (1977). Control of the Larynx in Speech. *Phonetica* 34, 280–288.

Fujimura, Osamu (1981). Body-Cover Theory of the Vocal Fold and its Phonetic Implications. In *Vocal Fold Physiology*, edited by Kenneth Stevens and Minoru Hirano. Tokyo: University of Tokyo Press.

Gandour, Jack (1974). Consonant Types and Tone in Siamese. In *Studies on Tone from the UCLA Tone Project. UCLA Working Papers in Phonetics* 27, 92-117.

Gandour, Jack (1975). Evidence from Lue for Contour Tone Features. *Pasaa* 2, no. 2, 39–52.

Goldsmith, John (1976). *Autosegmental Phonology*, Ph.D. dissertation, MIT.

Goldsmith, John (1990). *Autosegmental and Metrical Phonology.* Oxford: Basil Blackwell.

Guo, Jinfu (1993). *Hanyu shengdiao yudiao chanyao yu tanshuo (An Explication and Investigation of Chinese Tones and Intonation).* Beijing: Beijing Language Institute Press.

Halle, Morris (1983). On Distinctive Features and Their Articulatory Implementation. *Natural Language and Linguistic Theory* 1, 91–105.

Halle, Morris (1989). The Intrinsic Structure of Speech Sounds. Ms., MIT.

Halle, Morris (1990). An Approach to Morphology. Ms., MIT.

Halle, Morris (1992). Phonological Features. In *International Encyclopedia of Linguistics*, edited by William Bright. Oxford, Oxford University Press.

Halle, Morris (1995). Feature Geometry and Feature Spreading. *Linguistic Inquiry* 26, 1-46.

Halle, Morris, and Kenneth Stevens (1971). A Note on Laryngeal Features. *Quarterly Progress Report 101*, MIT.

Halle, Morris, and Jean-Roger Vergnaud (1980). Three Dimensional Phonology. *Journal of Linguistic Research* 1, 83–105.

References

Halle, Morris, and Jean-Roger Vergnaud (1982). On the Framework of Auto-segmental Phonology. In *The Structure of Phonological Representations*, part 2, edited by Harry der van Hulst and Norval Smith. Dordrecht: Foris.

Hammond, Michael (1988). On Deriving the Well-Formedness Condition. *Linguistic Inquiry* 19, 319–325.

Hashimoto, Mantaro (1991). Gu Hanyu shengdiao diaozhi gouni de changshi jiqu hanyi (An Attempt at the Reconstruction of Archaic Chinese Tone Values and Its Implications). *Yuyanxue Luncong* 16, 47–98.

Haudricourt, André G. (1954). De l'origine des tons en Vietnamien. *Journal Asiatique* 242, 69–82.

He, Wei (1984). Luoyang fang yan ji lui (Notes on the Luoyang Dialect). *Fangyan* 1984, 278–299.

He, Wei (1993). *Luoyang fangyan yanjiu (A Study of the Luoyang Dialect)*. Beijing: Social Science Documents Press.

Hewitt, Mark, and Allen Prince (1990). OCP, Locality, and Linking: the N. Karanga Verb. Ms., Brandeis University.

Hombert, Jean-Marie, John J. Ohala, and William G. Ewan (1979). Phonetic Explanations for the Development of Tones. *Language* 55, 37–58.

Hou, Jinyi (1980). Pingyao fangyan de liandu biandiao (Tone Sandhi in the Pingyao Dialect). *Fangyan* 1980, 1–14.

Hou, Jinyi (1983). Changzhi fangyan jilu (Notes on the Changzhi Dialect). *Fangyan* 1983, 260–274.

Hou, Jinyi, et al. (1986). Shanxi fangyan de feng qu (Distribution of Shanxi Dialects). *Fangyan* 1986, 81–92.

Hung, Tony (1987). Tianjin Tone Sandhi: towards a Unified Approach. *Journal of Chinese Linguistics* 15, 274–305.

Hyman, Larry (1975). *Phonology: Theory and Analysis*. New York: Holt, Rinehard and Winston.

Hyman, Larry (1985). Word Domains and Downstep in Bamileke-Dschang. *Phonology Yearbook* 2, 47–83.

Hyman, Larry (1986). The Representation of Multiple Tone Heights. In *The Phonological Representation of Suprasegmentals*, edited by Koen Bogers et al. Dordrecht: Foris.

Hyman, Larry (1993). Register Tones and Tonal Geometry. In *The Phonology of Tone: the Representation of Tonal Register*, edited by Harry van der Hulst and Keith Snider. Dordrecht: Foris.

Hyman, Larry, and Russell G. Schuh (1974). Universals of Tone Rules: Evidence from West Africa. *Linguistic Inquiry* 5, 81–115.

Inkelas, Sharon (1987). Tone Feature Geometry. *Northeast Linguistic Society* 18, 222–237.

Jakobson, Roman, Gunner M. Fant, and Morris Halle (1952). *Preliminaries to Speech Analysis*. Cambridge, Mass.: Acoustics Laboratory, MIT.

Jiangsu he Shanghai fangyan diaocha zhidao zu (Investigation Group of Dialects in Jiangsu Province and Shanghai City) (1960). *Jiangsu sheng he Shanghai shi fangyan gaikuang (An Outline of the Dialects in the Province of Jiangsu and the City of Shanghai)*. Nanjing: Jiangsu People's Press. Cited as Jiangsu.

Kao, Diane L. (1971). *Structure of the Syllable in Cantonese*. The Hague: Mouton.

Kennedy, George A. (1953). Two Tone Patterns in Tangsic. *Language* 29, 367–373.

Kenstowicz, Michael (1993). *Phonology in Generative Grammar*. Oxford: Basil Blackwell.

Kiparsky, Paul (1982a). From Cyclic Phonology to Lexical Phonology. In *The Structure of Phonological Representations*, part 1, edited by Harry van der Hulst and Norval Smith. Dordrecht: Foris.

Kiparsky, Paul (1982b). Lexical Morphology and Phonology. In *Linguistics in the Morning Calm*, edited by I.-S. Yang. Seoul: Hanshin.

Ladefoged, Peter (1973). The Features of Larynx. *Journal of Phonetics* 1, 73–83.

Laniran, Yetunde O., and George N. Clements (1996) Downstep as Regressive Upstep: Evidence from Yoruba. Ms., University of North Carolina, Chapel Hill, and CNRS, Paris.

Laughren, Mary (1984). Tone in Zulu Nouns. In *Autosegmental Studies in Bantu Tone*, edited by George N. Clements and John Goldsmith. Dordrecht: Foris.

Leben, William (1973). *Suprasegmental Phonology*. Ph.D. dissertation, MIT.

Lehiste, Ilse (1970). *Suprasegmentals*. Cambridge, Mass.: MIT Press.

Li, Fang Kui (1964). The Phonemic System of the Tai Lü Language. *Bulletin of the Institute of History and Philology* 35, 7–14.

Li, Paul J.-K. (1985). A Secret Language in Taiwanese. *Journal of Chinese Linguistics* 13, 91–121.

Li, Rong (1979). Wenling fangyan de liandu biandiao (Tone Sandhi in the Wenling Dialect). *Fangyan* 1979, 1–29.

Li, Xingjian, and Liu, Sixun (1985). Tianjin fangyan de lian du bian diao (Tone Sandhi in Tianjin Dialect). *Zhongguo Yuwen* 1985, 76–80.

Li, Xinkui (1994). *Guangdong de fangyan* (*The Dialects of Guangdong*). Guangzhou: Guangdong People's Press.

Li, Yongming (1959). *Chaozhou Fangyan* (*The Chaozhou Dialect*). Beijing: Zhonghua Shuju.

Li, Yongsui et al. (1959). Miao yu sheng mu he sheng diao zhong de ji ge wenti (Some Issues in the Consonants and Tones in Miao). *Yuyan Yanjiu* 4, 65–80.

Lin, Hwei-bing, and Bruno H. Repp (1989). Cues to the Perception of Taiwanese Tones. *Language and Speech* 32, 25–44.

Lin, Jo-wang (1994) Lexical Government and Tone Group Formation in Xiamen Chinese. *Phonology* 11, 237–275.

Lin, Yen-hui (1988). Nasal Segments in Taiwanese Secret Language. Ms., University of Texas, Austin.

Lin, Yen-hui (1989). Autosegmental Treatment of Segmental Processes in Chinese Phonology. Ph.D. dissertation, University of Texas, Austin.

Lü, Shuxiang (1980). Danyang fangyan de shengdiao xitong (The Tonal System of the Danyang Dialect). *Fangyan* 1980, 85–122.

Lü, Shuxiang (1993). *Danyang fangyan yuyin bian* (*The Sound System of the Danyang Dialect*). Beijing: Language Press.

Luo, Changpei, and Jun Wang (1981). *Putong yuyan xue ganyao* (*An Outline of General Phonetics*). Beijing: Commercial Press.

McCarthy, John (1979). *Formal Problems in Semitic Phonology and Morphology*. Ph.D. dissertation, MIT.

McCarthy, John (1981). A Prosodic Theory of Nonconcatenative Morphology. *Linguistic Inquiry* 12, 373–418.

McCarthy, John (1986). OCP Effects: Gemination and Antigemination. *Linguistic Inquiry* 17, 207–263.

McCarthy, John (1989). Linear Order in Phonological Representation. *Linguistic Inquiry* 20, 71–99.

McCarthy, John, and Allen Prince (1997). *Prosodic Morphology 1986*. Technical Report 32, Rutgers Center for Cognitive Science, Rutgers University.

Maddieson, Ian (1974). A Note on Tone and Consonants. *Studies on Tone from the UCLA Tone Project. UCLA Working Papers in Phonetics* 27, 18-27.

Maddieson, Ian (1978) Universals of Tone. In *Universals of Human Language: Phonology*, vol. 2, edited by Joseph H. Greenberg. Stanford: Stanford University Press.

Marantz, Alec (1982). Re Reduplication. *Linguistic Inquiry* 13, 483–545.

Matisoff, James A. (1973). Tonogenesis in Southeast Asia. In *Consonant Types and Tone, Southern California Occasional Papers in Linguistics* 1, edited by Larry Hyman. Los Angeles: University of Southern California.

Mei, Tsu-lin (1970). Tones and Prosody in Middle Chinese. *Harvard Journal of Asiatic Studies* 30, 86–110.

Meng, Zhaojie (1985). Yao zhu Bunu hua liandu biandiao wenti chutan (A Preliminary Investigation of Tone Sandhi in the Bunu Language of the Yao Nationality). *Yuyan Yanjiu* 8, 215–218.

Milliken, Stuart, Guangping Zhang, Xueyi Zhang, Zhiqi Li, and Ying Lü (1997). Resolving the Paradox of Tianjin Tone Sandhi. In *Studies in Chinese Phonology*, edited by Jialing Wang and Norval Smith. Berlin: Mouton de Gruyter.

Myers, Scott P. (1987). *Tone and the Structure of Words in Shona*. Ph.D. dissertation, University of Massachusetts, Amherst.

Newman, Paul (1986). Contour Tones as Phonemic Prime in Grebo. In *The Phonological Representation of Suprasegmentals*, edited by Koen Bogers et al. Dordrecht: Foris.

Newman, Paul (1995). Hausa Tonology: Complexities in an "Easy" Tone Language. In *Handbook of Phonological Theory*, edited by John Goldsmith. Oxford: Basil Blackwell.

Norman, Jerry (1989). *Chinese*. Cambridge: Cambridge University Press.

Odden, David (1986). On the Role of the Obligatory Contour Principle in Phonological Theory. *Language* 62, 353–383.

Odden, David (1988). Anti-gemination and the OCP. *Linguistic Inquiry* 19, 451–75.

Odden, David (1995). Tone: African Languages. In *Handbook of Phonological Theory*, edited by John Goldsmith. Oxford: Basil Blackwell.

Ohala, John J. (1972). How Is Pitch Lowered? *Journal of the American Society of Acoustics* 52, 124.

Ohala, John J. (1977). Speculations on Pitch Regulation. *Phonetica* 34, 310–312.

Ohala, John J. (1978). Production of Tone. In *Tone: A Linguistic Survey*, edited by Victoria A. Fromkin. New York: Academic Press.

Pike, Kenneth (1948). *Tone Languages*. Ann Arbor: University of Michigan Press.

Prince, Allen (1987). Planes and Copying. *Linguistic Inquiry* 18, 491–510.

Pulleyblank, Douglas (1986). *Tone in Lexical Phonology*. Dordrecht: Reidel.

Pulleyblank, Edwin (1978). The Nature of the Middle Chinese Tones and their Development to Early Mandarin. *Journal of Chinese Linguistics* 6, 172–203.

Pulleyblank, Edwin (1984). *Middle Chinese: A Study in Historical Phonology*. Vancouver: University of British Columbia Press.

Qian, Zengyi et al. (1982). *Yantai fangyan baogao* (*Report on the Yantai Dialect*). Jinan: Qilu Book Society.

Qiao, Quansheng (1996). Shanxi fangyan renchen daici de jige tedian (A Few Properties of the Personal Pronouns in Shanxi Dialects). *Zhongguo Yuwen* 1996, 27–30.

Ramsey, S. Robert (1987). *The Languages of China*. Princeton: Princeton University Press.

Sagey, Elizabeth C. (1986). *The Representation of Features and Relations in Non-linear Phonology*. Ph.D. dissertation, MIT.

Sagey, Elizabeth C. (1988). On the Ill-Formedness of Crossing Association Lines. *Linguistic Inquiry* 19, 109–118.

Sawashima, Masayuki, and Hajime Hirose (1983). Laryngeal Gestures in Speech Production. In *The Production of Speech*, edited by Peter F. MacNeilage. New York: Springer-Verlag.

Selkirk, Elizabeth, and Tong Shen (1990). Prosodic Domains in Shanghai Chinese. In *The Phonology-Syntax Connection*, edited by Sharon Inkelas and Draga Zec. Chicago: University of Chicago Press.

Shi, Feng, and Rong-rong Liao (1994). *Yuyin conggao* (*Essays on Phonetics*). Beijing: Beijing Language Institute Press.

Shih, Chi-lin (1986). *The Prosodic Domain of Tone Sandhi in Chinese*. Ph.D. dissertation, University of California, San Diego.

Snider, Keith L. (1988). Towards the Representation of Tone: A Three-dimensional Approach. In *Features, Segmental Structure and Harmony Processes*, edited by Harry der van Hulst and Norval Smith. Dordrecht: Foris.

Snider, Keith L. (1990). Tonal Upstep in Krachi: Evidence for a Register Tier. *Language* 66, 453–474.

Steriade, Donca (1982). *Greek Prosodies and the Nature of Syllabification*. Ph.D. dissertation, MIT.

Steriade, Donca (1986). Locality Conditions and Feature Geometry. *Northeast Linguistic Society* 17, 595–617.

Steriade, Donca (1988). Reduplication and Syllable Structure. *Phonology* 5, 73–155.

Stevens, Kenneth (1977). Physics of Laryngeal Behavior and Larynx Modes. *Phonetica* 34, 264–279.

Stevens, Kenneth (1981). Vibration Modes in Relation to Model Parameters. In *Vocal Fold Physiology*, edited by Kenneth Stevens and Minoru Hirano. Tokyo: University of Tokyo Press.

Tan, Fu (1987). Tone Sandhi in the Tianjin Dialect. *Journal of Chinese Linguistics* 15, 228–246.

Ting, Pang-hsin (1982). Some Aspects of Tonal Development in Chinese Dialects. *Bulletin of the Institute of History and Philology* 53, 629–644.

Ting, Pang-hsin (1989). Hanyu shengdiao de yanbian (Diachronic Change in Chinese Tones). *Proceedings of the Second International Sinology Conference*, 395–408. Taiwan: Academia Sinica.

Tsay, S.-C. Jane (1994). *Phonological Pitch*. Ph.D. dissertation, University of Arizona, Tucson.

Trubetzkoy, Nikolaj S. (1969). *Principles of Phonology*. Berkeley: University of California Press.

Wang, Fushi (1957). Guizhou Weining Miao yu liangci (The Classifiers in the Miao Language in Weining, Guizhou). *Yuyan Yanjiu* 2, 75–122.

Wang, Guosheng (1996). Hubei Daye hua de qingyi biandiao (Emotive Tone Sandhi in the Dialect of Daye, Hubei). *Zhonguo Yuwen* 1996, 355–360.

Wang, Li (1956). *Hanyu yinyun xue (Chinese Phonology)*. Beijing: Zhonghua Shuju.

Wang, Li (1957). *Hanyu shi gao (A History of Chinese)*. Beijing: Science Press.

Wang, Li (1979). *Hanyu shi lu xue (Chinese Poetics)*. Shanghai: Shanghai Education Press.

Wang, William S.-Y. (1967). Phonological Features of Tone. *International Journal of American Linguistics* 33, 93–105.

Wen, Duanzheng (1985) *Xinzhou fangyan zi (Notes on the Dialect of Xinzhou)*. Beijing: Language Press.

Wen, Duanzheng (1991). *Cangnan fangyan zi (Notes on the Dialect of Cangnan)*. Beijing: Language Press.

Williams, Edwin (1976). Underlying Tone in Margi and Igbo. *Linguistic Inquiry* 7, 463–484.

Woo, Nancy (1969). *Prosody and Phonology*. Ph.D. dissertation, MIT.

Wright, Martha (1983). *A Metrical Approach to Tone Sandhi in Chinese Dialects*. Ph.D. dissertation, University of Massachusetts, Amherst.

Wu, Zongji (1984). Putonghua sanzizu biandiao guilü (Sandhi Patterns of Three-Character Phrases in Mandarin). *Zhongguo Yuyanxue Bao* 2, 70–92.

Xia, Jianqin (1983). Liuyang Nanxiang fangyan jilue (A Brief Note on the Liuyang Nanxiang Dialect). *Fangyan* 1983, 47–58.

Xing, Xiangdong (1996). Shenmu fangyan de erhua biandiao (Tone Sandhi of Diminutive Affixation in the Shenmu Dialect). *Fangyan* 1996, 52–55.

Xu, Lin, and Yansun Zhao (1964). Bai yu gaikuang (An Outline of the Bai Language). *Zhongguo Yuwen* 1964, 321–335.

Yan, Sen (1981). Gao'an (Laowu Zhoujia) fangyan de yuyin xitong (The Sound System of the Gao'an (Laowu Zhoujia) Dialect). *Fangyan* 1981, 104–121.

Yip, Moira (1980). *The Tonal Phonology of Chinese*. Ph.D. dissertation, MIT.

Yip, Moira (1982). Reduplication and C-V Skeleta in Chinese Secret Languages. *Linguistic Inquiry* 13, 637–661.

Yip, Moira (1988). The Obligatory Contour Principle and Phonological Rules: a Loss of Identity. *Linguistic Inquiry* 19, 65–100.

Yip, Moira (1989). Contour Tones. *Phonology* 6, 149–174.

Yip, Moira (1992). The Spreading of Tonal Modes and Tonal Features in Chinese Dialects. In *Proceedings of the Special Session on the Typology of Tone Languages, Eighteenth Annual Meeting of the Berkeley Linguistic Society.* 157–166.

Yip, Moira (1995). Tone in Asian Languages. In *Handbook of Phonological Theory*, edited by John Goldsmith. Oxford: Basil Blackwell.

Yuan, Jiahua et al. (1960). *Hanyu fangyan gaiyao (An Introduction to Chinese Dialects).* Beijing: Language Reform Press.

Yue, Saiyue (1979). Guiyang Huaxi qu Jiading Miao hua de qianjia cheng fen (Prefixes in the Miao Dialect of Jiading, Huaxi District, Guiyang City). *Minzhu Yuwen* 1979, 199–205.

Yue-Hashimoto, Anne (1972). *Phonology of Cantonese.* Cambridge: Cambridge University Press.

Yue-Hashimoto, Anne (1986). Tonal Flip-Flop in Chinese Dialects. *Journal of Chinese Linguistics* 14, 161–182.

Zee, Eric, and Ian Maddieson (1979). Tones and Tone Sandhi in Shanghai: Phonetic Evidence and Phonological Analysis. *UCLA Working Papers in Phonetics* 45, 93–129.

Zhan, Bohui (1981). *Xiandai Hanyu fangyan (Modern Chinese Dialects).* Wuhan: Hubei People's Press.

Zhang, Chengcai (1980). Xining fangyan jilue (Notes on the Xining Dialect). *Fangyan* 1980, 282–302.

Zhang, Hongnian (1985). Zhenjiang fanyan de liandu biandiao (Tone Sandhi in the Zhenjiang Dialect). *Fangyan* 1985, 191–204.

Zhang, Zhengsheng (1987). The Paradox of Tianjin: Another Look. *Journal of Chinese Linguistics* 15, 247–273.

Zhang, Zhenxing (1982). Zhangping (Yongfu) fangyan de danzi diao (Lexical Tones of the Zhangping (Yongfu) Dialect). *Fangyan* 1982, 264–275.

Zhengzhang, Shangfang (1964a). Wenzhou yinxi (The Sound System of Wenzhou). *Zhongguo Yuwen* 1964, 28–49.

Zhengzhang, Shangfang (1964b). Wenzhou fangyan de liandu biandiao (Tone Sandhi in the Wenzhou Dialect). *Zhongguo Yuwen* 1964, 106–152.

Zhengzhang, Shangfang (1980). Wenzhou fangyan er-wei ci de yuyin bianhua (Sound Change of the *er* Suffix in the Wenzhou Dialect). *Fangyan* 1980, 245–262.

Zong, Fubang (1964). Guanyu Guangzhou hua yin ping diao de fenghua wenti (On the Split of the *Yin Ping* Tone in Cantonese). *Zhongguo Yuwen* 1964, 376–389.

Index